Over
One Hundred
Years Of
Fine Stringed
Instruments

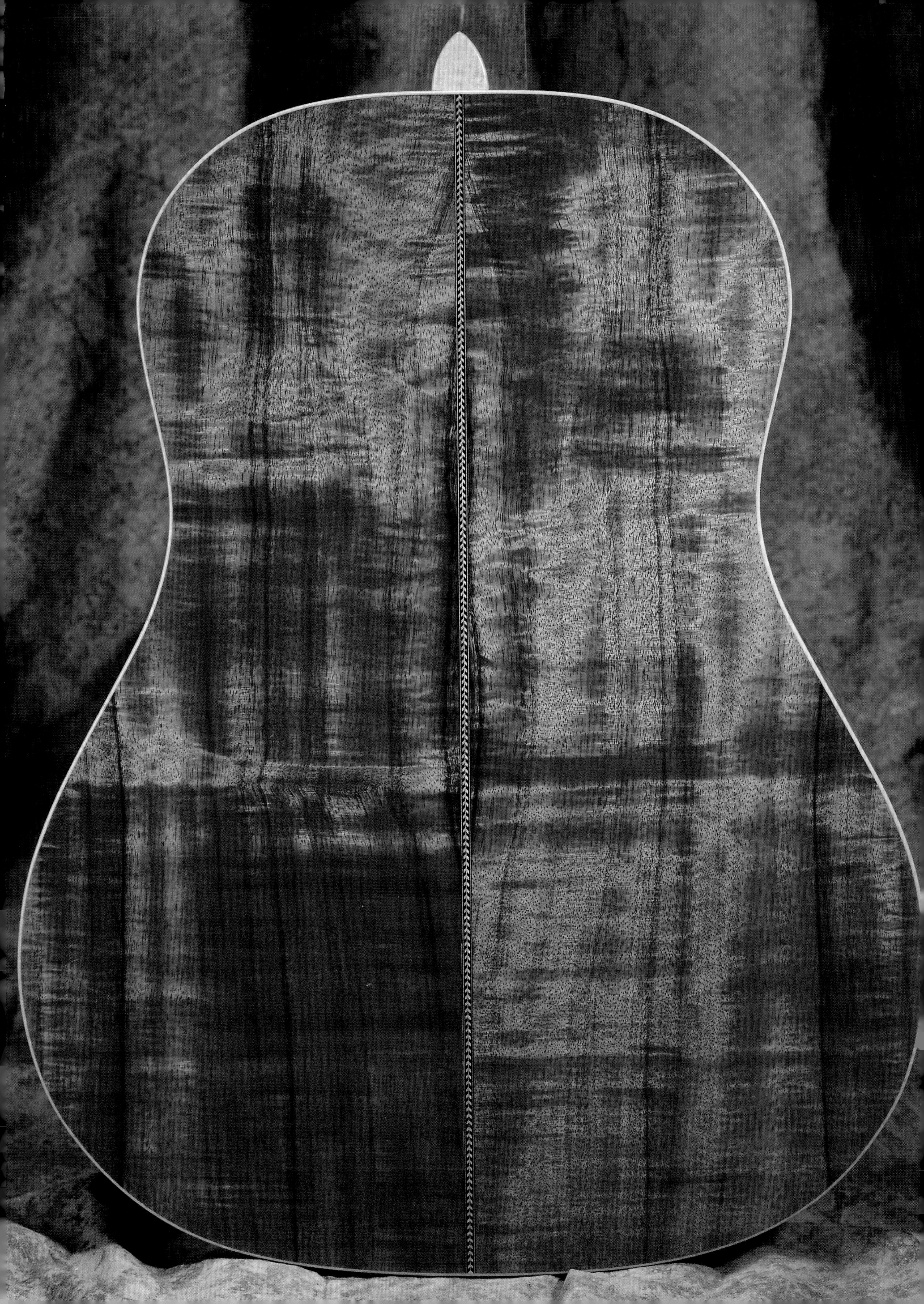

Over One Hundred Years Of Fine Stringed Instruments

By John Teagle

Music Sales Corp.
New York

Layout and Design: 20th Century Guitar/Seventh String Press
Cover Artwork: Idea To Image/Jeff Lynch
Cover Photos courtesy of Washburn International
except Model 308 courtesy Stan Jay/Mandolin Brothers, Ltd.
and Hawaiian Harp Guitar courtesy John Sprung.

Softcover:
Order No. AM 92230
US International Standard Book Number: 0.8256.1435.X
UK International Standard Book Number: 0.7119.4355.9

Hardcover:
Order No. AM 92231
US International Standard Book Number: 0.8256.1436.8
UK International Standard Book Number: 0.7119.4356.7

Exclusive Distributors:
Music Sales Corporation
257 Park Avenue South, New York, NY 10010 USA
Music Sales Limited
8/9 Frith Street, London W1V 5TZ, England
Music Sales Pty. Limited
120 Rothschild Avenue, Rosebery, Sydney, NSW 2018, Australia

Printed in the United States of America by
Vicks Lithograph and Printing Corporation

Washburn
WASHBURN
WASHBURN
WASHBURN
Cherokee
Washburn
washburn

Table of Contents

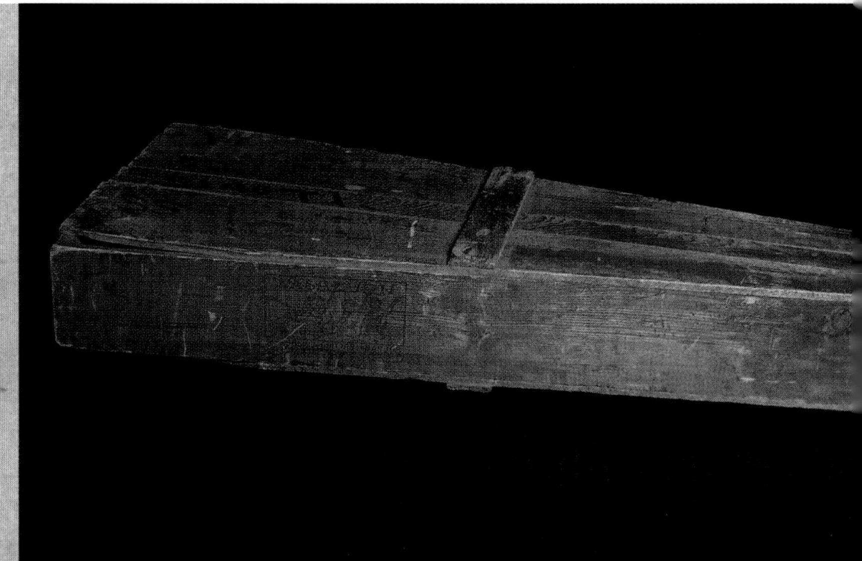

Table of Contents

Part 3: Modern Acoustic Instruments

Part 4: Electric Instruments

LANEY
LANEY
LANEY
LANEY
LANEY

Foreword

By Nuno Bettencourt

I started working with Washburn right around the time of Extreme's first album. The original N4 was designed and patterned after N2, the composite guitar I built for myself from a sawed-down Schecter body and Warmouth neck. The prototype Washburns were handmade for me just like the original. I had input on everything from the fret sizes and curvature of the fingerboard to the electronics. The Steven's Extended Cutaway is still one of the guitar's most unique features which we refer to as the "shark fin." The cutaway allows the fretting hand's thumb and palm to remain behind the neck all the way down to the last fret.

Today, the Washburn N4 is better than ever because now they've got Grover Jackson running the plant building some really great guitars. My new 6/12 custom double neck N4 grew out of a meeting I had with Grover in Chicago last year, which I needed for playing things like "Hole Hearted." It worked out that it's not as heavy as old double necks. It's actually light and comfortable which is how I like my guitars.

While recording Extreme's new album, "Waiting For The Punch Line," I said to myself, "Look, I'm in the studio, I'm looking for good, different sounds and I can use what I want," but I always end up coming back to my N4 which is pretty constant for me. That's the thing, you see - it's not as if I'm just doing an endorsement deal with any old company; I'm actually playing a guitar I designed, so I'm going to be happy.

Nuno Bettencourt - 1994

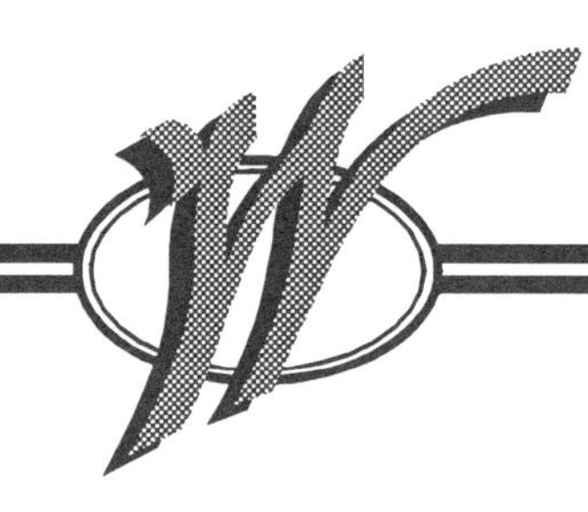

Foreword

By George Gruhn

In my conversations with John Teagle and review of sections of his manuscript, it has become clear that he is a careful researcher as well as a concise and entertaining writer. His presentation is unique - I know of no other comprehensive review of the Lyon & Healy company or its products.

At the turn of the century, Lyon & Healy of Chicago was one of the largest and most influential manufacturers, distributors and retailers of musical instruments in the world. Unfortunately, until the publication of this book, the company and its products have been poorly documented and frequently misunderstood. With the exception of a few catalog reprints and brief mentions in other books, information on Lyon & Healy instruments has been very limited.

I have been looking forward to the publication of John Teagle's book because I need it as much as anyone else. This book greatly expands my personal knowledge and appreciation of Lyon & Healy products and enhances my ability as a dealer to serve the public.

It is my expectation that proper documentation will increase public awareness of Lyon & Healy products and increase demand for these fine instruments. Had it been published ten years ago, I think demand for vintage Washburn instruments would be much greater today.

I expect this book to have a very positive effect on the market as well as providing a bridge linking the historically important vintage instruments with the modern Washburn company and the current product line.

About The Author

Born in Akron, Ohio "at the height of the original rock & roll era" and starting school "just before the British Invasion," John Teagle relates the majority of his life experiences in some way to music. "Blessed with parents who listened to Classical music 18 hours a day," he played clarinet and cello in grade school before becoming a "teenage record hound." Buying his first of many vintage guitars led to twenty years of playing in bands, running sound for other bands, producing and engineering studio sessions, teaching guitar, working in music stores, and repairing instruments. A self-taught ethnomusicologist, he collects catalogs, magazines, books and posters dealing with music, musical instruments and pop culture, as well as records and "cowboy" guitars. Currently residing in New York City with his wife and daughter, Mr. Teagle is a Senior Contributing Editor for 20th Century Guitar magazine and the author of "Fender Amps: The First Fifty Years."

Dedicated to Phillip G. Teagle
for all his help.

Acknowledgements

Writing this book has been a great joy and learning experience for me, so to all involved, my sincerest thanks. To all the kind folks in Chicago at Washburn; Rudy for sitting with me and pushing for a better book, Marianna for making me feel at home, Del Breckenfeld and Lisa Yucht for taking care of me during my visits, Marks Kinsman for getting me started, Grover Jackson for the tour of his past and the factory, and especially Rich Siegle for organizing the modern history and instruments. Also Christina from Lyon & Healy Harps and Terry Fife for her initial research.

To Nuno and George for taking the time to write words. Also to Mr. Gruhn for his encouragement and help along the way and especially for his early words of advice, "You should call Jim Bollman." Jim Bollman of the Music Emporium in Lexington, Massachusetts knows more about early American stringed instruments and manufacturers than anyone I've met and was more than willing to share his life-long accumulation of information, giving me the run of his file cabinet, his home and his store. To my hometown friend Tom Humphrey of Ross Music in Akron, Ohio for digging up surprise after surprise and for travelling a thousand miles with me and a car full of instruments. To Stan Werbin of Elderly Instruments in Lansing, Michigan for trusting me with a number of catalogs from his extensive collection, which he graciously offered to send me following a short conversation. These gentlemen all have a love of the folklore and the music that transcends their roles as vintage instrument merchants. A number of other collectors and dealers who were involved in making the book happen includes John Bernunzio of BVI, Scott Freilich of Top Shelf Music, author Jim Fisch, Dave Stutzman of Stutzman Guitar Center, G. E. Smith, Rocky and Deb Blakewood, Stan Jay of Mandolin Bros., Larry Wexer, Adam Kreiswirth, Jay Scott of Nutty Jazz Guitars, Mike Newton of Archer Music, Michael Katz, Walter Carter and Greg Gfell.

Finally, thanks to my bandmates, Tom Wheeler for his book American Guitars, Chad Crumm, all the helpful people at the NYC Public Library, Dan Courtenay, and Les Leiva, of Chelsea 2nd Hand Guitars in NYC for allowing me to use their store as my mail room, Larry and Jim Acunto of Seventh String Press and Steve Wilson of Music Sales for their patience, my family for their continual support.

Lastly to my tolerant wife who had to live with me and my papers for over a year, not to mention our numerous road trips, late night awakenings and endless phone calls.

Introduction

Before the Civil War, quality musical instruments were not easy to come by in America. Most were imported from Europe, which had a history of building fine instruments going back centuries. As more people came to the United States, the demand for music and musical instruments increased, as did the number of immigrants with experience building them. Some would set up shop and sell instruments by word of mouth, and/or through retail establishments and teachers. Many craftsmen would take on other vocations, building a few examples by hand in their spare time. The majority of the early American instruments were still rather crude in their construction.

Between the end of the Civil War and the beginning of the twentieth century, there was a steady increase in the quality of life for much of the American population. This provided more free time to pursue the joys of music as well as the discretionary income to purchase instruments. To accommodate this growing demand, small factories began replacing workshops, and craftsmen from across the sea flocked to Boston, New York and Chicago, early centers for the trade. By the end of the century, Chicago had become the U.S. center for musical merchandise, and this had become BIG business.

The leader of this community was Lyon & Healy, a retail and wholesale giant, as well as manufacturer. A modest portion of their operation was the building and selling of Washburn Stringed Instruments, the focus of this book. To help grasp the importance of Washburn and Lyon & Healy in the history of American Music, a number of related topics will also be approached in the following pages. References will be made to a number of other manufacturers and models will be compared with well known instruments, in particular, those of Martin and Gibson, industry leaders for much of the steel string era (Before the 1930s, most quality guitars came fitted with gut strings).

For many years these two companies, isolated in the remote Nazareth and Kalamazoo areas, were responsible for only a very small share of the market.The Martin factory averaged less than one instrument per day before WWI. Orville Gibson took between one week and a month to build an instrument and the Gibson Mandolin-Guitar Co. was almost bankrupt in the early 1920s. On the other hand, Lyon & Healy, an early pioneer of mass production, was averaging over one hundred stringed instruments per day!

Mass production techniques brought consistency to all the levels of work while allowing apprentices to grow into journeymen. Highly skilled workers could direct their efforts to the processes involved that were worthy of their time, leaving the less exacting work to those appropriately trained. The top of the line models benefited from more accurate rigs for cutting frets, neck joints, etc. Train cars full of quality wood were available to chose from, with lesser pieces finding their way into the construction of the lower models, helping to keep prices down. Homemade instruments began to be replaced with assembly line models that were affordable to all but the poorest, with a brand new bottom of the line guitar or banjo costing as little as two dollars. No frills and the cheapest materials, but built using tested methods and machinery.This mass production of musical goods would benefit everyone from the end user to the gainfully employed builders to the management and owners.

A friendly competitiveness allowed neighboring companies to buy and trade parts and subcontract work to each other. It was also not unusual for a craftsman to work for a number of different factories during his life, having closer ties to friends and family members in the trade than to his employer.Instruments no longer had to come from "the House of" In the big cities of America they came from "the Factory of." The proliferation of available instruments created an awareness of music that led to its more prominent role both in the home and at social functions.

Socio-economic considerations aside, this book will attempt to cover all the instruments that have been released over the last one hundred and eleven years bearing the Washburn name. A fascinating collection indeed! These include all kinds of guitars plus a variety of basses, the mandolin family, banjos of all styles, zithers, harps, pianos, violins, ukuleles and tiples. Also a look at who was building and who was selling Washburns, including Lyon & Healy, J.R. Stewart, Tonk Bros., Regal, Beckmen Musical Instruments, Fretted Industries, Washburn International, a number of builders in the orient and the new factories in Chicago and Nashville.

The Roots of Washburn

The long line of Washburn guitars, mandolins and banjos is a fine one, going back to Chicago over one hundred years ago! The company's roots go back even further, to Boston before the Civil War. The Oliver Ditson Co. started in the 1830s selling sheet music and the business grew to include publishing music and retailing musical instruments. Besides helping start the John Church Co. (Cincinnati, 1860) and the John C. Haynes Co. (Boston, 1865) to manufacture instruments, Ditson would establish outlets for his publishing business in three major cities. Two of these were operated by his sons, Chas. H. Ditson (& Co., New York, 1867) and J.E. Ditson (& Co., Philadelphia, 1875). A third was opened in Chicago in 1864 by one of his Boston employees and a clerk from another downtown Boston music store. Lyon & Healy, as they would be called, went on to become the world's

Lyon & Healy

largest music house, with the slogan "Everything Known in Music" describing the extent of their selection.

Oliver Ditson had picked his duo wisely, with the forty-four year old George Washburn Lyon's experience complementing the twenty-four year old Patrick Joseph Healy's ambition. Lyon, born in 1820, was a talented musician, playing a number of string and brass instruments as well as studying the harp. He also liked to tinker with and try to improve musical instruments. Healy, who was born in Ireland on St. Patrick's Day 1840, had over ten years' experience in music when he left Boston for Chicago. Coming to the U.S. at age ten, he would operate the pump for his church's organ and work as a clerk for G.P. Reed's music store, not far from Ditson's. The story goes that if Reed's did not have a particular item in stock, Healy would run to the other stores to procure it. He was of build so short and thin that he was rejected by the Union armed forces during the Civil War.

Traveling to three cities under consideration for the new store, San Francisco, St. Louis and Chicago, Healy came back to Boston with his mind made up. He and George Washburn Lyon were going to Chicago. As Healy, his wife and Lyon were about to leave the train station in May of '64, Mr. Ditson offered the encouraging words "If you have good luck, in ten years you will do a business of $100,000 a year." They would top that figure within the first year!

Early *Lyon & Healy*

Chicago was only thirty years old in 1864 but had quickly become the hub of the midwest, with train connections and access to the Great Lakes. During the Civil War, much of the Union's supplies passed through the docks and warehouses of the bustling, but rough and unrefined city.

On October 14th, 1864, the Lyon & Healy music store opened for business. Located at the corner of two muddy streets, Washington and Clark, the tiny store offered the best stock of sheet music in the area. Next door was Smith & Nixon, a music store that was the midwest distributor for Steinway Pianos. In less than ten years time, Lyon & Healy would buy Smith & Nixon out, gaining the Steinway franchise. It's interesting to compare one of the numerous later pictures of the "original" store that give the impression the whole building was Lyon & Healy's, and a more accurate picture from the actual time, which shows the numerous businesses surrounding the ground floor corner shop.

By the end of the decade, the company was beginning to wholesale certain items and needed more space for its retail business. Making the first of many moves, space was leased at the corner of Washington and Wabash Streets. Wabash was becoming the center for the musical merchandise business, not just of Chicago, but soon the whole country. Unfortunately, the entire block was destroyed by a fire on September 4th of 1870.

CORNER WABASH AVE. & WASHINGTON ST.
870-DESTROYED BY FIRE

Luckily for Lyon & Healy, they were insured and quickly back in business at a new location, 150 S. Clark Street. In October of '71 the infamous Chicago fire ravaged much of the city, including S. Clark Street. Healy would describe the events: "The Sunday evening of the Great Fire I had retired at eight o'clock. I had not been in bed long before an alarm of fire sounded, then a second, a third, and so on. I dressed and went downtown and upon reaching the river, I concluded that the business section of Chicago was doomed, and pressing forward I arrived at our store at No. 150 Clark Street about ten o'clock. I opened the safe, took out all the money, bills receivable, insurance policies and other valuable papers and carried them home." Following the first fire, a more thorough insurance policy had been taken and this allowed the

firm to totally recover its losses. Finding an available space proved difficult. The company set up first in a small shop at 287 W. Madison Street and shortly thereafter in a small church, on Wabash but clear down at 16th Street. Lyon & Healy finally settled into a permanent headquarters downtown at the corner of State & Monroe Streets. It was a difficult period between 1869 and the end of 1872, operating out of five different locations, but, unlike many Chicago businesses, Lyon & Healy ended up with a well stocked store in the downtown area.

The First Washburn Instruments

With considerably more room, Lyon & Healy expanded the scope of the retail section of the business and began a serious effort to become a major wholesaler, the Chicago location proving to have been a perfect choice. The country was booming and more and more people were moving inland from the coast, many to the great expanse around and to the west of Chicago. Buyers were sent to Europe, returning with a selection of instruments and accessories previously unavailable in the U.S. The 1870s saw Lyon & Healy prosper and expand, eventually taking over the rest of their building.

TRADE-MARKS.

[Certificates of registration of Trade-Marks numbered 8,191 and upward are registered under the act of March 3, 1881.]

15,173.—CHAMPAGNE AND OTHER WINES.—*Henri Abelé*, Rheims, France. Application filed December 15, 1887. Used since August 31, 1887.

"The words 'RUBY ROYAL.'"

15,174.—BLOCKS OF NATURAL SALT.—*Chicago Sawed Salt-Block Company*, Chicago, Ill. Application filed December 17, 1887. Used since November 1, 1887.

"The representation of a horse standing in a stall with a groom beside him with one arm outstretched toward the head of the animal, thus calling attention to the block of salt on a shelf over a manger, which the horse is licking, and above which are the words 'SAWED ROCK' and below it 'SALT-BLOCK.'"

15,175.—NATURAL MINERAL WATER AND SALT.—*The Eisner & Mendelson Company*, Philadelphia, Pa. Application filed September 29, 1887. Used since January 1, 1887.

"The representation of a lion issuant and the heraldic representation of a stream of water."

15,176.—CAPSULES CONTAINING MEDICINE.—*James W. Gedney*, New York, N.Y. Application filed December 28, 1887. Used since December 1, 1887.

"The words 'GEDNEY'S PEARLS.'"

15,177.—SPARKLING WINES.—*Gebrüder Hoehl*, Geisenheim, Prussia, Germany. Application filed December 5, 1887. Used since December 15, 1885.

"The word-symbol 'KAISER BLUME' and the representation of a bunch of flowers having blue petals and red centers, with green stalks and leaves."

15,178.—MEDICINE FOR THE CURE OF ALL THROAT AND LUNG DISEASES.—*George M. Brown* and *Joseph M. Hunnicutt*, Atlanta, Ga. Application filed December 27, 1887. Used since November 9, 1887.

"The letters and character 'H T & L C' in a diamond-shaped border, 'H' being in the left-hand angle of the figure and 'C' in the right-hand angle, and attached by a black line to the black rectangular figure which forms the background of the letters and character 'H T & L C.'"

15,179.—TEA.—*C. D. Lathrop & Co.*, Chicago, Ill. Application filed November 30, 1887. Used since May 1, 1887.

"The words 'FLOWER OF JAPAN.'"

15,180.—STRINGED MUSICAL INSTRUMENTS.—*Lyon & Healy*, Chicago, Ill. Application filed March 14, 1887. Used since November, 1883.

"The word 'WASHBURN.'"

Seeing no limits to what parts of the music business they could excel in, the company branched out again. Opening a factory at Michigan Avenue and Madison Street, the company wasted no time in developing a whole line of instruments whose quality, price, availability, etc., they could control. It also allowed Lyon & Healy to develop distinct lines which only they would sell.

The Washburn brand name was chosen to represent a group of high quality stringed instruments that included first guitars, then mandolines (old spelling) and zithers, followed in a few years with banjos. The name Washburn, and the logo of a guitar circled by a belt bearing the name George Washburn, were in use by the mid 1880s, showing up in magazine advertisements. An address for the factory was listed as 211-215 S. Canal Street. A trademark of the word Washburn was filed for in 1887 and granted in 1888. In the application it was stated that the name had been in use since November 1883 and this appears to be accurate.

For years there has been confusion surrounding the start of Washburn, with the years 1864, 1874 and 1876 all being mistakenly used in official promotion. The introduction date was just one of a number of misleading "facts" about the company that were carelessly released by Lyon & Healy's in-house advertising department over the years. This department was started in 1887, the first of its kind in the music industry, and it played a major role in the future successes of Lyon & Healy and Washburn. They surely had no idea at the time that their work would be scrutinized so intently one hundred years later.

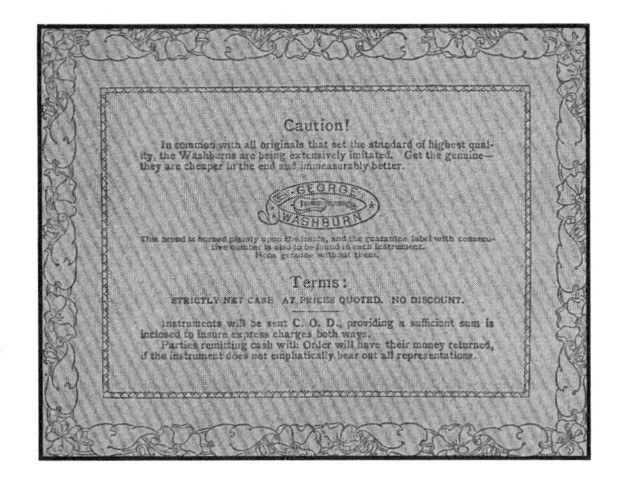

Caution!

In common with all originals that set the standard of highest quality, the Washburns are being extensively imitated. Get the genuine—they are cheaper in the end and immeasurably better.

GEORGE WASHBURN

This brand is burned plainly upon the inside, and the guarantee label with consecutive number is also to be found in each instrument. None genuine without them.

Terms:

STRICTLY NET CASH AT PRICES QUOTED. NO DISCOUNT.

Instruments will be sent C. O. D., providing a sufficient sum is inclosed to insure express charges both ways.

Parties remitting cash with Order will have their money returned, if the instrument does not emphatically bear out all representations.

Advertising

Lyon & Healy's strong commitment to advertising was a relatively fresh and daring use of funds at the time. Just six days into their new business, the little store placed its first ad, in the Chicago Tribune, with the results being sufficient to encourage them to continue the practice. Because of the Civil War, the public's awareness of the media, with up to date news via the telegraph (and some of the earliest photo journalism), had never been as acute. A quote attributed to Healy said "A good advertisement of a good thing in a good paper is a good investment." This attitude proved itself for the company repeatedly over the years, and still holds true today. Another quote attributed to Healy stated his reply of "The returns are not all in yet" to a query regarding the success of a band instrument campaign that had run a few years prior. Lyon & Healy invested in advertising not expecting the results to be seen immediately.

WASHBURN
Guitars, Mandolins & Zithers
in volume and quality of tone are the BEST IN THE WORLD. Warranted to wear in any climate. Sold by all leading dealers. Beautifully illustrated souvenir catalogue with portraits of famous artists will be Mailed FREE.
LYON & HEALY, CHICAGO.

It appears that Mr. Healy was the go-getter of the original duo and his later successes seem to bear this out. Unfortunately, much of the historical material available today was written following George Lyon's departure, with little mention of him, casting some doubt over Healy's apparent domination of the company's early business decisions. Healy was, however, always hard working and bright and would not have had his own business at the age of twenty-four, or enjoyed such great success later, if this were not the case.

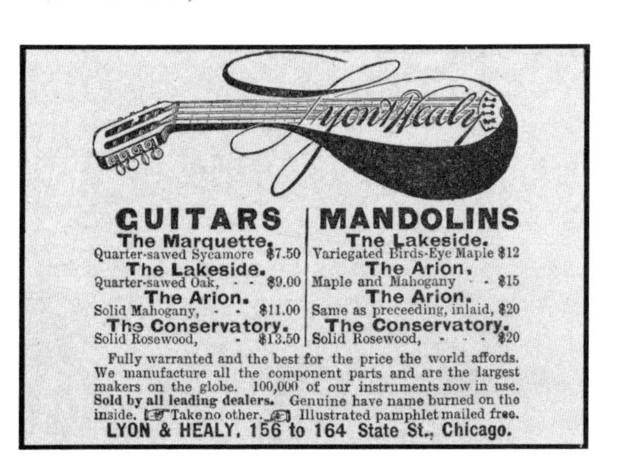

Lyon & Healy began publishing a catalog of all their goods in the 1870s. Included were the set prices and descriptions, often accompanied by illustrations. This was a dramatically different method of selling, compared to the usual technique of the time, i.e., salesmen showing samples and charging whatever they felt the buyer would pay. In later years, specific catalogs would be printed for the different lines and an all-encompassing hardbound "jobber book" was supplied to retailers.

Washburns were usually advertised as a brand, with no reference to specific models. An ad from 1886 showed a poorly rendered illustration of a plain, bottom line model. By the end of the century the artwork had improved greatly and the first of many ads featuring animals and small children with instruments were run.

In April of '89, an ad for Washburn guitars, mandolins and zithers ran in what is known today as Music Trades magazine. At the time, the magazine ran hundreds of ads for pianos, but none for guitars. Lyon & Healy's Washburn ad was a first for the magazine and was followed by the end of the year with ads for both Bay State and Martin Guitars (available exclusively from C.A. Zoebisch & Sons), two of Washburn's main competitors.

A famous ad of four babies with Washburns was somewhat bold for the time in that three of the children were white and the fourth was black, playing a banjo, of course. Interracial bands of adults were unheard of until the late 1930s and instrument catalogs rarely showed black artists in their endorsement sections (a few had separate pages for them). The Washburn ad was soon changed with the banjo going to one of the other children. This was probably part of a larger effort to make the banjo appeal more to those who could afford the new expensive and ornate models that were becoming "socially" acceptable at the end of the 1800s. Lyon & Healy ran these ads for five years before replacing the babies with a trio of slightly older children.

Later ads were more traditional, often times not showing any instruments at all. You had to send away for the souvenir catalog. Years later, Lyon & Healy would run a ground breaking ad for their new Style A mandolin in Crescendo, an early magazine devoted to the mandolin, guitar and harp. A full page color plate was bound into the magazine, showing the front and back of the instrument and a brief description. There was nothing printed on the back, making the picture suitable for framing.

Lyon & Healy were also early champions of the radio, sponsoring shows as early as April 1922, one being "The Duo-Art Piano and Orchestra Radio Program . . . Presented By Lyon & Healy . . .Weather Conditions Permitting."

COPYRIGHTED BY
LYON & HEALY, 1897
"That's my Washburn!"
If you have it in mind to buy either a Guitar, Mandolin or Banjo, let us send you our "Washburn Book." It tells why Washburns are by far the best instruments made; gives portraits and testimonials of over 100 artists, and quotes to you the net cash prices at which Washburns are sold everywhere. Address Dept. T, Lyon & Healy, 199-203 Wabash Ave., Chicago.

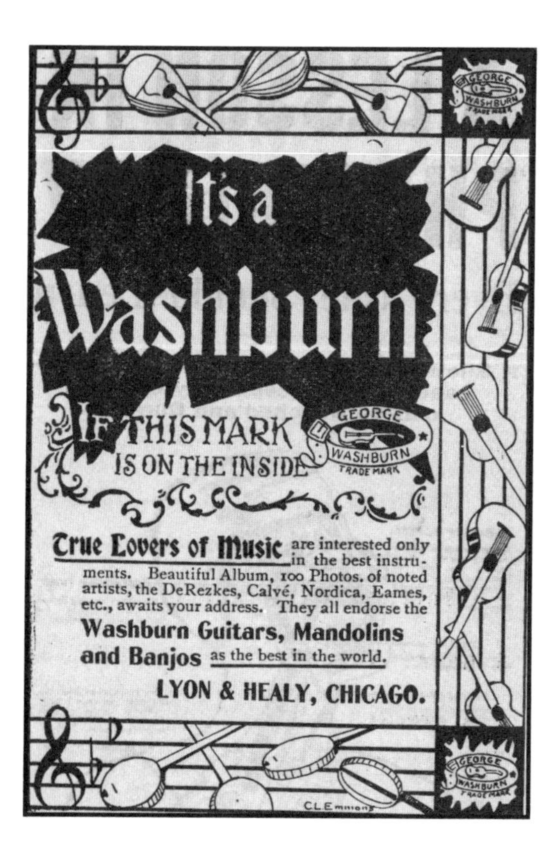
It's a
Washburn
IF THIS MARK
IS ON THE INSIDE
GEORGE WASHBURN
TRADE MARK
True Lovers of Music are interested only in the best instruments. Beautiful Album, 100 Photos. of noted artists, the DeRezkes, Calvé, Nordica, Eames, etc., awaits your address. They all endorse the
Washburn Guitars, Mandolins and Banjos as the best in the world.
LYON & HEALY, CHICAGO.

MUSICAL
Instruments
of Highest Quality
at Lowest Prices
WASHBURN
Mandolins,
Guitars and
Banjos.
We are manufacturers of the famous Washburns. We sell everything known in music, including pianos, organs, musical boxes, band and orchestra instruments, drums, violins, graphophones, sheet music, etc., etc. Annual output of our factories 100,000 instruments. In Lyon & Healy instruments alone you are assured of absolutely correct scales, thoroughly seasoned materials and genuine musical worth. They will outlast a life-time. All live music dealers sell Lyon & Healy goods but if your local dealer will not supply you write to us.
FREE—A catalogue containing hundreds of illustrations. In writing state kind of instrument wanted.
LYON & HEALY, 112 Adams St., Chicago, Ills.

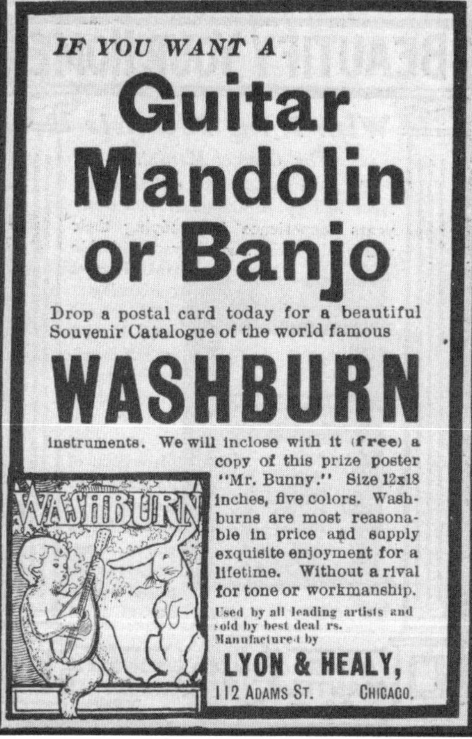
IF YOU WANT A
Guitar
Mandolin
or Banjo
Drop a postal card today for a beautiful Souvenir Catalogue of the world famous
WASHBURN
instruments. We will inclose with it (free) a copy of this prize poster "Mr. Bunny." Size 12x18 inches, five colors. Washburns are most reasonable in price and supply exquisite enjoyment for a lifetime. Without a rival for tone or workmanship.
Used by all leading artists and sold by best dealers.
Manufactured by
LYON & HEALY,
112 ADAMS ST. CHICAGO.
WASHBURN

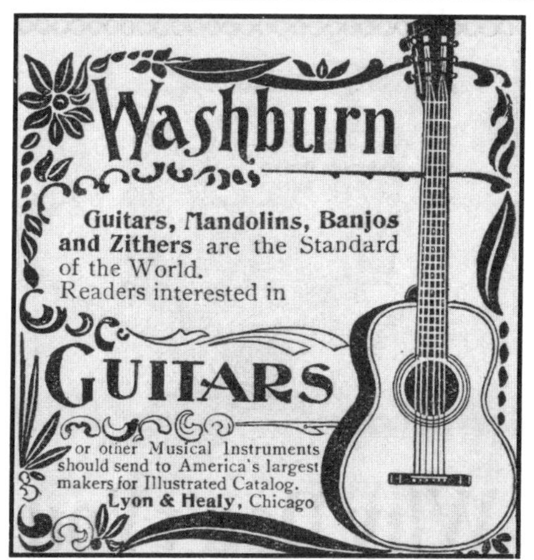
Washburn
Guitars, Mandolins, Banjos and Zithers are the Standard of the World.
Readers interested in
GUITARS
or other Musical Instruments should send to America's largest makers for Illustrated Catalog.
Lyon & Healy, Chicago

Endorsements & Catalogs

The use of catalogues as selling tools was still a relatively new idea in the 1880s, particularly in the musical instrument field. With the release of the Washburn Souvenir Catalog, the whole world could see just how grand these instruments were. Accompanying pictures and graphic descriptions of guitars, mandolins and zithers were pages devoted to Artist Endorsements featuring musicians from all over the country. From coast to coast, from Boston to New York City, Philadelphia, Baltimore, Pittsburgh, Cincinnati, Memphis, Kansas City, St. Louis, Denver, San Francisco, St. Paul, Lansing, Chicago . . . there was even a top-hatted gentleman from Middleton, Ohio. The endorsements were a rather novel promotional

approach for the time. There was no television or radio in the 1880s and no widespread magazines devoted to music. There wasn't even a medium for the reproduction of music as the record player was yet to be invented. Were the endorsers celebrities? How did anyone know who these people were unless they happened to live in one of the cities mentioned above? These were not mythical figures, as a number of them would show up in Twentieth Century publications. Arling Schaefer would publish a number of music books and William Foden would be recognized as one of the country's finest soloists, moving from St. Louis to New York and writing for Crescendo. Martin would gain his endorsement and make a series of Foden Special models from 1912-'17. The Noss Jollity Company would show up in many early Gibson catalogs as the Musical Nosses. Both the Washburn and the Gibson catalogs featured Ferd Noss, one of the more interesting names from the turn of the century.

The influence of the Washburn catalogs on other manufacturers was enough to cause Martin to print a similar style, issued in 1898 and somewhat regularly thereafter, as well as influencing the Gibson Mandolin-Guitar Co. to publish its one hundred-plus page diatribes almost annually, featuring only about twenty pages on the actual instruments. Today these catalogs offer a reasonably accurate representation of the models and styles available at the time. This book would not have been possible without them, as the people involved in the early company are now three and four generations gone. Even the people involved in the new company had to dig through storage vaults and personal memoirs to be able to accurately reconstruct the details of the last twenty years, with the catalogs offering positive proof of release dates and specifications.

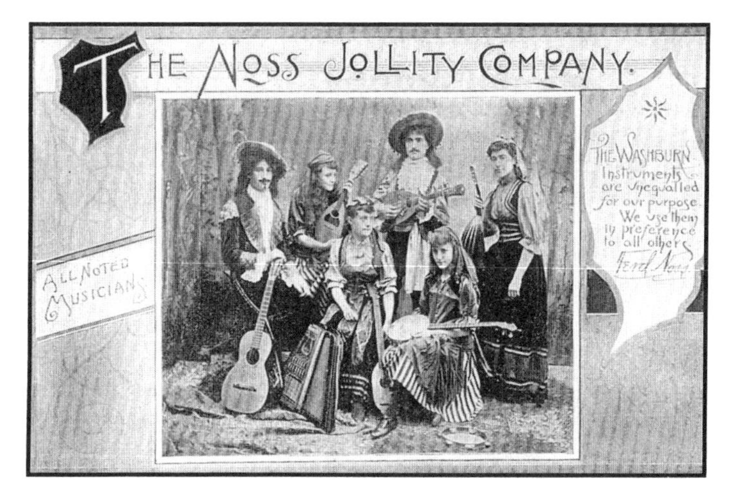

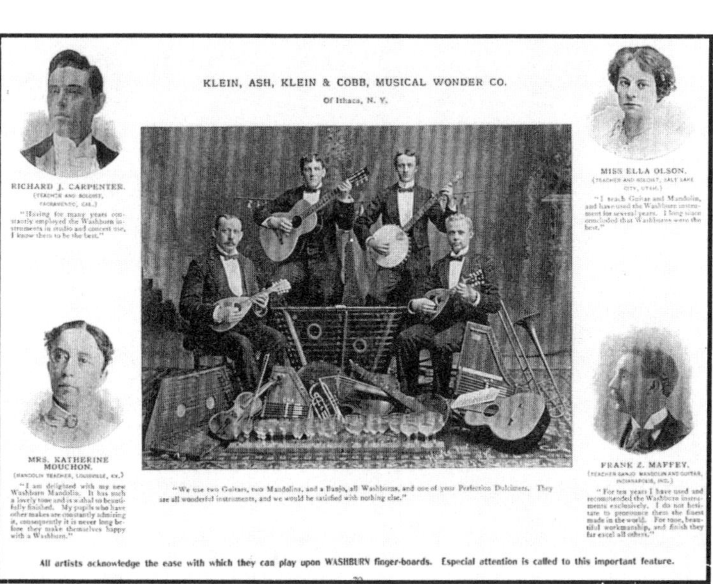

KLEIN, ASH, KLEIN & COBB, MUSICAL WONDER CO.

Of Ithaca, N. Y.

RICHARD J. CARPENTER.
(TEACHER AND SOLOIST, SACRAMENTO, CAL.)

"Having for many years constantly employed the Washburn instruments in studio and concert use, I know them to be the best."

MISS ELLA OLSON.
(TEACHER AND SOLOIST, SALT LAKE CITY, UTAH.)

"I teach Guitar and Mandolin, and have used the Washburn instrument for several years. I long since concluded that Washburns were the best."

MRS. KATHERINE MOUCHON.
(MANDOLIN TEACHER, LOUISVILLE, KY.)

"I am delighted with my new Washburn Mandolin. It has such a lovely tone and is withal so beautifully finished. My pupils who have other makes are constantly admiring it, consequently it is never long before they make themselves happy with a Washburn."

"We use two Guitars, two Mandolins, and a Banjo, all Washburns, and one of your Perfection Dulcimers. They are all wonderful instruments, and we would be satisfied with nothing else."

FRANK Z. MAFFEY.
(TEACHER BANJO, MANDOLIN AND GUITAR, INDIANAPOLIS, IND.)

"For ten years I have used and recommended the Washburn instruments exclusively. I do not hesitate to pronounce them the finest made in the world. For tone, beautiful workmanship, and finish they far excel all others."

All artists acknowledge the ease with which they can play upon WASHBURN finger-boards. Especial attention is called to this important feature.

ROYCE & LANSING MUSICAL COMEDY COMPANY

"We are using the Washburn Guitars, Zithers, and Mandolins constantly and tak pleasure in pronouncing them the finest we have ever seen or used."

G. W. Lyon Retires

Just twenty-five years after coming to Chicago (1889), Lyon & Healy was about to become the largest music house in the world, a position it would hold for almost forty years. Certainly neither Lyon nor the energetic young Healy could have imagined their little sheet music store growing into the giant it had become. The retail department had already taken over the whole building at State and Monroe and a new salesroom was also lying in the near future. The original factory at Michigan and Madison was about to become a warehouse for the wholesale department and a larger manufacturing facility had become a necessity.

It must have seemed like a good time for Lyon, approaching seventy years of age, to retire. He had seen his corner sheet music store expand and branch out repeatedly and had followed the enthusiasm of Patrick Healy through a quarter century of fast paced "gambling" in the business world. His name would live on, representing the line of guitars, mandolins, zithers, and harps he had helped develop. A reportedly amicable parting of the two founders netted Lyon a sizable amount of money and the rights to sell Steinway Pianos, an entirely more suitable position for his golden years. With E. A. Potter and the blessings of Steinway, "Lyon, Potter & Co." opened a multi-floor piano showroom not far from Lyon & Healy at 174-176 Wabash, where Lyon would work until his death on January 12, 1894.

A short-lived line of guitars bearing the name George W. Lyon were made during this period. These featured some novel improvements that today reinforce the idea of George Washburn Lyon's interest in guitar construction. The "Tone Chamber Duplex Bridge," a wooden box-like device fitted inside the body beneath the bridge, was patented January 5, 1892. The Virzi Bros. would take a similar approach nearly thirty years later with their "Tone Producer," fitted inside Gibson's F5 mandolins during Lloyd Loar's tenure. A second unique feature of the Lyon guitar was its recessed top (or raised binding) which helped keep the soundboard isolated from the player's body parts etc. This idea would be used in the late 1930s on the Loar-designed Vivi-Tone acoustics.

Meanwhile Lyon & Healy incorporated, with P.J. Healy as its President, maintaining the rights to use the "Lyon & Healy" and "Washburn" names. Whether new money was needed to buy Lyon out, or for the upcoming expansion, the control of the company stayed in Healy's hands until his death sixteen years later. Two of his children would grow up to head the company, implying a controlling interest was held by the family.

Shortly after Lyon's death, the Lyon & Healy headquarters moved from the building at State & Monroe it had occupied for the previous twenty-two years. Moving to 199-203 Wabash Avenue at the corner of Adams Street, the company joined the numerous music merchandisers, piano showrooms and publishing houses that made the street the center of American musical merchandising for much of the Twentieth Century. In 1898, Lyon & Healy purchased Lyon, Potter & Co., regaining the Steinway franchise and ending any confusion over the Lyon name.

THE NEW

LYON & HEALY BUILDING

OVER 100,000 SQUARE FEET. 150 WINDOWS FACING THE STREET.

Largest and Finest Musical Establishment in the World.

CORNER

WABASH AVENUE & ADAMS ST.

CHICAGO.

Although Lyon & Healy came to Wabash Avenue at the eleventh hour, they secured the finest corner. * * * There is no other building upon Wabash Avenue within a half dozen blocks that can show such a large window frontage. * * * In making this move the firm will be in a far better position to handle its trade than it is in its present location.

Chicago Evening Journal.

100,000 Musical Instruments

A new five story factory at the corner of Randolph Street and Ogden Avenue gave the "Corporation" the room and facilities necessary for full scale production. Almost every conceivable musical instrument would be made there, with the company's huge wholesale division being the perfect outlet for them. This was a win-win situation keeping the end price of Lyon & Healy products extremely competitive, consequently more orders for the factory. Building such a variety of goods required a large pool of laborers that could move from department to department as necessary. This helped smooth seasonal ups and downs and enabled the factory to accommodate trends without being left "holding the bag." The workers were gainfully employed and conditions were good for the time. A job at Lyon & Healy was a career.

The Washburn line was becoming one of the world's most respected and the Lyon & Healy Harp quickly established itself as the finest ever. In the early 1890s, the slogan "Annual production upward of 100,000 Musical Instruments" began to appear in ads and on the back covers of Lyon & Healy catalogs. That worked out to be "a musical instrument every other working minute." A picture of the mighty factory, with "Lyon & Healy Manufacturers of Musical Instruments" printed across the facade made the enormous production figures seem believable. In a bold, and not entirely ethical move, the picture was retouched for a late 1890s Washburn catalog, with "Washburn" replacing "Lyon & Healy" on the factory's front. Accompanying the altered picture was the somewhat misleading slogan "The annual production of the Washburn Factories is 100,000 Musical Instruments." While not entirely false, it implied an enormous number of Washburns were being manufactured which simply was not the case. "100,000 Musical Instruments" included violins, bugles, flutes, drums, musical bones and clappers, metronomes, tambourines, etc., as well as the cheaper makes of guitars, mandolins and banjos. These were sold in numbers many times that of the Washburn instruments, which were expensive and required a great deal of highly skilled handiwork. Considering Martin was making between 150 and 400 instruments a year prior to WWI, a figure of a thousand Washburns a year would seem more likely. Generous perhaps, though certainly feasible.

THE ANNUAL PRODUCTION

OF THE

Washburn Factories

IS

MUSICAL INSTRUMENTS

WASHBURN

100,000

Musical Instruments.

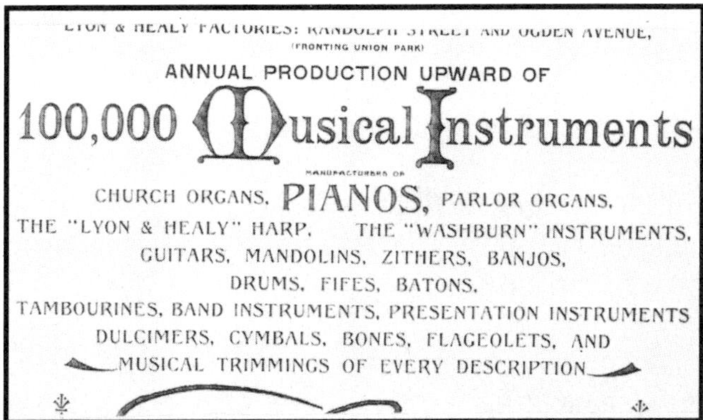

Awards

Not one to rely on previous successes, Healy saw the opportunity to show the whole world the variety of goods and services that were Lyon & Healy. If there was a P.T. Barnum of the musical instrument industry, it was P.J. Healy, who repeatedly was noted for his confidence in promotions. In 1893, Chicago hosted the Columbian Exposition (as in Christopher), similar in concept to the World's Fairs of the Twentieth Century. A brand new faux marble city was built along the Lake Michigan shore, featuring displays, food, rides (including the first Ferris Wheel, seating 1,400 and standing 264 feet tall) and entertainment from around the world. An average of 150,000 visitors passed through the Exposition's gates daily and Lyon & Healy was there with two stories of the grandest musical instrument display ever seen. An estimated 12 million people visited the Fair during its 179 day run (total admission was 27 million). Lyon & Healy paid for daily concerts six months running and had thousands of potential customers sign their guest register. The good will from these concerts elevated the status of the company in both the Chicago community and the music business.

Awards were given for excellence and Lyon & Healy "cleaned up," receiving a dozen medals for various instruments and designs. How qualified the judges were regarding instruments is questionable, but to the millions of people who marveled at the grandness of the Exposition, either in person or through an astounding amount of media coverage, these awards were seen as a great honor. The following year Lyon & Healy set up at the Antwerp International Exposition in Belgium and the Washburn line was again awarded the highest honors. Later advertisements and catalogs would devote pages to reminding people of the company's successes.

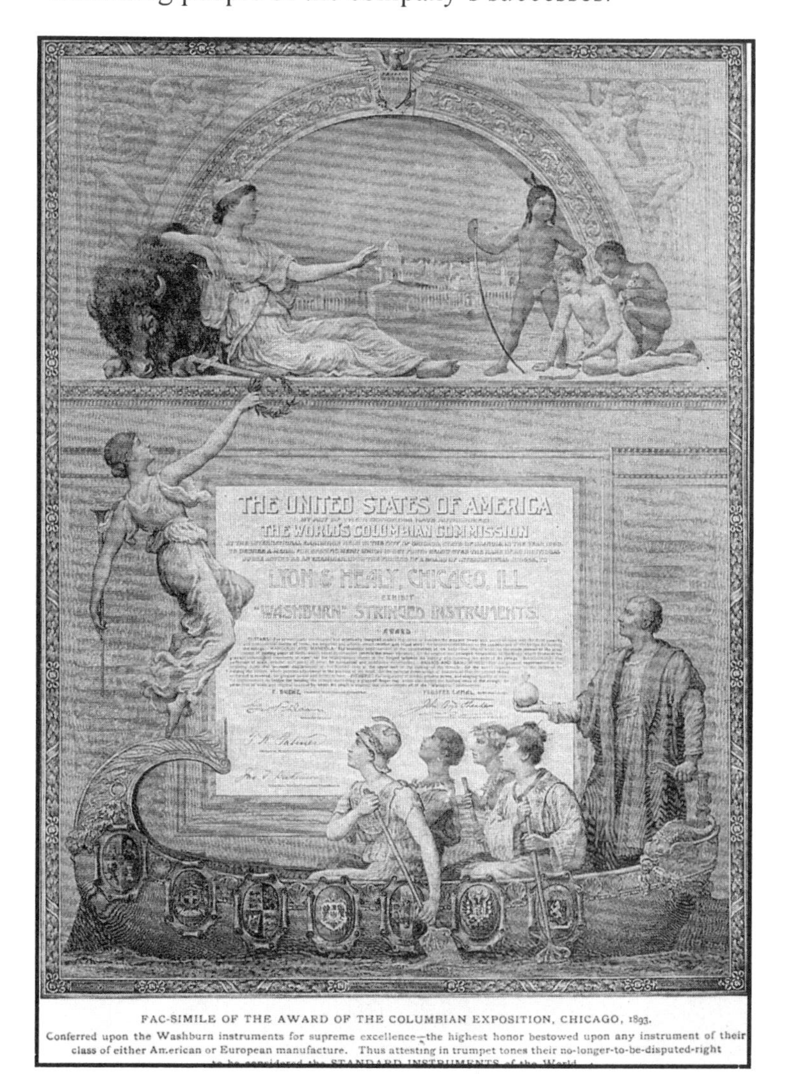

FAC-SIMILE OF THE AWARD OF THE COLUMBIAN EXPOSITION, CHICAGO, 1893.
Conferred upon the Washburn instruments for supreme excellence—the highest honor bestowed upon any instrument of their class of either American or European manufacture. Thus attesting in trumpet tones their no-longer-to-be-disputed-right to be considered the STANDARD INSTRUMENTS of the World.

FAC-SIMILE OF THE GRAND DIPLOMA OF HONOR, ANTWERP (Belgium) INTERNATIONAL EXPOSITION, 1894,
Which, with a Gold Medal, was awarded to the Washburn instruments for supreme excellence. The highest honors conferred upon any instrument of their class, of either American or European manufacture.

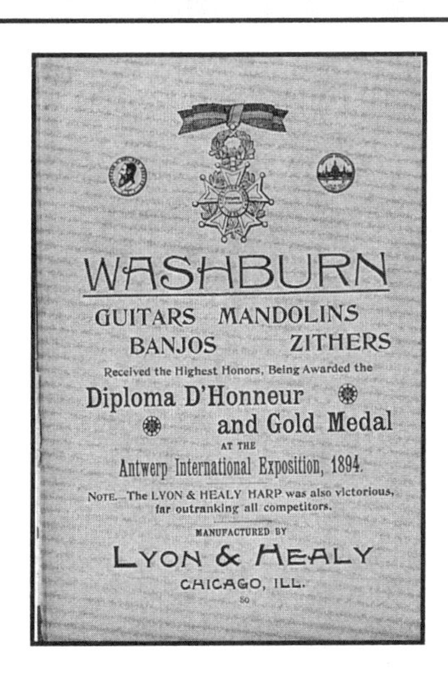

Death of Healy: 1905

Patrick J. Healey
President, 1889-1905

Charles N. Post
President, 1905-1908

Robert B. Gregory
President 1908-1911
and 1915-1918

Paul J. Healy
President, 1911-1915

As P.J. Healy approached his sixty-fifth birthday, he was stricken with a form of paralysis knows as Dr. Armitage's Disease. In a noble gesture to reward some of his closest employees, he issued $250,000 in stock and split it between his board of trustees and ten of his department heads. "I grow my captains" was an expression Healy used to explain his many loyal employees in key positions. Over one hundred workers had ten years or more service at the time, with thirty of them having twenty to forty years each.

Healy saw his sixty fifth birthday but died less than three weeks later on the morning of April 3rd, 1905. His company was in perfect order as longtime employee Charles Post became the new President. Healy left his second wife and eight of his ten children, two of whom would later become Presidents of the firm. He also left behind a legacy of helping Chicago become the center for American musical instruments and for starting Lyon & Healy, the World's Largest Music House.

The 1890s and the early years of the twentieth century had been a period of enormous growth for Lyon & Healy and Washburn. The company had also gotten behind the new record players and records which became big money-makers. Some musical instrument companies saw recorded music as a threat to their business, but Lyon & Healy looked at it to generate interest in music, which it certainly did.

Post was succeeded by longtime employee Robert B. Gregory in 1908. Gregory had been with the company since 1866, starting as a stock clerk and moving up the ranks. One of his duties had been traveling to Europe every year for twenty five years keeping abreast on what was happening overseas. Lyon & Healy earned their reputation of offering the latest in music related goods.

In 1911 Gregory retired, with the late Patrick Healy's son, Paul J. becoming President. With a Healy again in charge, a new piano factory was built in 1914 at the corner of Fullerton and Crawford Avenues. The following year Robert Gregory came out of retirement and replaced the young Healy as President. But before Healy stepped down, plans were made for a new building to house the retail showrooms and offices. This was not going to be just any music store, this was going to be a shrine!

The Lyon & Healy Building

In May of 1916 the new building, a magnificent granite faced, nine story tall, steel structure, was opened. This building still stands at the corner of Wabash Avenue and Jackson Blvd. and for years was a pillar of downtown Chicago. The first floor offered visitors the largest selection of sheet music and books in the world with close to 250,000 titles.

The first floor also housed the Concert Hall, which had a novel use during the day. From 10:00 AM until 5:00 PM daily, people could sit down and listen to a program of Victor Records at no charge. There was no radio yet and records were somewhat expensive at the time, making this service a treat to the building's many visitors. At night Lyon & Healy would stage concerts in the 200 seat hall. The second floor held the largest selection of records in the world, a medium Lyon & Healy had championed since the earliest days of the Victrola. The third floor offered nothing but pianos with over twenty-five brands, including the Lyon & Healy and Washburn brands of their own manufacture. Many of the makers were exclusive franchises, the most famous of which was Steinway. For most of forty years Lyon & Healy had been Steinway's agent for the Midwest. Band instruments, stringed instruments and drums had separate rooms on the upper floors, which also housed the administrative offices, repair shops and teaching studios.

This building operated continuously until shortly after CBS bought Lyon & Healy in the late 1970s. It now houses the administrative offices for DePaul University as well as a string of ground floor shops that includes a McDonald's and a Dunkin Donuts.

World War 1

As the world went to war, Lyon & Healy, the wholesaler, had to deal with a shut-down European music market and the inflation of prices on U.S. goods and services. The company, however, was awarded numerous U.S. Military contracts, supplying the troops with thousands of band and stringed instruments. The breadth and diversity of the organization helped it weather the difficult years of the war. Although it was far from business as usual during these years, the U.S. was not as greatly effected as it would be during WWII when production of almost all non-military goods was halted. Lyon & Healy was able to release a new line of Washburn instruments in 1915 and complete its new building in 1916 before the U.S. became officially involved in the war.

Robert Gregory died in 1918, having served the company for over fifty years. His replacement as President, James F. Bowers, had been with Lyon & Healy almost as long, joining in 1870. He would serve as President until 1921.

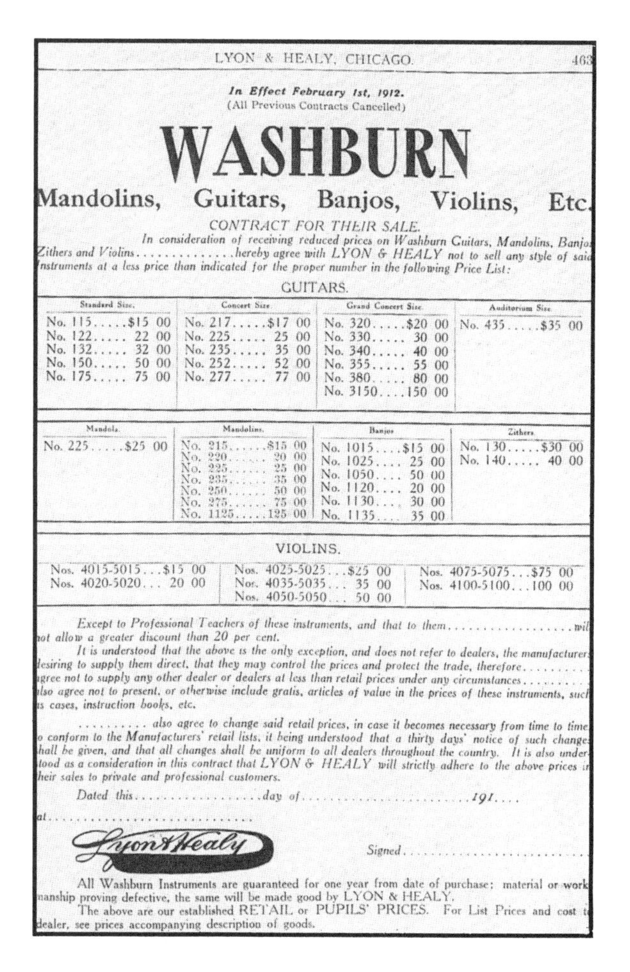

LYON & HEALY, CHICAGO. 463

In Effect February 1st, 1912.
(All Previous Contracts Cancelled)

WASHBURN

Mandolins, Guitars, Banjos, Violins, Etc.

CONTRACT FOR THEIR SALE.

In consideration of receiving reduced prices on Washburn Guitars, Mandolins, Banjos, Zithers and Violins................hereby agree with LYON & HEALY not to sell any style of said instruments at a less price than indicated for the proper number in the following Price List:

GUITARS.

Standard Size.	Concert Size.	Grand Concert Size.	Auditorium Size.
No. 115.....$15 00	No. 217.....$17 00	No. 320.....$20 00	No. 435.....$35 00
No. 122..... 22 00	No. 225..... 25 00	No. 330..... 30 00	
No. 132..... 32 00	No. 235..... 35 00	No. 340..... 40 00	
No. 150..... 50 00	No. 252..... 52 00	No. 355..... 55 00	
No. 175..... 75 00	No. 277..... 77 00	No. 380..... 80 00	
		No. 3150....150 00	

Mandola.	Mandolins.	Banjos	Zithers
No. 225.....$25 00	No. 215......$15 00	No. 1015....$15 00	No. 130.....$30 00
	No. 220...... 20 00	No. 1025.... 25 00	No. 140..... 40 00
	No. 225...... 25 00	No. 1050.... 50 00	
	No. 235...... 35 00	No. 1120.... 20 00	
	No. 250...... 50 00	No. 1130.... 30 00	
	No. 275...... 75 00	No. 1135.... 35 00	
	No. 1125.....125 00		

VIOLINS.

Nos. 4015-5015...$15 00	Nos. 4025-5025...$25 00	Nos. 4075-5075...$75 00
Nos. 4020-5020... 20 00	Nos. 4035-5035... 35 00	Nos. 4100-5100...100 00
	Nos. 4050-5050... 50 00	

Except to Professional Teachers of these instruments, and that to them..................will not allow a greater discount than 20 per cent.

It is understood that the above is the only exception, and does not refer to dealers, the manufacturers desiring to supply them direct, that they may control the prices and protect the trade, therefore.......... agree not to supply any other dealer or dealers at less than retail prices under any circumstances.......... also agree not to present, or otherwise include gratis, articles of value in the prices of these instruments, such as cases, instruction books, etc.

.... also agree to change said retail prices, in case it becomes necessary from time to time, to conform to the Manufacturers' retail lists, it being understood that a thirty days' notice of such changes shall be given, and that all changes shall be uniform to all dealers throughout the country. It is also understood as a consideration in this contract that LYON & HEALY will strictly adhere to the above prices in their sales to private and professional customers.

Dated this..................day of..........................191....

at..............................

Lyon & Healy

Signed..............................

All Washburn Instruments are guaranteed for one year from date of purchase; material or workmanship proving defective, the same will be made good by LYON & HEALY.

The above are our established RETAIL or PUPILS' PRICES. For List Prices and cost to dealer, see prices accompanying description of goods.

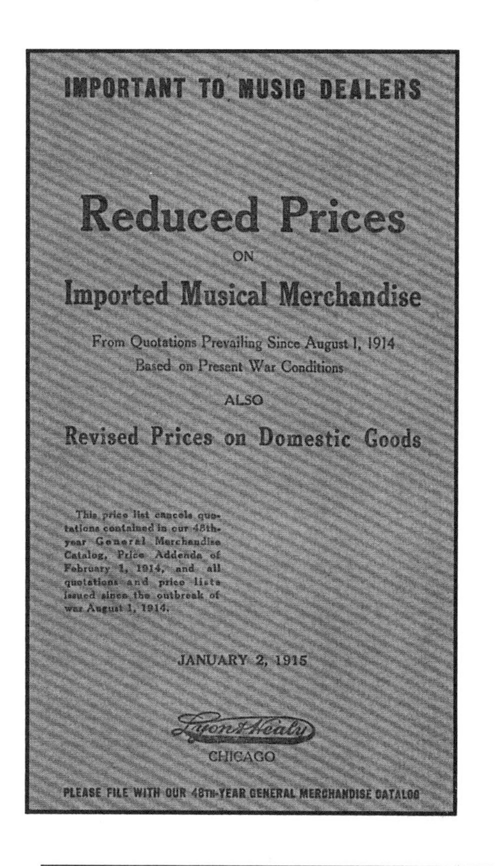

IMPORTANT TO MUSIC DEALERS

Reduced Prices

ON

Imported Musical Merchandise

From Quotations Prevailing Since August 1, 1914
Based on Present War Conditions

ALSO

Revised Prices on Domestic Goods

This price list cancels quotations contained in our 48th-year General Merchandise Catalog, Price Addenda of February 1, 1914, and all quotations and price lists issued since the outbreak of war August 1, 1914.

JANUARY 2, 1915

Lyon & Healy
CHICAGO

PLEASE FILE WITH OUR 48TH-YEAR GENERAL MERCHANDISE CATALOG

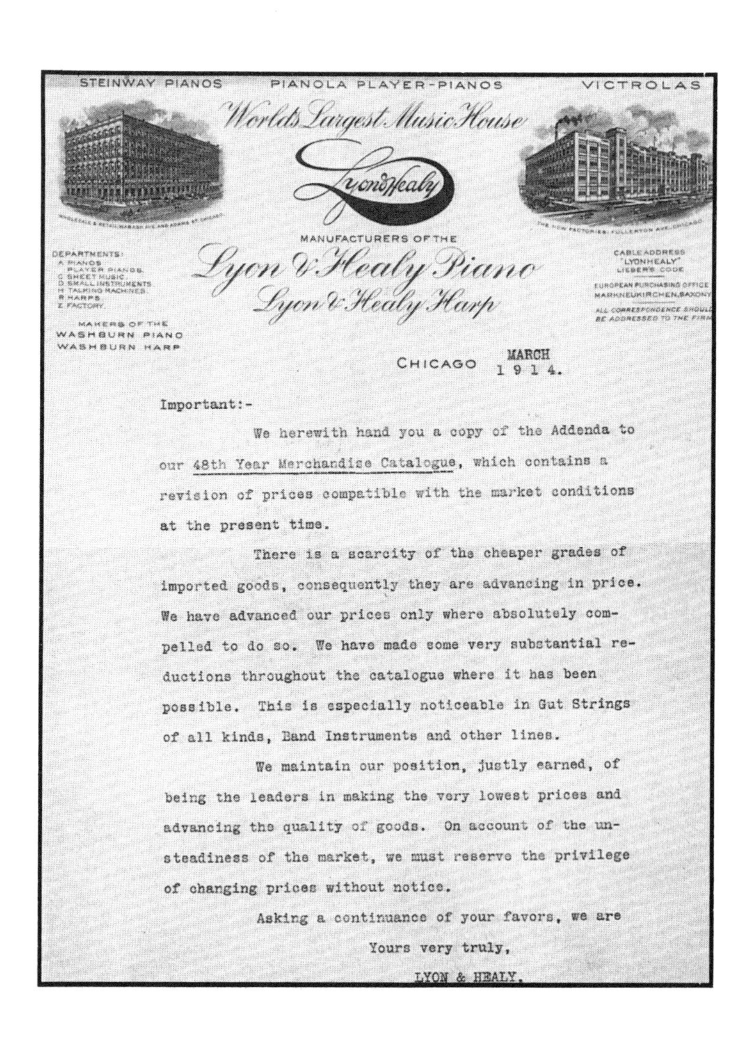

STEINWAY PIANOS PIANOLA PLAYER-PIANOS VICTROLAS

World's Largest Music House

Lyon & Healy

MANUFACTURERS OF THE
Lyon & Healy Piano
Lyon & Healy Harp

DEPARTMENTS:
A PIANOS
PLAYER PIANOS.
C SHEET MUSIC.
D SMALL INSTRUMENTS
H TALKING MACHINES.
R HARPS
Z FACTORY.

MAKERS OF THE
WASHBURN PIANO
WASHBURN HARP

CABLE ADDRESS
"LYONHEALY"
LIEBER'S CODE

EUROPEAN PURCHASING OFFICE
MARKNEUKIRCHEN, SAXONY

ALL CORRESPONDENCE SHOULD BE ADDRESSED TO THE FIRM

CHICAGO MARCH 1914.

Important:-

We herewith hand you a copy of the Addenda to our 48th Year Merchandise Catalogue, which contains a revision of prices compatible with the market conditions at the present time.

There is a scarcity of the cheaper grades of imported goods, consequently they are advancing in price. We have advanced our prices only where absolutely compelled to do so. We have made some very substantial reductions throughout the catalogue where it has been possible. This is especially noticeable in Gut Strings of all kinds, Band Instruments and other lines.

We maintain our position, justly earned, of being the leaders in making the very lowest prices and advancing the quality of goods. On account of the unsteadiness of the market, we must reserve the privilege of changing prices without notice.

Asking a continuance of your favors, we are

Yours very truly,

LYON & HEALY.

The Last Of Healy's "Captians"

James F. Bowers
President, 1918-1921

Marquette A. Healy
President, 1921-1925

Raymond E. Durham
President, 1925-1939

Following James Bower's retirement, Marquette A. Healy became the third and final Healy to head the company. He had been with the firm for nearly twenty years, running the enormous piano department. This section of Lyon & Healy would have been a good sized business by itself between the factory, the huge floor of pianos available to the public and midwest distributorship for a number of major brands.

Times were good in the Roaring '20s for Chicago and the giant store on the Loop, which moved a tremendous volume of goods. Band instruments for school programs, sheet music for the popular songs of the radio (and the radios to hear them on), records (and the phonographs to play them on), whole sets of drums (a relatively new idea for the time); these were just a few of the retail items that were making Lyon & Healy great profits.

The Washburn line of banjos, ukuleles and guitars were doing well, the mandolins were holding on, but the competition and profit margins of manufacturing instruments compared to retailing them would start the company on a new course by the end of the decade. Marquette Healy retired in 1927, "to devote more time to travel," following twenty-five years of service. He was the last of Patrick Healy's "captains." Like all the previous Presidents, Marquette had come up through the ranks and felt the positive influence of the company's founder.

A relative newcomer succeeded Healy as President in 1927, one Raymond E. Durham. Though never officially mentioned, it appears he was married to the daughter of former Lyon & Healy President Robert Gregory. According to later company history, Durham's promotion occurred in 1925, but the trade magazines noted Marquette Healy's retirement in July of '27. An article in the December '26 issue of Musical Merchandise magazine referred to Durham as Vice President and General Manager. Most relevant to Washburn was an article from April of '27 describing the mass production techniques used in their construction. The article discussed the new stringed instrument factory, taken over in June of '26, with 60,000 square feet of floor space. If Durham had become President in '25, there would *not* have been a new factory in 1926!

Sale of the Manufacturing Division

Raymond Durham's vision for the future of Lyon & Healy had no room for the building or wholesaling of Washburns. Retailing was Durham's plan for the future, his idea being a Lyon & Healy music store in every city. With strategies similar to the corporate raiders of the 1980s, large sections of the company were sold off, starting with the manufacturing division. In April 1928 it was announced that Lyon & Healy was selling its equipment for making band instruments to the Holton Co. In May the company announced that Washburns would now be manufactured by the J.R. Stewart Co. of Chicago.

The sale included all the machinery and the rights to manufacture Washburns, which would be exclusively distributed by Lyon & Healy's wholesale department. This was really nothing new as Lyon & Healy had regularly contracted work out to other builders in the past, possibly even for some of the Washburns. An article from 1926 stated that besides its own factories, Lyon & Healy "absorbs the output of other factories in Chicago and other parts of the world." The Stewart-made Washburns would "remain identical in design and manufacture and all distinctive features of the Washburn line will be continued."

May, 1928

Stewart Acquires Huge New Factory

As a result of the growing demand for fretted musical instruments, the J. R. Stewart Co. have taken new quarters in Chicago where there will be 22,500 square feet of manufacturing space available. The Stewart Co. recently took over the machinery and patent rights of the Lyon & Healy Washburn line of stringed instruments.

The new Stewart factory is at the corner of Twenty-Second and Rockwell Streets, Chicago, in a modern three-story building. It is fully daylight construction and is laid out in the most efficient manufacturing arrangement.

J. R. Stewart organized his business on a small scale about three years ago and his rapid success is a tribute to his energy and skillful ability in manufacturing and marketing quality instruments. A year after his first instrument was made, he had to greatly enlarge his factory and now he is in charge of one of the largest plants devoted to stringed instruments. The company manufactures a full line of fretted musical instruments.

Stewart had started his business in 1925, building ukuleles. The LeDomino line of ukuleles, with dominoes stenciled on the face of the instruments, had become a trendy little item, necessitating a larger factory for the company.

With the Washburn machinery and his ukulele company's, Stewart moved into a new 22,000 square foot factory. Whether the workers were former Washburn builders is unsure, but the instruments appear to have made the transition with no major problems.

May, 1928

Stewart to Manufacture Washburn Line

Following the new developments in Lyon & Healy announced in last month's Musical Merchandise, the entire line of Washburn stringed instruments will in future be manufactured by the J. R. Stewart Co., Chicago, and exclusively distributed by Lyon & Healy. This is in line with the Lyon & Healy policy of discontinuing all manufacturing endeavor excepting in the field of harps.

Patent rights for the manufacture of the Washburn instruments, manufacturing machinery, tools, dies and jigs have been sold to the Stewart Company. The instruments will remain identical in design and manufacture and all distinctive features of the Washburn line will be continued.

Lyon & Healy recently closed their La Porte factory and sold the machinery for the manufacture of band instruments to the Frank Holton Co.

ANOTHER factor that will be of great assistance in increasing business is the creation of the new Lyon & Healy chain store system. This well-known organzation is confining its energies to retail distribution and into the formation of a national chain of music stores. We feel sure that these stores will show a marked increase in the volume of musical instruments.

Sale of the Wholesale Division

Much goes on behind closed doors during major business transactions and whether J.R. Stewart was aware of Lyon & Healy's next phase when he bought the Washburn machinery is uncertain. In August of '28, just three months after Stewart and Lyon & Healy signed their exclusive wholesale distribution contract for all the Washburns made, it was announced that Lyon & Healy's entire wholesale division had been sold to the Tonk Bros. Co. of Chicago! Whether this was known in advance, as part of Raymond Durham's grand scheme, or came as a surprise to Stewart is unclear. Fortunately, perhaps, Tonk Bros., who had acquired the rights to the Washburn name, and Stewart would continue the relationship started with Lyon & Healy. This arrangement left Lyon & Healy with its retail store and harp manufacturing division, Stewart with a new partner for the Washburns, and Tonk Bros. as the largest wholesaler in the country. The Lyon & Healy store would continue to sell Washburns, but whether they bought them from Stewart or Tonk Bros. is a mystery. By 1930 Lyon & Healy catalogs featured both Washburn and Martin guitars and in 1934 a giant window display at the Lyon & Healy headquarters featured only the Martins, with no sign of any Washburns.

22 MUSICAL MERCHANDISE *August, 1928*

Tonk Buys Lyon & Healy Wholesale Division

Lyon & Healy, Inc., Chicago, have sold that portion of their wholesale business including small goods and tuners' supplies, to the Tonk Bros. Company, also of Chicago. Lyon & Healy, Inc., has been undergoing extensive reorganization during the past three years. Within that time, there have been important additions to the personnel, the retail premises have been completely remodeled, they have disposed of their piano, band instrument and string instrument factories. Now, with

Paul Moennig

the announcement of the disposal of their wholesale small goods departments, the reorganization of the company is fully completed.

Lyon & Healy, Inc., will continue to operate the wholesale piano, radio and sheet music departments, and to manufacture the famous Lyon & Healy Harp, which is dominent throughout the world. Meanwhile, Lyon & Healy's retail activities have been expanding through the enlargement and opening of branch stores in Chicago and Evanston, and the recent purchase of the Dreher Piano Company in Cleveland, where Lyon & Healy will operate a complete music store.

Tonk Bros. Company was organized in 1893, and is under the able management of Paul Moennig, who has been in charge of the business for the last 15 years. The company has grown rapidly and met with marked success. The transfer by Lyon & Healy of their wholesale small goods interest, which will now be owned and operated exclusively by Tonk Bros. Company, will make the latter concern the largest wholesale musical jobbing house in the United States.

Mr. Moennig, who will direct Tonk Bros. Company's expanded interests, was born in Markneukirchen, Germany, where for generations the Moennig family have been engaged in the manufacture of musical merchandise. Upon his first coming to Chicago, Mr. Moennig began work with Lyon & Healy and he has been in the musical instrument business continuously during his entire business career. He took complete charge of the Tonk Bros. Company 15 years ago when only 21 years old and no concern in their line of business has made more progress and won greater success. Mr. Moennig's ability is widely known throughout the trade. Tonk Bros. Company has enjoyed an enviable reputation for integrity and fair dealing and Lyon & Healy can be congratulated upon being able to place the interests disposed of in the hands of a concern with so promising a future.

Tonk Bros.

Tonk Bros. had started in Chicago in 1893, headed by Charles J. Tonk (1856-1918). In 1913 Tonk retired, turning the operation over to a twenty-one year old gentleman named Paul Moennig. Moennig (later Monnig) was born in Markneukirchen, Germany, the European center for musical merchandise. His family had been in the musical instrument business for many generations and Paul was actually born in a violin factory! He would run Tonk Bros. until 1947 when it merged with Continental Music. Tonk Bros. became the country's largest "jobber," or wholesaler, shortly after acquiring Lyon & Healy's wholesale division in 1928 and the Artophone wholesale company of St. Louis in 1929. Their network at one time included over 7,000 dealers.

By the end of 1928 Tonk Bros. issued a hardcover dealer catalog that featured the unchanged Washburn line. Times were good and Tonk Bros. boasted of 5,600 orders filled in June of '29, with 98.5% of them filled the same day as received. In September the orders filled increased to 7,200. Then came October of '29 and Black Friday. Things would change drastically.

Bankruptcy of Stewart

The Great Depression hit fast and it hit hard. Of all the businesses involved with Washburn in the 1928 changeover, the young J.R. Stewart Co. fared the worst. Having overextended itself with a new factory, and the payroll and mortgage to go along with it, the five year old company had nothing to fall back on. The exclusive Washburn contract probably had no minimum order requirement, leaving Stewart's future totally in Tonk Bros. hands. Tonk Bros., unsure of the near future, held off ordering, leaving Stewart to deal with an unsympathetic bank.

In March 1930, the J.R. Stewart Co., makers of the world famous Washburn Guitars, had no one to sell them to and went into receivership. The company was put up for sale but no one made a satisfactory bid, including Stewart's "partner" in the Washburns, Tonk Bros.

Bankruptcy was declared and the assets were then auctioned off with Tonk Bros. paying nickels on the dollar for the existing stock as well as the Stewart and LeDomino trade names. Tonk Bros. held on to their Washburn name, but sold the Stewart and LeDomino trade names to the Regal Musical Instrument Co. of Chicago. Regal immediately announced that it was manufacturing and selling the Stewart and LeDomino brand instruments. J.R. Stewart, like many American small businessmen, was left with nothing. They even took his name.

April 1930

Stewart Co., in Bankruptcy, Business Is for Sale

A receiver has been appointed for the firm of J. R. Stewart Co., Chicago, Ill., manufacturers of fretted musical instruments. The business is for sale and all bids will be received by receiver Frank M. McKey at his office up to nine-thirty o'clock in the forenoon of Thursday, April 3rd, 1930. In the event no satisfactory bid is received the business will be sold at auction for the benefit of creditors.

May 1930

Tonk Bros. Buy Stewart Co. at Receiver Sale

Paul Monnig, head of Tonk Bros. Co., Chicago, leading Mid-Western jobbers and importers of musical merchandise, purchased all of the stock and trade-mark names of the defunct J. R. Stewart Co. of Chicago.

Mr. Monnig sold to the Regal Musical Insrument Co., Chicago, the manufacturing and selling rights of the popular trade-mark names Le Domino and Stewart for ukuleles, guitars, tenor-banjos, banjo-mandolins and other string musical instruments.

Regal Now Makes and Sells LeDomino and Stewart Lines

The Regal Musical Instrument Co., Chicago, has sent out a notice to the trade to the effect that they are now manufacturing and selling the Le Domino and Stewart lines of fretted musical instruments.

Max Monnig, Bud of Paul, To Sail on Bremen, May 18

Max Monnig of the firm of Tonk Bros. Co., Chicago, jobbers and wholesale distributors of everything in musical merchandise, will sail for Europe on the Bremen, May 18th. Mr. Monnig will visit the leading countries of Europe and hopes to return to his office in about two months. Max Monnig is the brother of Paul Monnig, the trade's most popular and best-thought-of "guy" in the big windy city of Chicago.

Regal

The history of the Regal Instrument Co. is nearly as convoluted and misunderstood as that of Washburn and the two companies' paths crossed on a number of occasions. A whole book could be devoted to just this company. Prior to WWII Regal built hundreds of thousands of instruments, most bearing the brandnames of others. After the war they did not fare as well and in 1954 fixtures and tradename were sold to Harmony of Chicago who used the name on a line of lower-priced instruments. In the late-'50s, Fender licensed the name for a series of Harmony-made flattops and acoustic electric hollow bodies. This arrangement and the use of the Regal name ended in the mid-'60s when Fender began building their own flattops and the Coronado series. A line of imported resonators have appeared recently bearing the Regal name.

It's what Regal did before WWII that makes it a major part of the Washburn history. And one of the most confusing. The line was started by an Indianapolis retailer/wholesaler named Emil Wulschner in the 1880s. In the early 1890s his stepson became the "Son" in Wulschner & Son. A factory was opened c.1896 to build guitars and mandolins under the Regal, University and 20th Century names. At the time of Wulschner's death in 1900 the company employed close to one hundred workers. The factory became part of a larger corporation and when the economy floundered a few years into the new century, the moneymen bailed out. This was the end of the original Regals.

Martin made half as many guitars in 1904 and 1905 as in the preceding and following years and a number of other companies folded, including Thompson & Odell of Boston, who had made thousands of instruments since 1887 and the John Brandt Musical Instrument Co. of Chicago, which was purchased by Lyon & Healy. Brandt would continue to build instruments, particularly bowlback mandolins, but as an employee of Lyon & Healy. A satirical Gibson ad from 1908 claimed their thin bodied mandolins were responsible for a number of companies going out of business, including Regal and Brandt. It's doubtful the eighteen-month old Gibson had much to do with Regal or Brandt going out of business in 1904.

In November 1904 Lyon & Healy purchased thousands of Regals; completed instruments, the work in progress, a

stockpile of raw materials and the company's trade names. What Lyon & Healy did with Regal the next few years is unclear. They retired their own Marquette, Columbus and Arion brands of budget instruments that had been named after three of Healy's children. The Lakeside, Jupiter and American Conservatory lines were also temporarily discontinued. Replacing them were the College Line instruments, much more like the Washburns of the time. In 1908 there was a new Regal company based in Chicago and probably tied to Lyon & Healy, who would have had no apparent reason to simply sell the name off. Around this time the College Line was retired and the student-quality Lakeside, Jupiter and American Conservatory lines returned to Lyon & Healy's line of guitars.

Regal marketed ukuleles, and in the '20s the new Tiples and tenor guitars, but supposedly no six strings. That Regal made guitars for other companies in the teens and '20s is generally accepted, the name being associated with Bruno, Weyman, Stahl and others. The double neck Lyon & Healy American Conservatory models are seen with other brand names and are usually regarded as Regal-made. Around the time of Washburn's deal with J.R. Stewart, Regal announced their own six-string guitars, to be sold through an exclusive group of jobbers that included Tonk Bros. in Chicago, Grossman in Cleveland, Ditson in Boston and Carl Fischer in New York. Perhaps there had been an agreement between Lyon & Healy and Regal not to compete in the six-string market.

There was very little difference between mid-'20s Washburns "made in the Lyon & Healy Factory," the models of 1928-1930 made by J.R. Stewart, and the early-'30s Tonk Bros. models which were almost certainly made by Regal. There are rumors that a fire at the Washburn factory in the early '20s stopped production and that all the instruments that followed were Regal made, but this seems doubtful. Were the same craftsmen bounced from factory to factory? If Regal had built Washburns for Lyon & Healy and later, Tonk Bros., what happened between 1928 and 1930?

By the mid-'30s, Regal was licensing Dobro resonators for use in a line of guitars, and following National-Dobro's move to Chicago, Regal acquired the rights to manufacture and market all the Dobro brand instruments. The engraved Dobros, the Regal Esquire, Prince, Troubadour and Bacon & Day Ne Plus Ultra archtops, the big bodied Washburn No. 5257 1/2 flattops and the high-end Washburn banjos show the quality of instruments Regal was capable of building in the '30s. In 1938 the company announced it was joining the name brand guitar builders that sold direct to dealers. This policy could possibly have led to temporary changes in the later Tonk Bros.-era Washburn design and production, however, the last Washburns also appear to have been Regal-made.

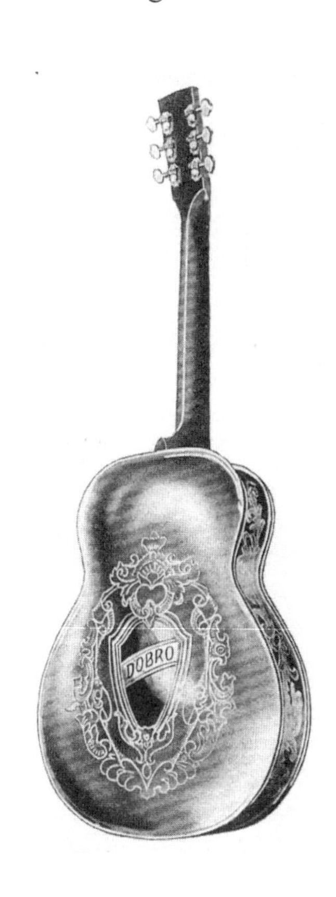

May 1929

Regal Musical Instrument Co.

A first showing of Regal custom built mandolins will be made at the Hotel Drake, rooms 208 and 209, by the Regal Musical Instrument Co., Chicago, Ill., manufacturers. In addition to this latest creation in the fretted instrument business a complete line of Regal custom built guitars will be exhibited as well as several styles of Octophones and their regular lines of tenor-guitars and banjos. A. Hunter, vice-president of the Regal Musical Instrument Co., will be in charge of this elaborate exhibit. A real surprise will be awaiting those dealers visiting the Regal Musical Instrument Co.'s display.

The End

With the addition of Lyon & Healy's wholesale division, Tonk Bros. had become a giant in the musical instrument world and the prestigious Washburn name added an element of credibility to the company's offerings. The long-running Sterling brand of inexpensive student instruments had previously been Tonk Bros. top-of-the-line. In the 1928 & 1930 hard-bound "counter copy" catalogs, which offered the complete Tonk Bros. line, the Washburn instruments were proudly displayed, with some models given entire pages. Even considering this preferential treatment, fifteen of every sixteen pages in the 250 page book were for "non-Washburn" items. By 1935 twenty-four of every twenty-five pages were for "non-Washburn" items, showing what a small role the high-quality instruments played in the day-to-day operation at Tonk Bros.

Looking back, it seems inevitable that Washburn would flounder under the circumstances. Tonk Bros. was simply not dedicated to promotion or research and development. When Tonk Bros. advertised, they advertised themselves, occasionally listing the availability of the Washburn line (along with numerous others), rarely the individual instruments. The actual builder of the Washburns was kept secret from the public, therefore it would have been inappropriate for them (Regal, etc.) to advertise. The last chance for exposure was the local retailer, and most of these across the country were "mom and pop" operations, unable to provide a quality ad for such a small part of their business. Besides, many of the guitar companies were running major advertising campaigns during the '30s, with Gibson, Epiphone, Gretsch, Vega, National and others regularly taking large ads in music magazines such as Downbeat and Metronome, as well as the trade magazines.

Orders for Washburns, not surprisingly, dwindled. Tastes had changed and the instruments hadn't. The introduction of Washburn archtops and big body flattops in the mid-'30s came too late. The apparent involvement of the Gibson company (and possibly Harmony) around this time, no matter how inconsequential, implies Tonk Bros. was no longer totally satisfied with their arrangement with Regal. Gibson records reportedly show an association between the two companies but whether the products went any further than the prototype stage is unclear. Production would have to have been very low due to today's lack of existing examples. The last Washburns appear to have been Regal-made and not in large quantities. Whether it was the war that stopped production (as with all guitar manufacturers), or that Tonk Bros. gave up on the line, it appears the Washburn instruments were retired with absolutely no fanfare, bringing to an unceremonious end a long, rich tradition.

In the late '30s, the "Purchasers Guide to the Music Industries," which lists trade names, dealers, and retail stores, showed a listing for Tonk Bros. that included Washburn. The listing ran unchanged every year until 1942, being replaced with a differently worded one, again mentioning Washburn. This listing ran unchanged through 1947 when Tonk Bros. merged with Continental Music, the wholesale division of C.G. Conn. (January 2, 1947). Continental's listing for 1947 read "now exclusive dealer for . . . Sterling and Fascinator fretted instruments . . ." The Sterling and Fascinator instruments were long-running Tonk exclusives implying the Continental listing was up to date and official. A March 1947 ad for Continental also listed Sterling and Fascinator instruments, again with no mention of Washburn. This seems to imply that Continental chose not to revive the Washburn line or that Paul Monnig of Tonk Bros. had held on to the name . . .

Another section of the Purchasers Guide listed trademark names and their associated companies. The Sterling and Fascinator names were shown with Tonk Bros. through 1947 and Continental from 1948 through at least the mid-'50s, once again implying the list was accurate. From the '30s through 1947 the Washburn trademark was shown for Tonk Bros. as would be expected. However, from 1943 to 1947 the Washburn trademark was also assigned to Lyon & Healy! In 1948 and 1949, following Continental's purchase of Tonk Bros., the Washburn name was shown for Lyon & Healy only, no Tonk Bros., no Continental. Starting in 1950 there was no listing for Washburn. It would seem odd for Lyon & Healy to have bought the Washburn trademark back and not done anything with it. It appears that Tonk Bros. had only licensed the name but never really owned it. The consensus today among collectors and cognoscenti is that no Washburns were made between WWII and the early seventies.

Post-Washburn Lyon & Healy

As for Lyon & Healy, Raymond Durham would head the company until his death in 1939. Looking back at his decision to streamline the company in '28, it seems as though he had predicted the events of '29 and saved the giant from being hit triply hard. When Black Friday came, all but the retail stores and the harp factory had been converted to cash, a commodity that would soon be very hard to come by. Although the Depression slowed things down, Lyon & Healy did manage to open retail stores in (besides Cleveland, 1928) New York (1930), Los Angeles (1933), Omaha (1935), Akron, Dayton, and St. Paul (1937), Columbus (1938), Youngstown, Davenport, Rockford and Lafayette (1939) as well as a number of suburban Chicago branches of the downtown headquarters.

Around 1935 Gibson's first amplifier, the EH-150, was designed at Lyon & Healy by one of it's employees, John Kutalek. The experimenting may have taken place in the company's extensive repair shop which, considering Lyon & Healy's policy of repairing everything they sold, undoubtedly was equipped to fix radios and phonographs. According to Alvino Rey, "Gibson wanted to devise some electric instruments and they put up a laboratory in the Lyon & Healy warehouse for us to experiment with pickups and design a steel guitar." Noted expert Andre Duchossoir writes in his book *Gibson Electrics*, "The making of the amp nonetheless remained entrusted to Lyon & Healy" and "(the EH-150 steel guitar) sold for $150 as a complete outfit with a matching namesake amp built by Lyon & Healy." Where and by whom the production models were made is not totally clear. A company history published in 1964, however, stated, "Lyon & Healy temporarily entered into the manufacture of radio amplifiers for the armed forces . . . This was done so effectively that in 1944 the company received the Army-Navy 'E' award for its efforts."

Durham was succeeded by Louis G. LaMair who had been Vice President and General Manager since 1932. LaMair would become President of both NAMM and the American Music Conference, which he co-founded. He set up the Education Division to encourage band programs and classes, as well as private lessons through the stores. LaMair retired after thirteen years, being followed for a short period by Mark S. Massel, the company's attorney. In 1953 R. Gregory Durham, son of Raymond Durham and grandson of Robert Gregory, became President, a position he held until 1977. In 1964 the company employed 425 people and operated thirteen stores. The harp division was still building the finest in the world. A giant anniversary bash was held, featuring entertainment by Johnny Smith and a feast for the employees and their families, as well as the press. One hundred years after opening the tiny sheet music shop on the corner of two muddy streets it looked like the company would last a hundred more . . .

The '70s saw the retail music business turn into a cut throat market, with huge discounts expected and technology changing faster than most stores could keep up with. A number of Lyon & Healy's suburban stores closed in the mid-'70s and in August 1977 the entire company was purchased by CBS Musical Instruments. Within a few years all the stores were closed including the headquarters at the corner of Wabash and Jackson which had served the Chicago area since 1916. CBS let the harp division run itself at the old factory on Ogden Avenue, finally selling it in 1985 to the Swiss concern LAM who own it today. The Lyon & Healy harp is to this day one of the world's greatest musical treasures and the skilled hands that build them represent a true American tradition. No one could be prouder of their work than the l group of craftsmen that carry on the legacy of what was once "The World's Largest Music House," Lyon & Healy.

Louis G. LaMair
President, 1939-1952

R. Gregory Durham
President, 1953-

The Seventies

The Washburn name resurfaced in 1974, following an extended period of nonuse. Ads in the trade magazines for a Beckmen Musical Instruments, Inc. promoted a line of guitars, mandolins and banjos bearing the traditional Washburn name. No mention of the country of origin was made in the ads or of a full-sized catalog published that year. A small range of Dreadnought Flattops started with a basic plywood body, adjustable bridge model and ran up to a solid wood construction D-45 copy. These guitars were made in Japan by the Tarada company and were similar to the lower priced Venturas etc. on the bottom end and the better quality Tamas, etc. on the high end. A pair of mandolins and a small line of 5-string banjos, similar to the Iidas, etc. completed the offerings. Most of the instruments had the 1930s style Washburn logo inlaid into the peghead. Standard 1970s imports, no more, no less.

Beckmen Musical Instruments, Inc. of 2925 S. Vail, Los Angeles, CA was started in July of 1972 by Thomas L. Beckmen to distribute the Boosey & Hawkes brand of woodwinds. In 1973 they acquired the rights to the Camco Drum Co., and shortly thereafter, the Washburn name. The company's big success however, was their

partnership as U.S. distributor for the Japanese electronics firm Roland. "Rolandcorp U.S." was soon operating out of the S. Vail address and would go on to become a HUGE business in the 1980s.

To devote his energies to Roland, Beckmen sold the rights to the Washburn name to a small Chicago business call Fretted Industries Inc. An agreement was made on December 20th, 1976 to turn over the existing inventory of guitars, parts, promotional supplies, etc. on January 21, 1977. At the time, reported annual sales figures were approximately $300,000 for between two and three thousand instruments. This was the humble beginnings of the modern Washburn company.

Fretted Industries, Inc. was a small wholesaling project that operated out of the Soundpost Music Store, located at 101 W. Prospect, Mt. Prospect, Illinois. This was actually the second Soundpost, having opened in 1972. The first had been opened in 1970 by a musician named Rick Johnstone and an instrument builder named Rudy Schlacher. These two would run Washburn for ten years, with Schlacher finally buying Johnstone out, the company now being run by Schlacher and his family. Annual sales figures are currently approaching the $60,000,000 mark for approximately 200,000 instruments!

The first product marketed by Fretted Industries was a line of guitar strings called Nashville Straights, released in 1974 and packaged in long boxes. This method kept the strings free from the damages normally incurred by coiling them to fit into standard packets. Good reviews in Guitar Player Magazine brought the company moderate success. The next item was called the FretSling, which was a guitar strap cut in a shape that helped distribute the weight of the instrument more evenly.

Following the purchase of Washburn, the remaining instruments from Beckmen were sold and a new line was drawn up. These were built by a number of different Japanese, and later Korean, builders, depending on the grade. A brand new headstock logo distinguished the new models and the old George Washburn logo of a belt surrounding a guitar was again burned into the back stripe on the inside of the guitars. These instruments were of a noticeably better quality than the preceding models.

Classical guitars were added to the line, ranging from handmade solid wood versions based on the designs of Ignacio Fleta and Hermann Hauser, to mid-priced plywood models. The banjos were upgraded and featured two new professional quality five strings, a raised head model and the B-16 flathead. The B-16 was endorsed by John Hartford and is still offered, basically unchanged, close to twenty years later. The mandolin line featured the first signature models, the Jethro Burns Standard and Deluxe. To accommodate expansion, space was leased at 1234 Sherman Avenue, Evanston, Illinois.

The new company put their cards on the table in their first catalog, released in 1978, writing, "Our designs are translated by Japan's most experienced craftsmen assuring the consistent quality and workmanship for which they are known." This was at a time when the American guitar-making craft had dropped to an all time low and guitars by Japanese companies such as Ibanez and Yamaha were beginning to be used by a growing number of professionals. Washburns first electric guitars, the Wing Series solid bodies, were released later that

year. These featured a number of popular designs and up-to-date, for 1978, hardware, including neck through body construction, brass nut and saddles, push-pull volume controls/coil taps and exposed coil pickups. Early endorsers included Randy California of Spirit, Jim Peterik of Survivor and Randy Hansen. The use of artist endorsements, a practice started by Washburn in the 1880s, would play a most important role for the company in the 1980s.

Fretted Industries again moved to larger quarters in late 1978, leasing a building at 1415 Waukegan Road, Northbrook, Illinois. The rapidly expanding business purchased the bankrupt Oscar Schmidt company in 1979, acquiring the rights to the Autoharp. This has been a steady seller for the company, mainly for use by schools and churches, and before Sears and Roebuck discontinued their catalog, the Autoharp was the longest running instrument it offered.

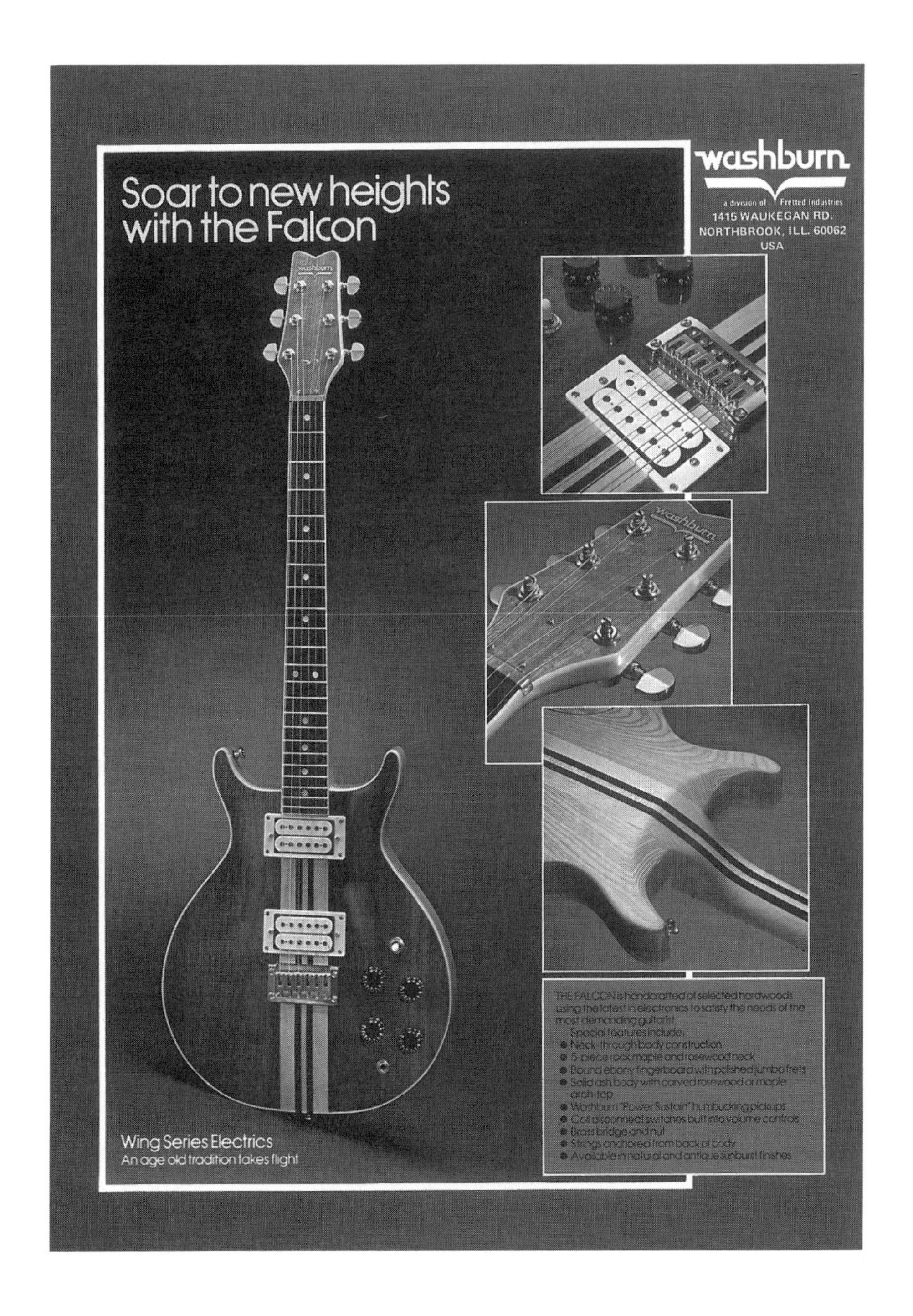

The Eighties

1980 saw the release of what is arguably the most trendsetting instrument the modern Washburn company has developed. The Festival Series of cutaway, thin-bodied flattops with built-in bridge pickups and controls, has gone on to become somewhat of a standard for live performances. The 12-string version was endorsed early-on by the well respected John Lodge of the Moody Blues, his gleaming white guitar showing up in concerts and advertisements for years. Countless Country and Rock artists have used these instruments over the last fifteen years, including Bob Dylan, Greg Allman, George Harrison and Jimmy Page, and the design has been copied by a number of other companies.

Chief designer of the new Washburns was co-owner Schlacher, who had been schooled in Austria, where he studied violin and guitar building for seven years. He received two degrees and achieved "master level" in constructing and repairing acoustic instruments. An appreciation of solid wood instruments led to an expanded line of higher grade flattops that changed the way many players looked at Washburn. In 1986 Mr. Page appeared on the cover of Guitar World with one of these and his brown B-Bender Tele, an unofficial endorsement that spoke volumes.

Using a destroyed Ramirez as a model, another handmade classical joined the Hauser and Fleta-inspired guitars. A fancier Wing Series electric, the all white Eagle, showed up in the hands of Nancy Wilson of Heart and John Goodsall of Brand X (shown in the catalog with Brand X drummer Phil Collins). Washburn now had a line of stringed instruments built to their own specifications and a rapidly growing number of credible endorsers. In less than five years, the company had become a major player in the international musical instrument trade. A network of dealers had been established in Australia, Canada, Denmark, U.K., France, Germany, Japan, Holland, Norway, Portugal, Sweden and Switzerland as well as the U.S. All this without having to invest in a factory . . . The reason this method of operation worked for Fretted Industries and not for Tonk Bros. is the new company was entirely devoted to developing a distinct line and keeping it up to date, finding reliable subcontractors to build them and working overtime on artists and promotions.

The remainder of the '80s saw the Washburn arrangement continue, with expansion in all directions. Thin semi-solid bodies, electric jazz boxes, outrageously shaped and colored Heavy Metal axes, solid body classicals and steel strings, electric basses, both solid and hollow . . . these were just a few of the new guitars. Besides their original designs, a number of models were basically copies of popular instruments (Les Pauls, Teles, etc.) and the company had licensing agreements with Steinberger and

Rob Green of the Status Bass, popular in England and Europe. The prices were about half that of an original. Besides the Washburn "Wonderbar" tremolo system, a number of popular hardware items were licensed and incorporated into Washburn guitars, including Floyd Rose Tremolos, Seymour Duncan Pickups and Stephen Davies' "Stephens Extended Cutaway." If it was currently popular, there was room in the line for it. Artist models were built for Rudy Szarzo (of Ozzie Osbourne and Quiet Riot) and Ace Frehley (Kiss), as the list of official and unofficial endorsers (users) continued to grow.

Branching out into amplifiers and P.A. systems, the company purchased BFI-SoundTech of Elkhart, Indiana in 1984. Manufacturing is still done in the same factory, with the offices now a part of Washburn headquarters. For a short time the English-made Laney amps were distributed by Washburn. Stompbox effects pedals and Washburn-brand strings were a few of the other extracurricular activities.

The company moved to bigger quarters at 230 Lexington Drive, Buffalo Grove, Illinois in 1985 and in 1987 changed the company's name to Washburn International. Around this time Rick Johnstone left the organization. As sole owner, Rudy Schlacher would continue his role designing instruments, ending the '80s with the release of the hollow body electric basses. These would become the standard "acoustic" basses in the '90s. At the end of the decade Washburn was a multi-million dollar international business with distributors all over the world.

The Moody Blues & Washburn
John Lodge Performs with the Washburn Festival Series
Tanglewood 12-String
The Festival acoustic electric guitar is intended to perform to the highest possible standards acoustically, and electrically without feedback, genuinely giving the best of both worlds.
Hand finished in the prestigious Washburn factories, their oval soundholes and florentine cutaways give a distinctive appearance, with the added ability to reach the higher register.
Washburn
Washburn Dept. F-G 1415 Waukegan Rd. Northbrook, IL 60062 USA
Photo: Lissa Wales

The quality of guitar building had greatly improved in the '80s, both in America and overseas. New ownership revived the slumping Gibson and Fender companies who both began making their best instruments in years. An interest in vintage guitars led both these companies and the venerable Martin Company to examine their old models and methods, which in turn brought on numerous reissues. The popularity of these guitars and Custom Shop models, as well as the success of better independent companies like Taylor and Jackson, showed that the public had high expectations for new instruments.

WAYNE'S WORLD STARS Mike Myers and Dana Carvey personally autographed 50 Washburn guitars given as a promotion for the film. Myers appears with a Washburn on each "Wayne's World" segment of TV's "Saturday Night Live."

Washburn Teams Up With *Wayne's World*

Washburn has been front-and-center on television's "Saturday Night Live" ever since the introduction of the popular segment "Wayne's World." Wayne, played by Mike Myers, appears in each segment with his Washburn electric guitar.

For the feature-length movie based on the TV segment, Washburn coordinated a national radio campaign, launched in 50 major markets and featuring a contest for listeners. The results were incredible, according to Washburn. Contest winners received tickets to their local *Wayne's World* premier and a Washburn guitar similar to the one used by Myers.

The winners' guitars were specially reworked in Washburn's Chicago factory and were personally signed by the film's stars, Myers and Dana Carvey. *Wayne's World* became the country's highest grossing film, and Washburn cites the film's success as a factor in achieving the most successful quarter in the company's history.

The Ninties

In the summer of 1991, Washburn began building guitars in America. Shortly thereafter the offices moved to 255 Corporate Woods Parkway, Vernon Hills, Illinois, just outside of Chicago. A small factory was opened on the north side Chicago to serve the company in a number of ways. Designed to build high-end electrics, the factory also became the home for the Research and Development Department allowing them to work closely with artists on custom instruments. This was done, not as a money making "custom shop," but for the learning experience and promotional rewards. Another reason for the factory was to test the waters, to experience the manufacturing process on a small level before diving in.

Once the basic operation was set up, including the hiring of staff, setting up a network of suppliers, etc., it was time to get serious. In March of 1993 Grover Jackson was hired to fine tune the operation. Jackson was responsible for the early Charvels and, of course, the Jackson guitars that had been considered "the" solid body guitar in the mid-80s. Having lost control of his own company by taking on partners for expansion, Grover had retired a frustrated man. The opportunity to work with a well-financed organization willing to invest in a brand new venture, enticed him to move from California to Chicago (where it is COLD in the winter!). The "partnership" appears to be working out great for both sides.

By July of 1993 the factory was producing their popular N4 Nuno Bettencourt model and by the start of 1994 the revised MG series guitars. These were soon joined by a pair of top-of-the-line basses.

By the NAMM show of '94, a few custom-made U.S. acoustic models began working their way into the line. Plans have now been made to open a brand new climate controlled, nine-million dollar facility in Mt. Julliette, Tennessee, just outside of Nashville, with production of acoustics and electrics set to begin there sometime in 1996. The plan is for more and more of the Washburn production to shift to Nashville, with guitars in the

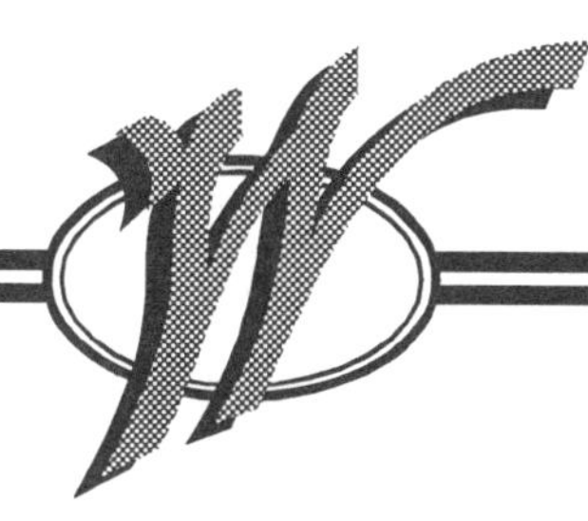

$800.00 to $5,000.00 range available in 1996 and eventually the entire line coming from Music City, USA.

With the recent acquisition of the Randall company, Washburn is looking to become a major player in the ever changing guitar amplifier field. Joining Washburn's line of small imported guitar amps (aimed at the student market), the Randall line will be used for a series of amps, professional in both size and sound. Tube and solid state models are currently being built at the SoundTech plant in Elkhart, which in recent years has been manufacturing power amplifiers and powered mixers, as well as speaker cabinets. Both SoundTech and Randall will end up in Nashville shortly, along with the first wave of full scale production U.S. made Washburn guitars. If these are anything like the models currently coming out of Chicago, Washburn International may achieve its unwritten goal: to become the largest musical instrument company in the world.

WASHBURN'S TV AD CAMPAIGN is now running nationwide in the U.S. and throughout Europe. The spots feature Greg Bennett, Washburn's director of marketing.

as an increase in the number of different spots.

Washburn Launches Nationwide TV Ad Campaign

Washburn began a nationwide television campaign in the U.S. this year, beginning in January, with a similar European campaign starting in April.

Last fall Washburn and key dealers in 50 markets worked together on a program to test the power of television advertising in each local market. The results were tremendous; overall sales experienced a major increase, and dealers experienced improved profit margins and an increase in the sale of high-ticket guitars. Based on these results, the national campaigns were scheduled.

Greg Bennett, director of marketing and featured artist in the commercials, commented, "After 13 million households turned into the Eric Clapton special on 'Unplugged' and saw the Washburn commercial, there was no doubting the power of television to create awareness and sales." Bennett foresees Washburn's continued expansion in television advertising as well

Photo Gallery

Prewar Instruments

49. Style 308. Non-original bridge courtesy Stan/Jay/Mandolin Bros. & Chinery Collection.
50. Presentation Model Guitar c.1900 courtesy Dave Stutzman/Stutzman's Guitar Center.
51. Presentation Model Guitar c.1910 courtesy Chinery Collection.
52. Deluxe Guitar c.1928 courtesy Washburn International.
53. Bell Guitar c.1928 courtesy San Werbin/Elderly Instruments.
54. Hawaiian Harp Guitar c.1928 courtesy Thom Humphrey/Ross Music photos: Roger Weston.
55. No. 5257 1/2 Guitar c.1936 courtesy Thom Humphrey/Ross Music photos: John Sprung.
56. No. 80 Mandolin c.1892 courtesy Jim Bollman/Guitar Emporium Lexington MA photos: John Sprung. No. 175 Mandolin c.1897 courtesy Scott Freilich/Top Shelf Music photo: Jim Fisch.
57. Left: Lyon & Healy Style C Mandolin c.1920 courtesy Rocky & Deb Blakewood. Center: Lyon & Healy No. 275 Mandolin Banjo c.1920 courtesy Rocky & Deb Blakewood Top right: Mandolin (model and year unknown) courtesy Washburn International. Bottom right: No. 1435 Mandolin c.1917 courtesy Washburn International.
58 & 59. Lyon & Healy Style A Mandolin c.1920 courtesy Rocky & Deb Blakewood.
Washburn Deluxe Mandolin c.1925 courtesy Rocky & Deb Blakewood.
Washburn Deluxe Mandolin c.1928 courtesy Thom Humphrey/Ross Music photos: John Sprung.
60. Lyon & Healy Professional Banjo c.1890 courtesy Jim Bollman/Guitar Emporium Lexington Ma photos: John Sprung.
61. Washburn Presentation Banjo c.1892 courtesy J.R. Westbrook.
62. Washburn Shrine Guitar, Tenor Guitar & Ukulele c.1927 courtesy Stan Werbin/Elderly Instruments.
63. Shrine c.1927, Super Deluxe c.1930 & Superb c.1935 Ukuleles courtesy Thom Humphrey/Ross Music photos: John Sprung.
64. Lyon & Healy Harp #501 c.1889 courtesy Lyon & Healy. Washburn Piano c.1912 courtesy Washburn International.

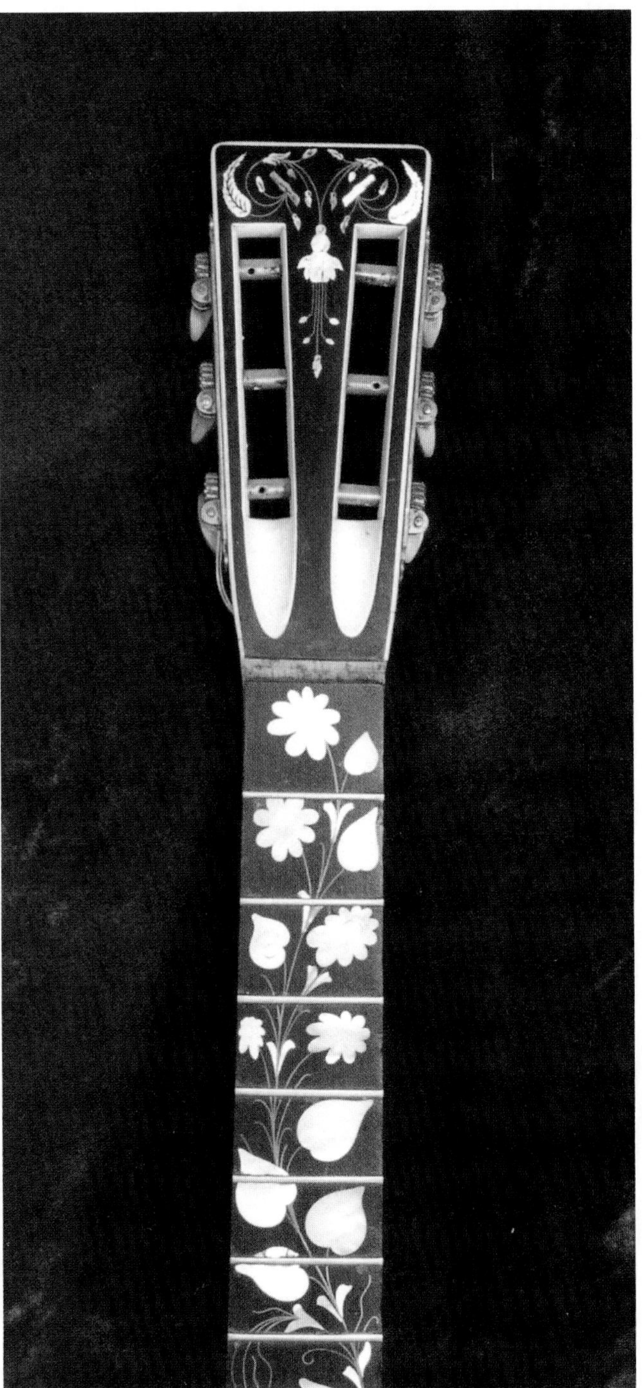

WASHBURN

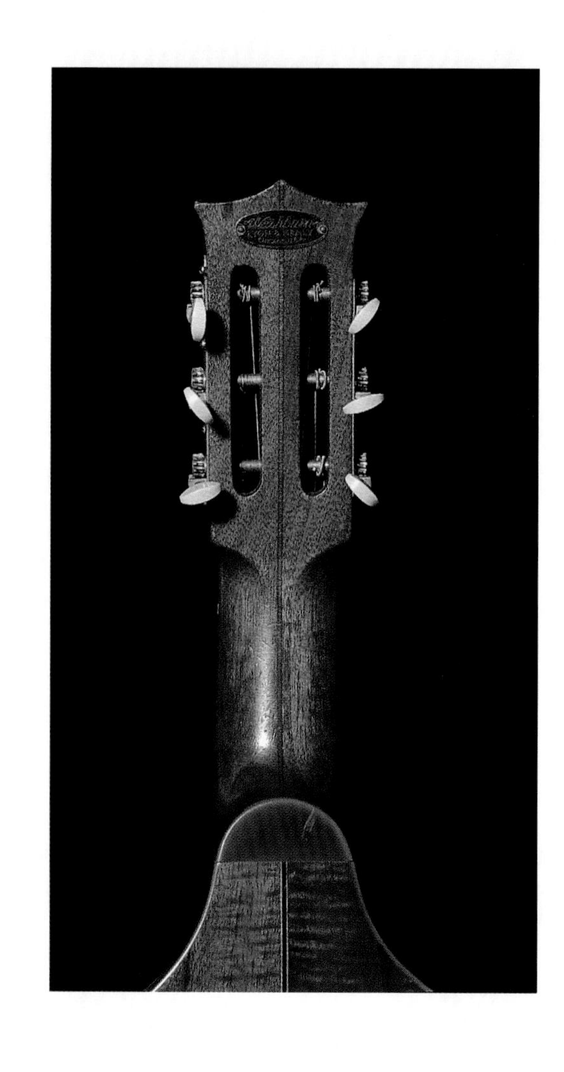

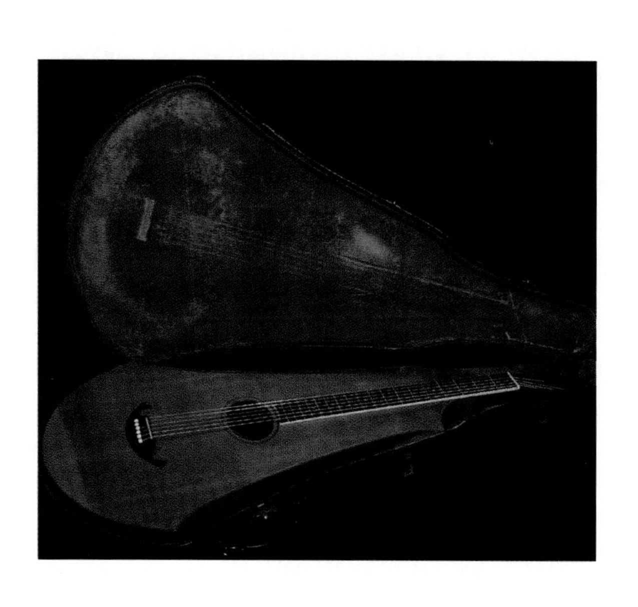

WASHBURN

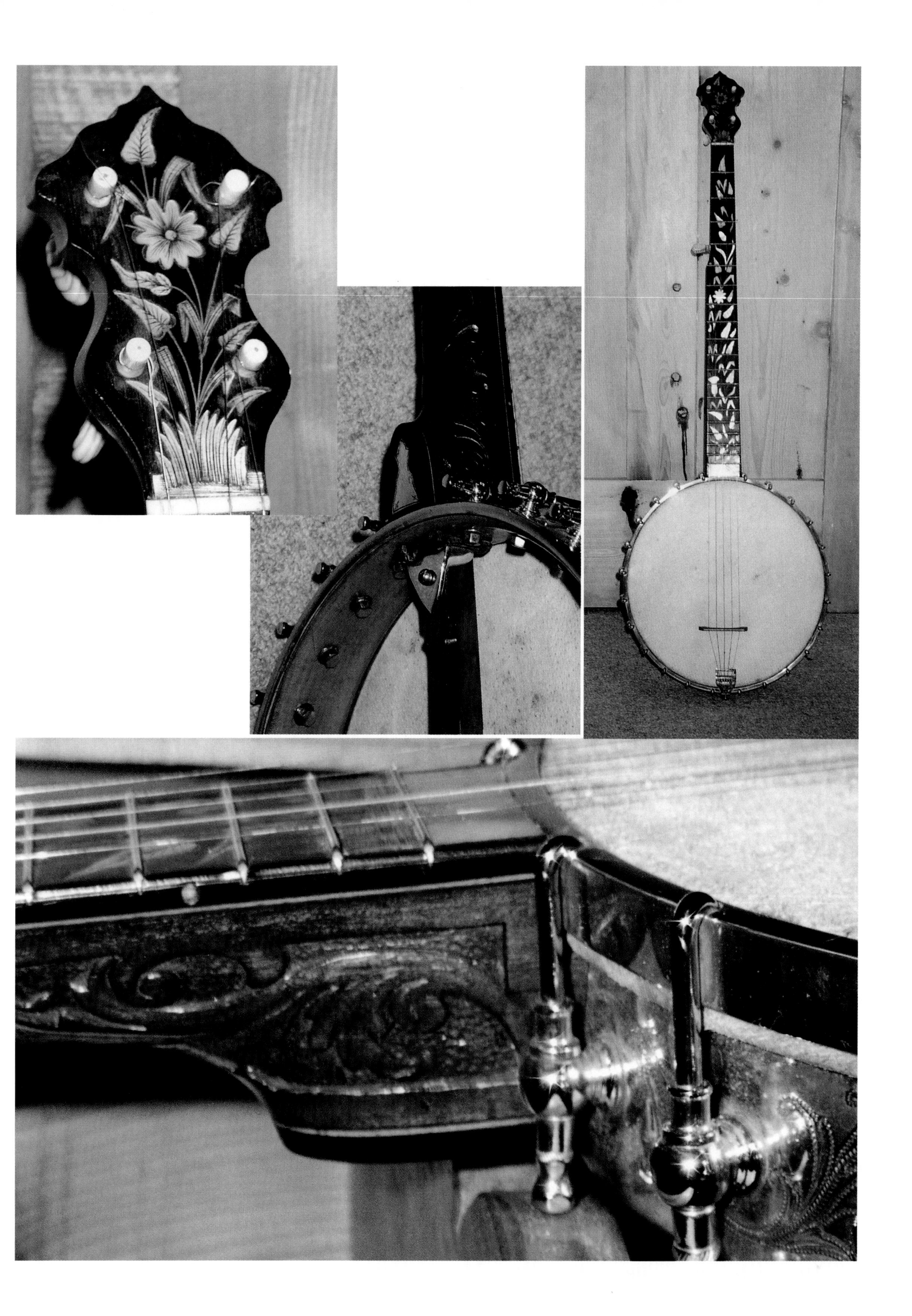

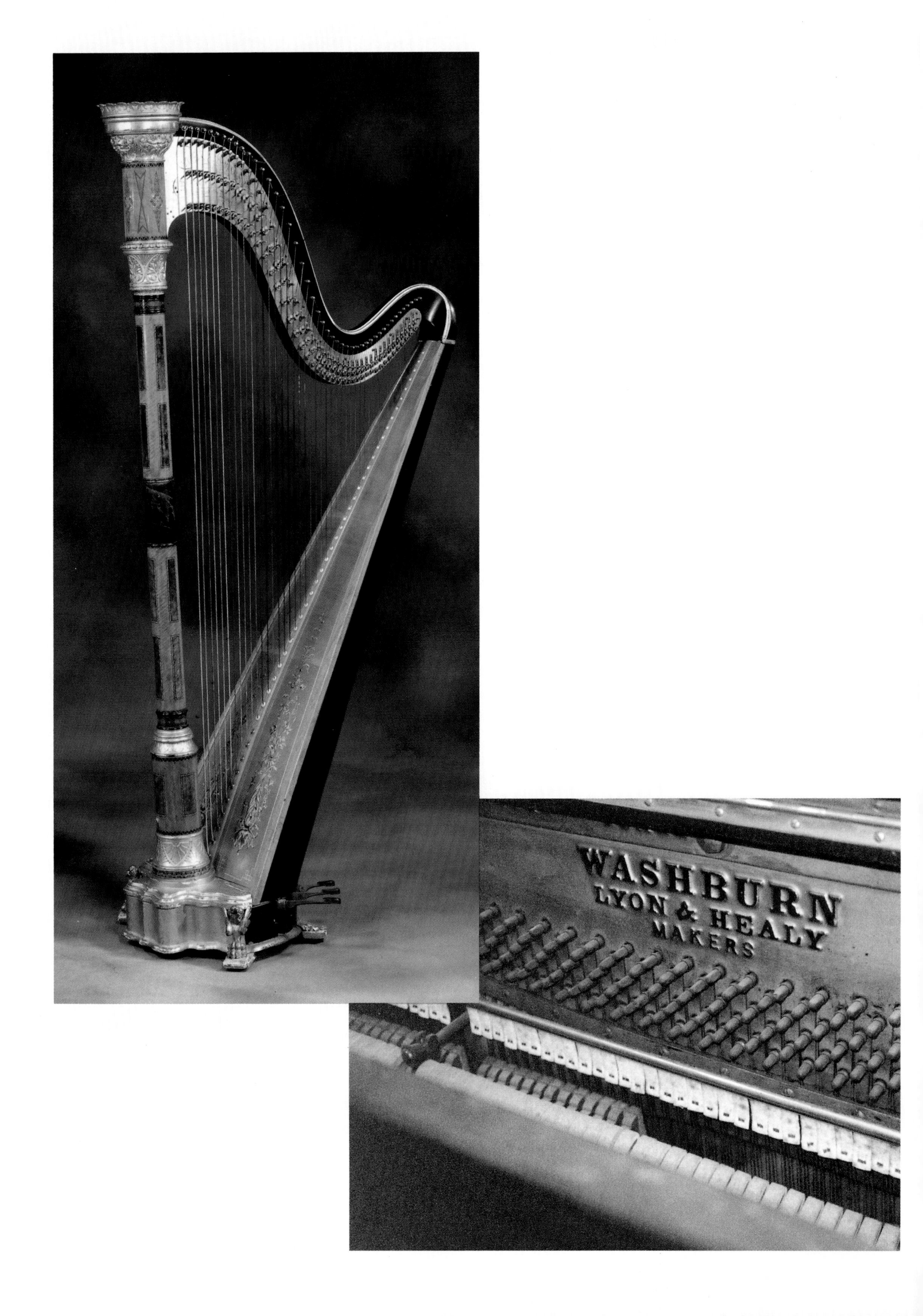
WASHBURN
LYON & HEALY
MAKERS

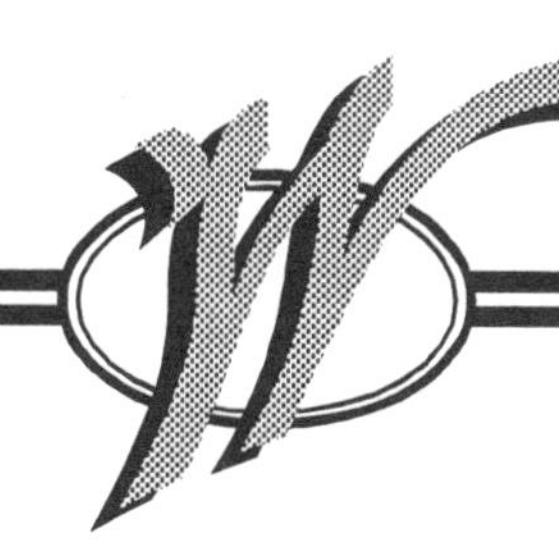

Prewar Instruments

Washburn Stringed Musical Instruments date all the way back to November, 1883, according to a patent application filed in 1887. The earliest printed information found on Washburn is from a Christmas 1885 catalog of Lyon & Healy which featured a line of guitars, but no other Washburn instruments. The prices ranged from $20 to $75 and the George Washburn logo of a belt encircling a guitar (still in use today) was pictured. The guitar in the ad was constructed with a slotted headstock and geared tuning pegs, as were all the following models until the 1930s.

Apparently, the very earliest models were constructed with solid headstocks and friction pegs. These instruments were also branded with the George Washburn logo and would seemingly date to 1883-'84. Rumors exist of earlier guitars bearing the name G.W. Lyon, which would appear to be the first Lyon & Healy made guitars, but these more likely date to the Lyon & Potter-era guitars of the early 1890s (see p.24).

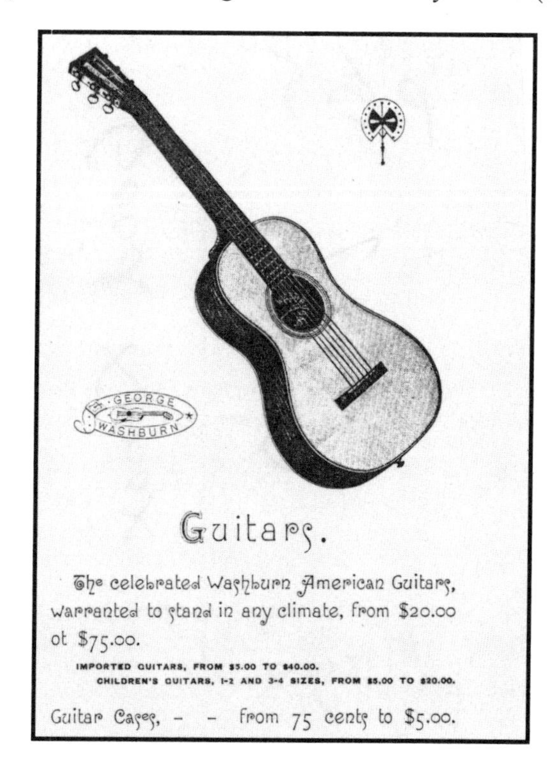

GEORGE
WASHBURN
Guitars.
The celebrated Washburn American Guitars, warranted to stand in any climate, from $20.00 ot $75.00.
IMPORTED GUITARS, FROM $3.00 TO $40.00.
CHILDREN'S GUITARS, 1-2 AND 3-4 SIZES, FROM $5.00 TO $20.00.
Guitar Cases, - - from 75 cents to $5.00.

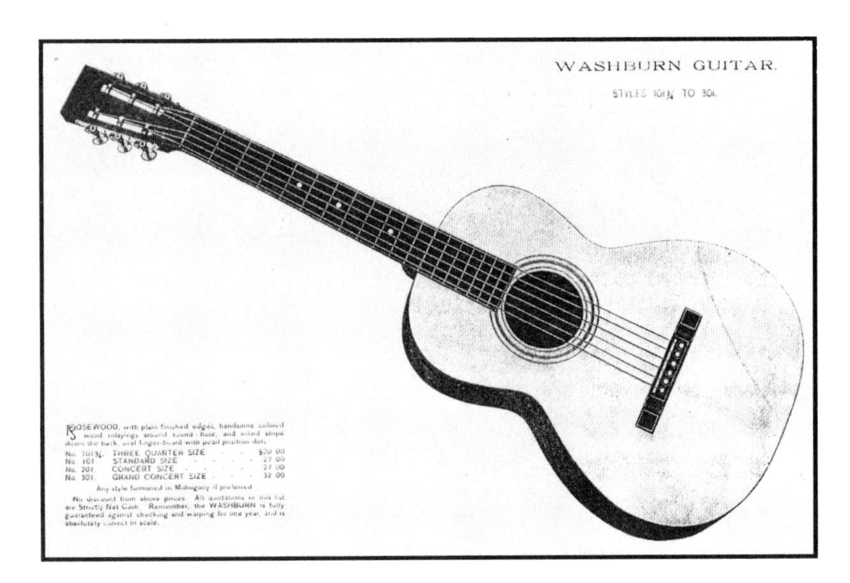

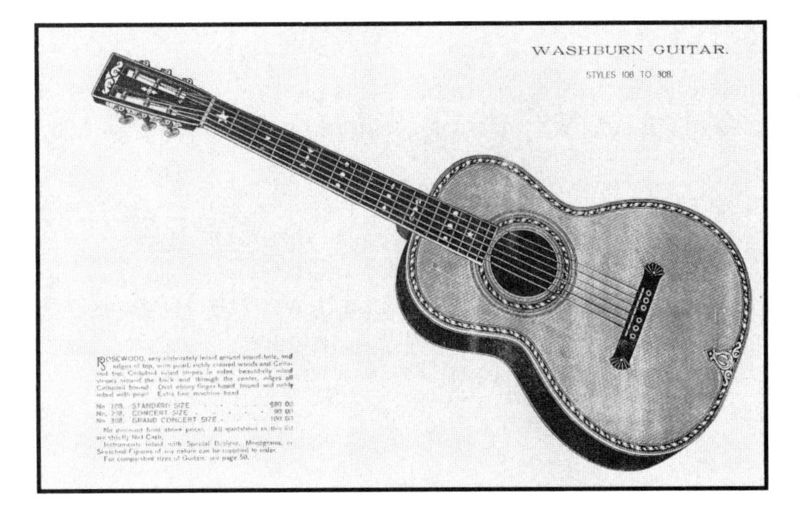

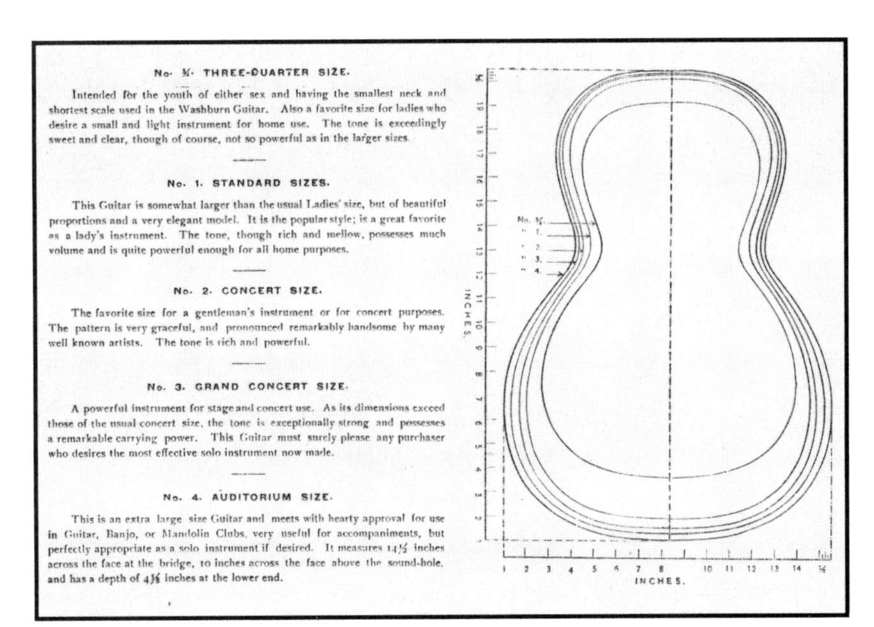

No. 3/4. THREE-QUARTER SIZE.

Intended for the youth of either sex and having the smallest neck and shortest scale used in the Washburn Guitar. Also a favorite size for ladies who desire a small and light instrument for home use. The tone is exceedingly sweet and clear, though of course, not so powerful as in the larger sizes.

No. 1. STANDARD SIZES.

This Guitar is somewhat larger than the usual Ladies' size, but of beautiful proportions and a very elegant model. It is the popular style; is a great favorite as a lady's instrument. The tone, though rich and mellow, possesses much volume and is quite powerful enough for all home purposes.

No. 2. CONCERT SIZE.

The favorite size for a gentleman's instrument or for concert purposes. The pattern is very graceful, and pronounced remarkably handsome by many well known artists. The tone is rich and powerful.

No. 3. GRAND CONCERT SIZE.

A powerful instrument for stage and concert use. As its dimensions exceed those of the usual concert size, the tone is exceptionally strong and possesses a remarkable carrying power. This Guitar must surely please any purchaser who desires the most effective solo instrument now made.

No. 4. AUDITORIUM SIZE.

This is an extra large size Guitar and meets with hearty approval for use in Guitar, Banjo, or Mandolin Clubs, very useful for accompaniments, but perfectly appropriate as a solo instrument if desired. It measures 14½ inches across the face at the bridge, 10 inches across the face above the sound-hole, and has a depth of 4⅝ inches at the lower end.

A souvenir catalog released in 1889 showed the early Washburn line in detail, from the $20 Model No. 101-3/4 to the $100 No. 308. Considering Lyon & Healy had guitars for as low as $5, the $20 Model No. 101-3/4 was not cheap for the time. Although the guitar was plainly appointed, it was constructed of solid spruce top and rosewood back and sides, (Brazilian of course, which was not as difficult to obtain then) with a decorative stripe up the back.

No. 308 was the finest American guitar made, surpassing all preceding models. A Grand Concert-sized body of finest rosewood and spruce was trimmed with multiple layers of binding and pearl inlay. A bound ebony fingerboard and headstock overlay were also elaborately inlaid with pearl. A small decorative pearl lyre was set into the top, suggesting a deep musical heritage, with a European inspiration. This was not a Cowboy Gee-tar! Lyon & Healy went to great efforts to bring culture to the Midwest, the 308 being a shining example.

The first number of the model referred to the size, ranging from the Standard size 1 to the Auditorium size 4. The last number identified the grade, or level of fanciness, ranging from the plain style 1 to the pearly style 8, which was far grander than the Martin top-of-the-line style 42. The smaller guitars were considered more appropriate for solo playing and were offered in all styles. The size 4 was only offered in styles 2, 3 and 4, implying the larger guitars were for playing situations where the ornateness of the higher models would be inappropriate, or the only people who needed loud guitars couldn't afford the DeLuxe models. In today's "bigger is better" market, it defies logic.

Washburn also made a 15" wide by 5" deep Model 503 Contra Bass Guitar, "intended especially for accompaniment." Whereas most Washburns of the time were intended to be strung with gut strings, the 503 came with steel strings and it was suggested that the guitar, with it's 27-1/2" scale, be tuned down to C. The company felt the guitar was "too large for successful solo use." This would be the first of many attempts by Lyon & Healy to expand the size, and likewise the role, of the steel string acoustic guitar.

All the guitars from Style 4 up were fitted with a patented ebony bridge designed by shop foreman George Durkee. The strings wrapped around the bridge pins, the treble side clockwise and the bass side counter-clockwise. This necessitated a gap between the D and G string pins, but the strings were evenly spaced. It is not unusual to see instruments with this charming bridge replaced by a standard bridge or with the strings wrongly placed in the bridge pin holes, leaving a gap between the treble strings and the bass. Styles 6 (recently reissued) and 8 (there was no style 7 until c.1897) had this bridge with a sea shell pattern carved into the ends, making the top-line "Durkee Bridge" one of the most appealing to connoisseurs.

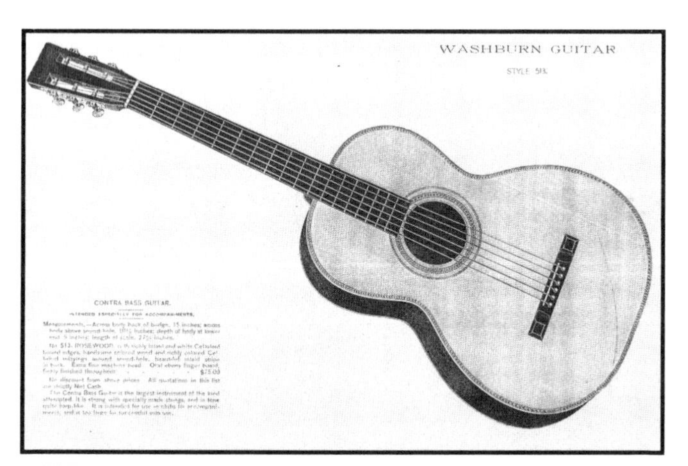

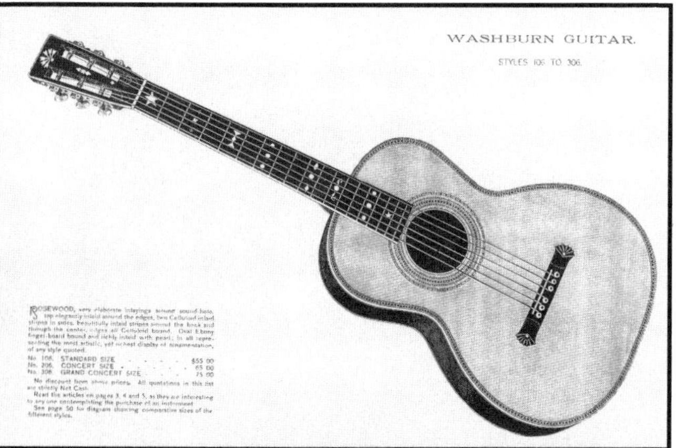

All the Washburns of this era had spruce tops, mahogany or cedar necks, ebony fingerboards and bridge (except style 1) and Brazilian rosewood bodies. The company was pushing mahogany as a better wood, being less susceptible to cracks and finish checking. While this may be true, the public expected rosewood and that's what they got. Gut strings were standard on the guitars although wire strings could be used if the guitar was ordered with the necessary bracing to accomodate the extra tension. (It is unfortunate that many of the original instruments and Durkee bridges have been damaged or ruined by having had steel strings mistakenly installed because of the pin bridge (instead of the tie bridge normally associated with gut or nylon strings).

The amount of inlays and binding on the better guitars was beyond that of any other production model guitar, then or now. "Altogether the most gorgeous instrument yet offered," a subtitle in the 1889 Catalog stated. And that was describing a standard model! Another subtitle offered, "The makers of Washburn Guitars are prepared to supply extra fine instruments to order for presentation or other purposes."

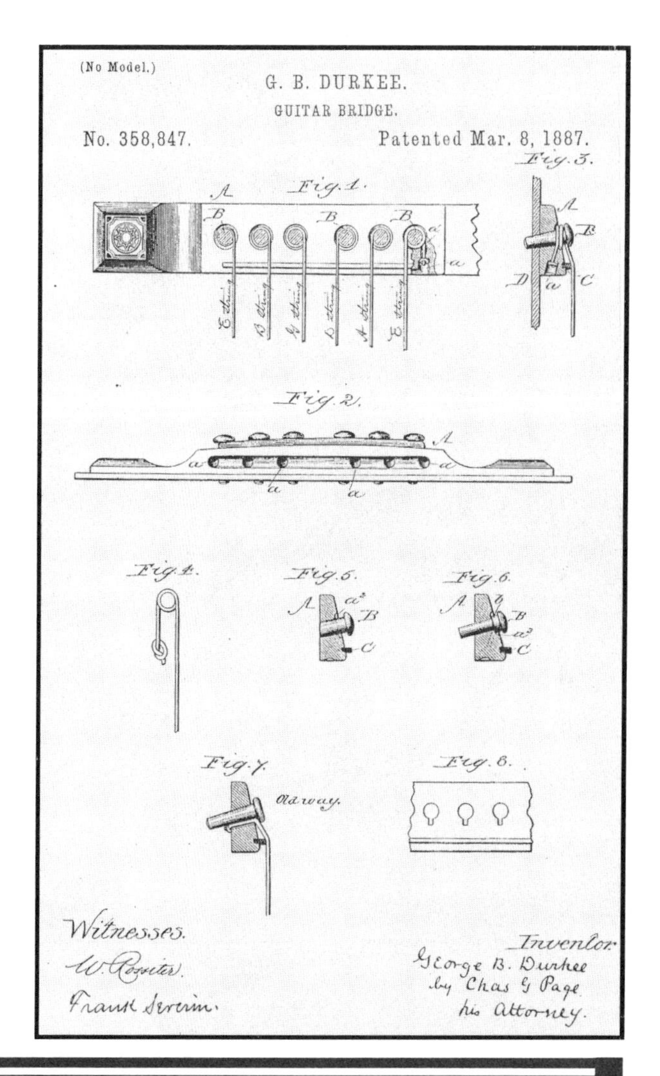

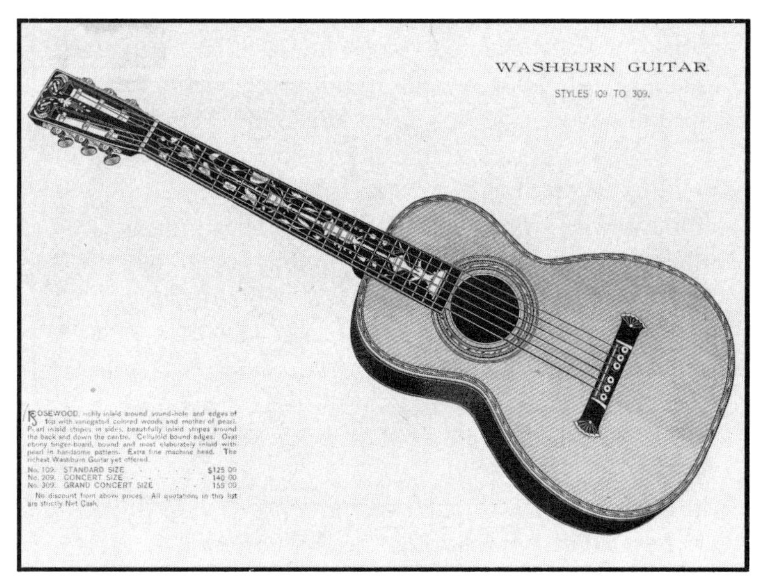

WASHBURN GUITAR.

STYLES 109 TO 309.

ROSEWOOD, richly inlaid around sound-hole and edges of top with variegated colored woods and mother of pearl. Pearl inlaid stripes in sides, beautifully inlaid stripes around the back and down the centre. Celluloid bound edges. Oval ebony finger-board, bound and most elaborately inlaid with pearl in handsome pattern. Extra fine machine head. The richest Washburn Guitar yet offered.

No. 109. STANDARD SIZE $125 00
No. 209. CONCERT SIZE 140 00
No. 309. GRAND CONCERT SIZE . . . 155 00

No discount from above prices. All quotations in this list are strictly Net Cash.

By 1892 an even fancier model, the Style 9, was offered at $155 for the Grand Concert size Model 309. This cost over 50 percent more than the Style 8 so you can imagine. . . pearl stripes on the sides, an incredible pattern inlaid into the fingerboard, stripes of multi-colored marquetry around the pearl inlaid edges, "the richest Washburn Guitar yet offered." As if that wasn't enough, the company made the offer "instruments inlaid with Special Designs, Monograms, or Sketched Figures of any nature can be supplied to order." These Presentation models predate today's "custom shop" instruments by a hundred years.

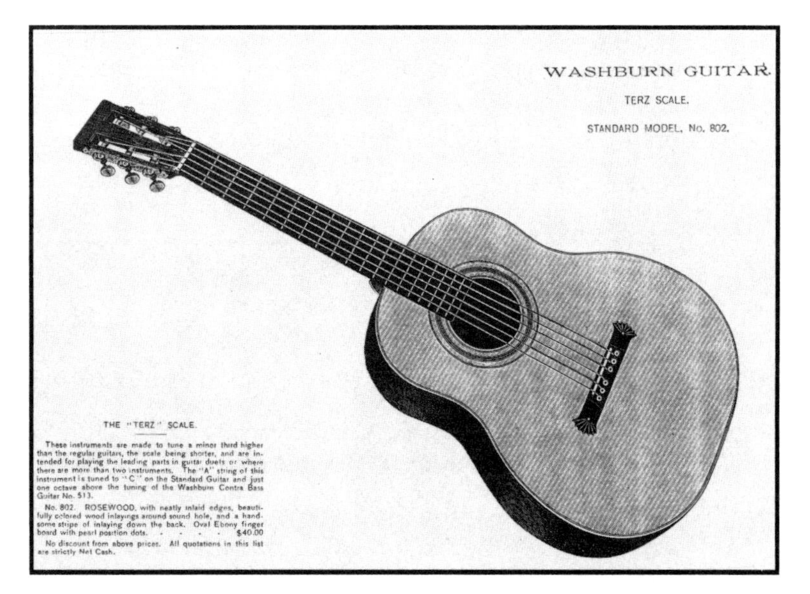

WASHBURN GUITAR.

TERZ SCALE.

STANDARD MODEL, No. 802.

THE "TERZ" SCALE.

These instruments are made to tune a minor third higher than the regular guitars, the scale being shorter, and are intended for playing the leading parts in guitar duets or where there are more than two instruments. The "A" string of this instrument is tuned to "C" on the Standard Guitar and just one octave above the tuning of the Washburn Contra Bass Guitar No. 513.

No. 802. ROSEWOOD, with neatly inlaid edges, beautifully colored wood inlayings around sound hole, and a handsome stripe of inlaying down the back. Oval Ebony finger board with pearl position dots. $40.00

No discount from above prices. All quotations in this list are strictly Net Cash.

Two Terz-scale instruments were made available, designed to be tuned 1-1/2 steps higher than a standard guitar. Standard Model No. 802 was shaped like a small guitar, while Lyre Model No. 804 had protruding upper bouts (with small f-holes) that extended up to the peghead, as sometimes seen on Harp Guitars. The two bouts were connected to the headstock by the "arms" of a man whose head was carved into the top of the headstock. At least one of these was made, as the photo on page 23 shows.

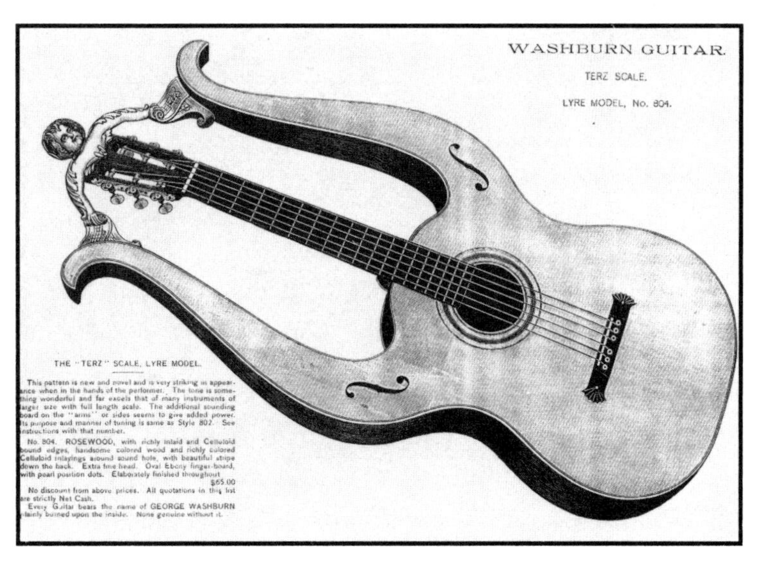

WASHBURN GUITAR.

TERZ SCALE.

LYRE MODEL, No. 804.

THE "TERZ" SCALE, LYRE MODEL.

This pattern is new and novel and is very striking in appearance when in the hands of the performer. The tone is something wonderful and far excels that of many instruments of larger size with full length scale. The additional sounding board on the "arms" or sides seems to give added power. Its purpose and manner of tuning is same as Style 802. See instructions with that number.

No. 804. ROSEWOOD, with richly inlaid and Celluloid bound edges, handsome colored wood and richly colored Celluloid inlayings around sound hole, with beautiful stripe down the back. Extra fine head. Oval Ebony finger-board, with pearl position dots. Elaborately finished throughout $65.00

No discount from above prices. All quotations in this list are strictly Net Cash.

Every Guitar bears the name of GEORGE WASHBURN plainly burned upon the inside. None genuine without it.

The numbering scheme was changed slightly in the mid-1890s, with the first number (size) and last number (grade) staying the same. The second number, which had always been zero, was now one number less than the grade, e.g. 145, 356, etc. A Style 7 was introduced by 1897, available in three sizes, 167, 267, and 367. The totally revamped Style 8 would have the second number match the third, as would Style 9. A full pearl fingerboard set Models 188, 288 and 388 apart from all others and the position markers were inlaid with a contrasting color of pearl. More pearl around the body edges and soundhole created a glowing appearance. The Style 9 guitars stayed the same except became Models 199, 299 and 399. In an endorsement, soloist and author Arling Shaeffer referred to the unchanged Style 9 as "The perfect model so long standard." The other models were also dressed up a bit with inlays at the ends of the bridge and fancier fingerboard inlays.

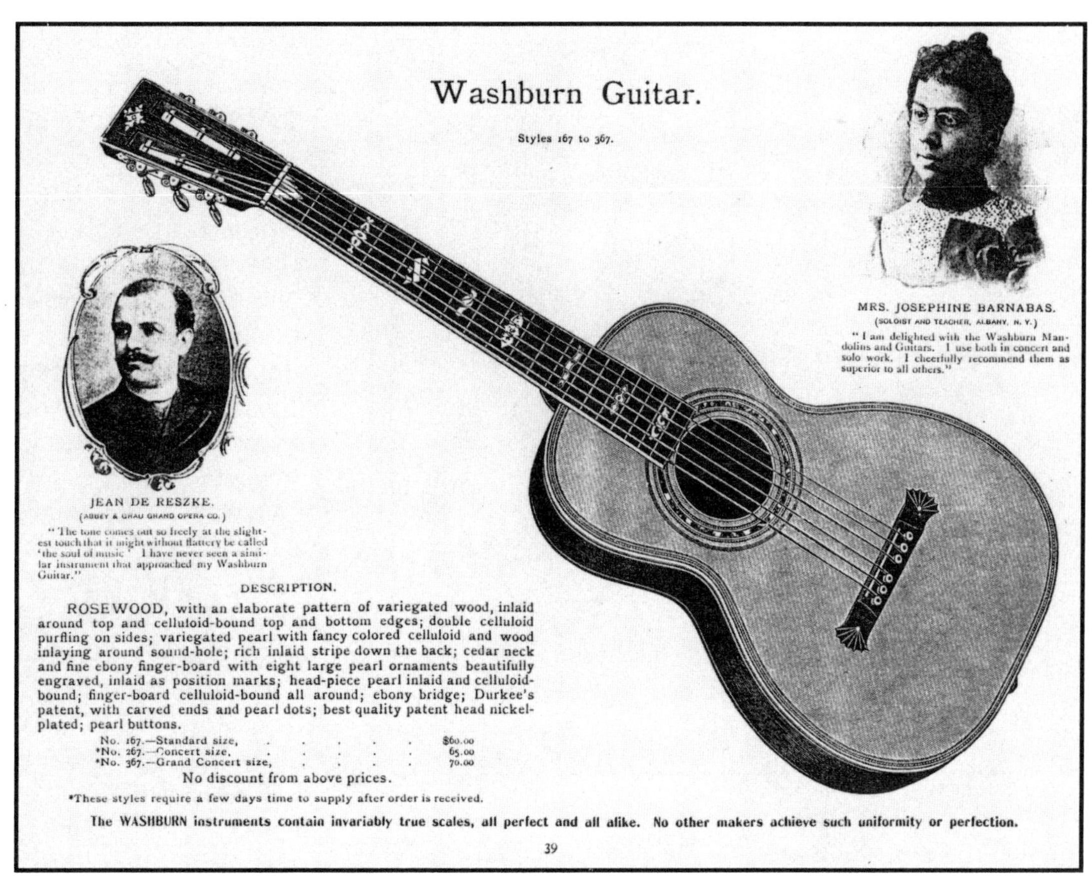

Washburn Guitar.

Styles 167 to 367.

MRS. JOSEPHINE BARNABAS.
(SOLOIST AND TEACHER, ALBANY, N. Y.)

"I am delighted with the Washburn Mandolins and Guitars. I use both in concert and solo work. I cheerfully recommend them as superior to all others."

JEAN DE RESZKE.
(ABBEY & GRAU GRAND OPERA CO.)

"The tone comes out so freely at the slightest touch that it might without flattery be called 'the soul of music.' I have never seen a similar instrument that approached my Washburn Guitar."

DESCRIPTION.

ROSEWOOD, with an elaborate pattern of variegated wood, inlaid around top and celluloid-bound top and bottom edges; double celluloid purfling on sides; variegated pearl with fancy colored celluloid and wood inlaying around sound-hole; rich inlaid stripe down the back; cedar neck and fine ebony finger-board with eight large pearl ornaments beautifully engraved, inlaid as position marks; head-piece pearl inlaid and celluloid-bound; finger-board celluloid-bound all around; ebony bridge; Durkee's patent, with carved ends and pearl dots; best quality patent head nickel-plated; pearl buttons.

No. 167.—Standard size,	$60.00
*No. 267.—Concert size,	65.00
*No. 367.—Grand Concert size,	70.00

No discount from above prices.

*These styles require a few days time to supply after order is received.

The WASHBURN instruments contain invariably true scales, all perfect and all alike. No other makers achieve such uniformity or perfection.

39

Washburn Guitar.

Styles 188 to 388.

CHAS. H. LEWIS.
(TEACHER, CINCINNATI, O.)

"The Washburn instruments are perfectly true in scale, durable in workmanship and finish, and possess the most powerful, yet sweet and mellow tone of any like instruments I know."

H. A. WEBBER.
(SOLOIST AND TEACHER, PORTLAND, ORE.)

"I have used the Washburn instruments for six years, and can highly recommend them. My Washburn Guitar is especially a source of delight to me, and I could not be induced to part with it."

DESCRIPTION.

ROSEWOOD, with a very rich variegated pearl and celluloid pattern of inlay around top; celluloid-bound top and bottom edges; double celluloid purfling on the sides; variegated pearl with fancy colored wood and celluloid inlaying around sound-hole; rich inlaid stripe in back; solid Sidney pearl finger-board; beautifully engraved position marks of contrasting pearl; head-piece inlaid with pearl and celluloid-bound; celluloid-bound finger-board; Durkee's patent bridge with carved ends, inlaid with pearl; finely French polished; extra fine patent heads; silver-plated, with pearl buttons.

*No. 188.—Standard size,	$80.00
*No. 288.—Concert size,	85.00
*No. 388.—Grand Concert size,	90.00

No discount from above prices.

*These styles require a few days time to supply after order is received.

To insure a positive standard of excellence the makers of the WASHBURN instruments make all the component parts, including the patent heads.

41

Catalogs from 1898 and 1900 show the line unchanged except for the prices. By 1905 a smaller number of guitars were offered, with a numbering scheme that reflected the size (first number) and the "Pupils Net Price" (second and third numbers). The $15 Model 115 (also 217 and 320) was quite fancy for a bottom-line instrument, with spruce top, rosewood body, ebony fingerboard and fancy trim around the edges. The top-of-the-line No. 380 (also 175 and 277) was, at $80, considerably less-costly than the retired No. 399. It was more like the discontinued No. 388 in its engraved full pearl fingerboard and pearl body trim. No. 355 (also 150 and 252) had a stunning fingerboard, inlaid with a vine pattern using metal for the vine and pearl for the leaves. The bridges were square on the ends and had decorative stars inlaid in pearl. In between the bottom and the top two styles were two other groups. Nos. 3/4-24, 125, 227, 330 and the only auditorium size offered, No. 435, had bound fingerboards with delicate inlays at frets 1, 5, 7 and 9. A slightly fancier group, Nos. 135, 237 and 340 completed the line. These guitars had larger inlays all the way up the neck, a bound headstock with a small pearl decoration and inlays at the ends of the bridge. Catalogs from 1905, through WWI show the models basically unchanged but since the models had no names, keeping track of what was actually available during the era is somewhat confusing. Nos. 125, 227, 330, 135, and 237 became Nos. 122, 225, 333, 132 and 235 respectively, showing that identical guitars from different years could have different model numbers.

Back and Front Views of No. 3150.

A new addition to the line in the 1912 and '13 catalogs was the $150 No. 3150, costing almost twice the price of the previous top-of-the-line 380 (the list price was $237.50). The short-lived 3150 revived the Durkee bridge's shape and was fitted with gold plated tuners. Everything else on this guitar was pearl, featuring different colors and variations. The nut, saddle, tuner buttons, bridge pins and end pin were all pearl, as was the fingerboard. Stripes of pearl were laid next to stripes of pearl, finely cut pieces of pearl were inlaid into larger pieces of pearl, the soundhole was trimmed in pearl, the top was trimmed in pearl, the sides were inlaid with pearl, the pearl fingerboard was bound with contrasting pearl. . . goldfish pearl, mother-of-pearl, Abalone pearl, Japanese pearl, green pearl. . . One cannot imagine a finer instrument. By comparison, Martin's finest Pre-WWI instrument was the $120 000-45, a classic today for many reasons, but nothing like the Washburn 3150.

Besides the Washburn line, which was the finest group of instruments Lyon & Healy could make, a number of other brand names were used, including Jupiter, Columbus, Lakeside, College Line and American Conservatory. All these instruments were either made by, or expressly for, Lyon & Healy. They ranged from inexpensive (although there was always some cheaper American-made guitars at the bottom-of-the-line) to ALMOST a Washburn, in the case of the American Conservatory Line. A number of progressive, interesting and influential instruments came from these lower lines, which could afford to be less traditional than Washburn.

A turn of the century catalog featured an outrageous looking instrument in the American Conservatory line of guitars. The Harp Guitar featured two necks, one standard fretted and one fretless, attached off-center in what appears to have been an afterthought. The bridge was placed off-center and the neck attached well down the curve of the guitar's upper bout. An aluminum head piece held the six bass string tuners and also two brackets that extended from the fretless neck over to and across the standard guitar neck's headstock, where they were screwed in. The Harp Guitar was later referred to as the "12-String Bass Guitar with Supplementary Aluminum Head Piece" and was available through the mid-teens. Though never catalogued, Washburn had made harp guitars with only three extra strings in the late 1800s using a similar head piece.

A different style followed from the mid-teens into the mid-'20s that was considerably more symmetrical, with the bridge and the two necks centered on the body. A new "Supplementary Ebonized Head Piece" tied the two pegheads together. These appear to have been made by Regal.

Early Lyon & Healy single neck 12-string guitars were way ahead of their time and appear to predate the famed Oscar Schmidt Stellas by a number of years. A less influential variation was the Eleven String, which had four pairs on the bass and three single strings on the treble for a total of seven courses. How they were tuned is a mystery. Both the 11-string and the 12-string were referred to as "Mexican Style" guitars.

No. 1210

12 String Bass Guitar with Supplementary Aluminum Head-Piece.
"THE AMERICAN CONSERVATORY" LARGE AUDITORIUM SIZE.

No. 1210. 12 Strings. Rosewood Back and Sides. Beautifully Hand Polished. Spruce Top. Fancy Colored Wood Inlaying around Sound-Hole and Edge. Top and Back Edges bound with White Celluloid. Fancy Colored Wood Stripe in Back. Mahogany Neck. Supplementary Aluminum Head-Piece, Ebony Finger-Board with Pearl Position Dots, Ebony Bridge. Length, 20½ inches; Depth, 5¼ inches; Width across Bridge, 16¼ inches.............Each $52.50

12 String Bass Guitar with Supplementary Ebonized Head-Piece
"The American Conservatory"—Large Auditorium Size

No. 1210. 12 strings, rosewood back and sides, beautifully hand polished, spruce top, fancy colored wood inlaying around sound-hole and edge, top and back edges bound with white celluloid, fancy colored wood stripe in back, mahogany neck, supplementary head-piece, ebonized finger-board with pearl position dots, ebony bridge. Length, 20½ inches; depth, 5¼ inches; width across bridge, 16¾ inches............Each $109.38

"The Lakeside" Bass Guitar
12 Strings, Jumbo Size

No. 1740. Birch back and sides, rosewood finish, spruce top, fancy broad inlayings around top and back sound-hole, top and back edges bound with white celluloid, fancy stripe inlaid down the back, mahogany finished necks, ebony veneered bridge, ebonized finger-board, pearl position dots, nickel plated patent heads, 12 strings...............Each $83.25

Nos. 1740-1210

11 and 12 String Guitars (Mexican Style)

"The Jupiter"
11 Strings, Standard

No. 1480. Mahogany finish back and sides, spruce top, fancy colored wood inlaying around sound-hole, fancy colored decalcomanie stripe on back, neck mahogany finish, finger-board with pearl position dots, our own nickel plated patent head, metal tail-piece, nickel plated, strung with steel strings....Each $20.63

"The Lakeside"
11 Strings, Standard Size

No. 1725. Birch back and sides, rosewood finish, spruce top, broad fancy colored corded wood inlaying around sound-hole and top and back edges, both edges bound with white celluloid, fancy colored stripe in back, body grained a rich rosewood and beautifully finished, neck mahogany finish, veneered head-piece, ebonized finger-board, pearl position dots, our own nickel plated patent head, nickel plated tail-piece, strung with steel strings..........................Each $28.75

"The Lakeside"
12 Strings, Concert Size

No. 1860. Beautiful Danish oak back and sides, hand polished, spruce top, broad fancy colored wood inlaying around sound-hole, top edge inlaid with broad fancy colored wood, both edges bound with white celluloid, inlaying down center of back, neck mahogany finish, ebonized finger-board, pearl position dots, our own nickel plated patent head and bridge, strung with steel strings..............................Each $30.63

No. 1725

One of the most interesting Lyon & Healy instruments was the 22-1/4" wide, 5" deep "Monster Bass" guitar, first available in 1908. While too extreme for the Washburn line, it would be, like the Washburn Contra Bass Guitar of the late 1800s, one of the many Lyon & Healy-made guitars attempting to expand the role of the guitar beyond solo work played on small instruments. "Wonderfully effective in heavy orchestra and club work," The Monster Bass No. 2089 was made-to-order only and required four weeks to build. It was not mentioned in the 1912 dealer's catalog but was offered in the 1913 and 1917 Lyon & Healy catalogs. It became extinct following WWI. The building of these behemoths could have been performed by Lyon & Healy or possibly farmed out to local craftsmen. In the '30s, at least one similar model was built by the Larson Bros. and was outfitted with their internal steel support rod system.

L. H. LELAND GUITAR-MANDOS.

The Guitar-Mandos possess a large, brilliant tone of great carrying power, equally adapted for solo or accompaniment.

Back and Sides are made of Finest Mahogany, Rosewood Finish; Front of best Seasoned Spruce; Neck, Mahogany, with Veneered Head-Piece; Finger-Board, Genuine Ebony, with Pearl Position Marks; German Silver Frets; Inlaid Stripe around Top Edge; Inlaid Sound-Hole; Top Edge bound with White Celluloid; Best Quality Nickel Plated Patent Head. Handsomely made throughout.

No. 731.
Length, 37 inches.
Depth, about 2 inches.

Prices:

No. 731 .... $32 50
No. 733 .... 25 00

No. 733

Two short-lived, thin-body flattops were made with the L.H. Leland name and were part of the Mandolin Orchestra line that also featured one of the earliest fretted basses. The Mando-Guitars looked like regular guitars from the front, but were only 2" deep (for side view, see p.87). The idea was that they would "cut" the way the thin Gibson mandolins cut.

Lyon & Healy College Line Monster Bass Guitar, G 2089.

(Made to order only)

G 2089

To satisfy the fast growing demand for a giant size instrument we have created facilities for building to order a tremendously large bass guitar.

The dimensions are:

Width across bridge, 22 1/4 inches.
Length of body..... 20 3/4 inches.
Depth of body...... 5 inches.

General description is like that of G 2088, and the same high standard of excellence in material and workmanship prevails. The tonal depth, volume and carrying power are enormous. Wonderfully effective in heavy orchestra and club work. Such a guitar will always be a source of pride and pleasure to the performer and excites wonder and enthusiasm wherever seen and heard.

Price only.................................... $60.00

G 2090 Same size as G 2089, but with six extra strings, like G 2088. Price............. 75.00

Canvas, leather bound case for either G 2089 or G 2090.............................. 5.00

N. B.—We require about four weeks time in which to build either G 2089 or G 2090.

G 2089

The 1912 catalog introduced what today is probably THE most important guitar that Lyon & Healy made, although at the time it didn't even warrant a picture, only a description. The steel-string Lakeside Jumbo Size guitar measured 16-1/4" wide by 5-1/4" deep by 20-1/2" in length, making it essentially THE FIRST DREADNOUGHT! That's right, by 1912 Lyon & Healy was making a steel-string guitar with dimensions approximately the same as what has long been considered the original, pre-dating Martin's D-1 and D-2 by at least 19 years and the Ditson 111, 222 and 333 models by at least five years! The folks at Ditson, who were authorized Lyon & Healy dealers, surely must have been aware of these guitars when they began drawing up plans for their version.

The body shape, bridge position and bracing patterns are different on the 12 and the 14-fret Martin D models, yet both are considered Dreadnoughts. The Ditson models that preceded them are reportedly "Spanish" or "fan" braced, suggesting they were not even intended to be strung with steel strings! Yet they are considered Dreadnoughts. In the history of the guitar, the big-bodied steel-string has played a major role for over sixty years. Martin's Dreadnoughts from the '30s are certainly classics for their execution of this design, but not for originating it. Credit for the original design must be given to Lyon & Healy, period. Starting with the Contra Bass Guitar in the late 1880s, going a bit overboard with the Monster Bass Guitar and finally finding a compromise between too big and too small, the company's experiments with steel-string guitars were ground-breaking. At the time however, the majority of the instruments used and sold were traditional gut string, and public demand for these progressive steel strings was small.

The Lyon & Healy Lakeside Jumbo guitar was offered in company catalogs into the mid-1920s, suggesting they were sold at least in small quantities for about a dozen years. Gibson would use the name in the '30s for a series of similar instruments.

Dimensions in Inches	Lakeside Jumbo	Martin 12 fret Dreadnought	Difference
Length of Body	20 1/2	20 15/16	-7/16
Total Length	39 1/2	39 9/16	-1/16
Width Upper Bout	12	11 1/2	+1/2
Width Lower Bout	16 1/4	15 5/8	+5/8
Depth	5 1/4	4 3/4	+1/2

1912

MANDOLINS, GUITARS, BANJOS, ETC.

Lakeside Bass Guitar

Jumbo Size

Style G2740

IZE — Length of body, 20½ inches; width at upper end, 12 inches width at lower end, 16¼ inches; total length, 39½ inches.

osewood finished birch back and sides. Spruce top. Highly polished

road, fancy wood inlaying around top edge, soundhole and down center of back.

op and back edges bound with white celluloid.

eck, mahogany finish, with veneered headpiece.

osewood fingerboard with pearl position dots.

ickel plated patent head with white celluloid buttons.

trung with best steel strings.

osewood bridge with bone saddle and ebony bridge pins with pear dot.

very handsome instrument, possessing a powerful tone and grea carrying quality. Indispensable to the up-to-date mandolin an guitar club.

1917

L. & H. GUITARS.

"THE LAKESIDE."

STANDARD SIZE.

No. — Each.

725. Birch Back and Sides, Rosewood Finish, Spruce Top, Broad Fancy Wood Inlaying around Sound-Hole and Edge, Top and Back Edges Bound with White Celluloid, Fancy Stripe in Back, Body Grained a Rich Rosewood and Beautifully Finished, Neck Mahogany Finish, Veneered Head-Piece, Rosewood Finger-Board, Pearl Position Dots, Nickel Plated Patent Head, Tail-Piece, Nickel Plated, Strung with Steel Strings..............$ 8 63

720. Same description as No. 725, but has plain Head-Piece, lighter Inlay, and Ebonized Finger-Board........... 7 50

JUMBO SIZE.

No. — Each.

740. Same description as No. 725, but Extra Large, with Rosewood Bridge. Length 20½ inches. Depth, 5¼ inches. Width across Bridge 16¼ inches.......................$18 75

84 LYON & HEALY, CHICAGO

Washburn Guitars

The **standard** of quality and relative excellence of the **Washburn** line has been maintained throughout a period of over thirty-five years. When changes in the line were made each style presented an improvement over its predecessor and over all others, so that today, as in the past, the Washburn leads in all that contributes to the making up of an ideal musical instrument.

No. 2123. Enlarged Model: Dull oil finish, selected mahogany back and sides, inlaid stripe in back, spruce top, sound hole with bound edge and inlaying as shown in illustration of No. 2132, both top and back edges bound with black fibre—the top edge binding is flanked by a strip of white and black, Spanish cedar neck, ebonized fingerboard, 3 pearl position dots, bone nut, rosewood veneered headpiece, good quality nickel-plated patent heads, ebonized bridge, strung with steel strings. Each $34.50

No. 2128. Standard size; rosewood back and sides; selected spruce top; top edge bound with black celluloid and inlaid with three line black and white wood stripe inlaying; sound hole bound with black celluloid and inlaid with three rings of black and white wood; ebony bridge with bone saddle; ebony bridge pins and end pin; top edge of side inlaid with faint line of white celluloid; inlaid strip in center of back; mahogany neck; rhodium headpiece; rhodium wood fingerboard inlaid with four pearl position dots; Liberty silver frets; bone nut; highest grade nickel-plated patent heads; strung with gut strings and silk center wound bass strings. Price.............$42.00

No. 2231. Same as above—Concert size. Price $46.50

No. 2333. Same as above—Grand Concert Size. Price $49.50

No. 2135

No. 2135. Standard size; same description as No. 2128 but with both top and back edges bound with black celluloid; top edge ornamented with one faint line of white celluloid next to black celluloid edge and inlaid with three strips of black and white wood inlaying; top and back edge of sides inlaid with faint line of white celluloid; ebony fingerboard bound with black celluloid with faint line of white celluloid inlaying. Price........................$52.50

No. 2238. Same as No. 2135—Concert size 57.00

No. 2342. Same as No. 2135—Grand Concert size 63.00

No. 2444. Same as No. 2135—Auditorium size 66.00

Three-quarter Size Washburn Guitar

No. 3136. Dimensions: Total length, 33 inches; length of body, 15¼ inches; width at lower bout, 11 inches; at upper bout, 8 inches; fingerboard, 14½ inches; depth, 3¼ inches. For details of construction, see description of Guitar No. 2132. Price $54.00

The guitars described above are constructed for the use of either steel or gut strings

Note.—The two final figures of stock numbers of Washburn Instruments represent in dollars the retail prices at which these are sold in Chicago. For example, Guitar No. 2128 sells at $28.00; No. 3136 at $36.00, and so on throughout the line.

LYON & HEALY, CHICAGO 85

Washburn Guitars

No. 2146

Standard size, selected handsomely figured rosewood back and sides, choicest selected well-seasoned white spruce top, highly finished, top and back edges bound with black celluloid, both top and back edges of sides inlaid with a faint line of white celluloid, top ornamented with a faint line of white celluloid next to black celluloid edge, and inlaid with black and white marquetry, sound-hole bound with black celluloid and inlaid with three rings of black and white marquetry, ebony bridge and bridge pins, bone saddle, back edge inlaid with faint line of white celluloid. Fancy wood marquetry strips in center of back, mahogany neck, rhodium wood headpiece, ebony fingerboard inlaid with six fancy pearl position dots on side, edge of fingerboard bound with black celluloid with faint line of white celluloid inlaying, Liberty silver frets, bone nut, ebony heel with faint line of white celluloid inlaying, highest grade nickel-plated engraved patent heads, strung with best quality gut strings and silk center wound bass strings. Price $69.00

No. 2250. Same as above—Concert size. Price $75.00

No. 2354. Same as above—Grand Concert size. Price $81.00

No. 2165

Standard size, carefully selected, handsomely figured rosewood back and sides, choicest selected white spruce top, highly finished, top and back edges bound with black celluloid with faint line of white celluloid. Sound hole bound with black celluloid, inlaid with four rings of black and white marquetry, ebony bridge inlaid with handsome pearl ornament, pearl saddle, rich mother-of-pearl bridge pins, pearl head end pin, top and back edge of sides inlaid with faint line of white celluloid, top edge inlaid with two rows of artistic marquetry of black and white, back edge inlaid with faint line of white celluloid, strip of two rows of black and white marquetry inlaid in center of back, mahogany neck of special design, ebony headpiece bound with black celluloid with faint line of white celluloid and inlaid with three pearl ornaments, ebony fingerboard inlaid with fourteen fancy pearl position ornaments on top and five inlaid position dots on the side, edge of fingerboard bound with black celluloid with faint line of white celluloid, Liberty silver frets, pearl nut, nickel-plated engraved patent heads with pearl buttons, ebony heel trimmed with faint line of white celluloid inlaying, strung with best quality gut strings and silk wound bass strings. Price..$ 97.50

No. 2165

No. 2270. Same as No. 2165. Concert size 105.00

No. 2375. Same as No. 2165. Grand Concert size. Price.................................... 112.50

Three Quarter Size Washburn Guitar

No. 3148. Dimensions: Total length, 33 inches; length of body, 15¼ inches; width at lower bout, 11 inches; at upper bout, 8 inches; fingerboard, 14½ inches; depth, 3¼ inches. For details of construction, see description of Guitar No. 2146..........................$72.00

The two final figures of stock number of Washburn Instruments represents, in dollars, the retail price in Chicago. For example, No. 2128 retails in Chicago at $28.00, No. 2146 at $46.00.

(It was the author's original intention to list only dates as chronological markers, avoiding the reference to WWI and WWII in the discussion of things musical. Unfortunately society is greatly changed during and following a war, in particular the work force and economy, even for non-military related goods). WWI disrupted, amongst other things, the production of musical instruments, including Lyon & Healy's. The fancy Washburns of the previous era became history, the magnificent pearl encrusted boxes being replaced by a new line of guitars for the post-war market.

The top-of-the-line No. 2375 had tastefully simple appointments including pearl tuner buttons, nut and saddle, as well as decorative headstock, fingerboard and bridge inlays. The bridge was squared off at the ends as was standard Washburn practice through the early-'20. Black binding on a rosewood and spruce body added a modern touch stylistically, and matched that of the Style A mandolins. Thin white trim accented the black binding and a strip of herringbone completed the edge treatment. A headstock volute was nicely carved and the front of the peghead was bound in black with thin white trim, making these guitars somewhat fancier than Martin's herringbone Style 28. Washburn no longer offered a pearl-bordered model to compete with Martin's Styles 42 and 45.

Four other styles of Washburn guitars were offered in Standard (2123, 2128, 2135, 2146 and 2164), Concert (2231, 2238, 2250, 2270) and Grand Concert (2333, 2342, 2354, 2375) sizes. Auditorium Model 2444 and three-quarter size models 3136 and 3148 completed the line. The first two digits of the model numbers designated the size, the last two were the selling price. In a patriotic upgrade, the German Silver fretwire used before the war was changed to Liberty Silver.

Having the model number reflect the price during inflationary times could make raising prices and keeping track of models difficult. A slightly changed line was released in the early '20s, using the designations A ($100) through G ($15). The top-of-the-line A would become the "Deluxe" and ran through the early '30s, introducing the "gold leaf flowery design" patterns on the face of the instrument. The method of applying gold leaf was completely different from cheap stenciling and was popular with fine furniture makers. Close examination is necessary to fully appreciate its beauty. All the models were equipped with "smile" bridges, the shape being great Industrial Design; functional, attractive and easily identifiable. It would be a standard appointment on all the Lyon & Healy Washburn guitars and most of the Tonk Bros. flattops that followed.

In the mid 1920s, Lyon & Healy began using another four digit numbering system to identify the different Washburns. The first two were common to all of a certain instrument, e.g. 52_ _ were guitars, 51_ _ were banjos and 53 _ _ covered mandolins and ukuleles. The last two digits designated the individual models. This numbering system would continue through the Tonk Bros. era and the discontinuing of the Washburn line. The first guitars using this system were the No. 5200 Inspiration, No. 5201 Classic, No. 5202 Aristocrat, and the top-of-the-line No. 5203 DeLuxe. These guitars were all Concert size and were offered in Grand Concert size as Nos. 5235, 5236, 5237, and 5238. The Inspiration and Classic guitars were mahogany bodied and plainly appointed. The $79 Aristocrat had a rosewood body and was somewhat fancier, although it would have been near the bottom of the line before WWI. Washburn was definitely concentrating its focus on playability and sound with a description reading "the Aristocrat has been built primarily for tone."

At the top of the line was the $140 DeLuxe, featuring an elaborate gold leaf pattern on the face of the guitar. Gold-plated tuners with pearl buttons, ebony fingerboard, peghead overlay, and bridge, multiple bound rosewood body and a solid spruce top gave the DeLuxe a simple elegance. The sides of the DeLuxe and the Aristocrat were specified as three ply laminated rosewood. This was NOT rosewood veneer and the gluing, bending and drying processes were described in a 1926 Musical Merchandise Magazine article with great pride. Ukuleles with similar style gold leaf (see p.108 & 109) were available for those wanting matching instruments. Lyon & Healy would release a number of Washburn guitar/ukulele "mates" during the mid-to-late '20s.

LYON & HEALY, CHICAGO

The
WASHBURN "DE LUXE"
Guitar

[H]ere is the instrument for the concert artist who knows the value of appearanc[e an]d for the amateur who takes the greatest pride and interest in his art and in h[is in]strument. The WASHBURN *"DeLuxe"* possesses a richness of appearance an[d] finished beauty that is distinctively its own.

[U]ntil the advent of the WASHBURN *"Bell,"* the WASHBURN *"DeLuxe"* wa[s th]e premier guitar in this famous line. It still stands as the most beautifully tone[d in]strument that can be purchased at anywhere near its price. In it is embodied th[e s]um total of our years of experience and research in the construction of guitars. [It h]as continuously held the undisputed lead among fine guitars, and is to be found toda[y i]n the hands of a large number of the country's leading artists.

[B]ody—Selected rosewood sides of three-ply laminated construction; two-piece selecte[d r]osewood back with stripe of inlaying through center; fine grained white spruce to[p, c]ross ribbed; top and back edges bound with white and black celluloid; raised ivor[y ce]lluloid soundhole ring; Lyon & Healy improved ebony bridge with bone saddle[; b]one fingerboard nut; ivory celluloid bridge pins; ivory celluloid end pin. Top orn[am]ented with gold design. Hand rubbed satin finish throughout.

[N]eck—Genuine mahogany neck; convex ebony fingerboard; artistically designed pea[rl i]nlaying in ebony headpiece; gold-plated patent heads with pearl buttons.

[C]ase—Beautiful black seal grain Keratol covered three-ply wood body; silk plu[sh li]ned; side opening; nickel-plated brass trimmings, lock and clasps; steel valanc[e; l]eather handle; compartment for accessories.

Concert Size

No. 5203 .... *Complete with case $140.00*

Grand Concert Size

No. 5203 .... *Complete with case $140.00*

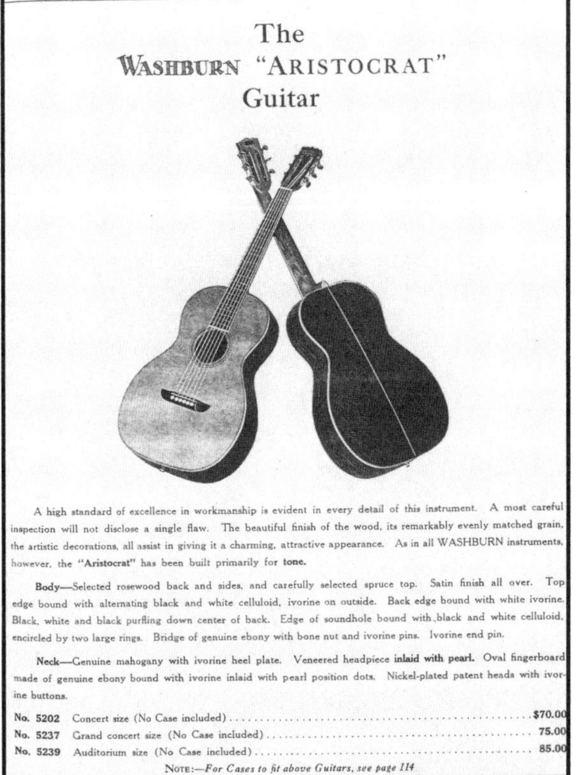

TONK BROS. CO., — — CHICAGO, ILLINOIS

The
WASHBURN "ARISTOCRAT"
Guitar

A high standard of excellence in workmanship is evident in every detail of this instrument. A most careful inspection will not disclose a single flaw. The beautiful finish of the wood, its remarkably evenly matched grain, the artistic decorations, all assist in giving it a charming, attractive appearance. As in all WASHBURN instruments, however, the **"Aristocrat"** has been built primarily for **tone.**

Body—Selected rosewood back and sides, and carefully selected spruce top. Satin finish all over. Top edge bound with alternating black and white celluloid, ivorine on outside. Back edge bound with white ivorine. Black, white and black purfling down center of back. Edge of soundhole bound with black and white celluloid, encircled by two large rings. Bridge of genuine ebony with bone nut and ivorine pins. Ivorine end pin.

Neck—Genuine mahogany with ivorine heel plate. Veneered headpiece **inlaid with pearl.** Oval fingerboard made of genuine ebony bound with ivorine inlaid with pearl position dots. Nickel-plated patent heads with ivorine buttons.

No. 5202 Concert size (No Case included) **$70.00**
No. 5237 Grand concert size (No Case included) **75.00**
No. 5239 Auditorium size (No Case included) **85.00**

NOTE:—*For Cases to fit above Guitars, see page 114*

Tenor Guitars

The Tenor Banjo became *the* Banjo following WWI, with the once popular 5-string, or Regular Banjo as it was known, becoming somewhat passé. The approach to playing the Tenor Banjo was considerably different, with chords being strummed in a rhythmic fashion, as opposed to the picking of melody and harmony/grace notes on the 5-string.

Washburn designed an instrument that would be instantly adaptable to the throngs of Tenor Banjoists. In the mid-twenties the first Tenor Guitar was released, probably with the hope that every Tenor Banjo player would buy one, immediately being able to double on the Guitar. The tuning and scale length of the Tenor Guitar was identical to that of the Tenor Banjo, even the tuning pegs were the same. Washburn's idea of having rhythm parts played on an instrument with "the same fingerboard as the Tenor Banjo. . . the tonal beauty of the Guitar" was a good one and the Tenor Guitar *did* play a direct role in the transition from Tenor Banjo Rhythm to Orchestra Guitar Rhythm in the late-'20s and early-'30s. For a short time, there seemed to be a majority of bands pictured with Tenor guitarists. However, a few influential players, and the extra range of the 6-string guitar, brought the 6-string to prominence in the big bands of the '30s, keeping the Tenor Guitar from becoming the standard that it *almost* did.

Washburn's early (c.1926-'28)Tenor Guitar No. 5265 was pear shaped, with flat top and back. The top was spruce with a round soundhole, the back and sides were mahogany. A mandolin-style tailpiece secured the strings and the floating bridge was made of ebony. The body shape had been used on cheaper Lyon & Healy guitars in the early-'20s. Regal offered a similar model Tenor guitar and an ad from 1926 made the claim/reference "which was designed by this Co." Both companies claimed to have invented the instrument, which, in a way, is probably true.

For a short time a Tenor guitar version of the Shrine Ukelele (see p.108 and 109) was available. Around the transition between Lyon & Healy and Tonk Bros., a guitar shaped body replaced the earlier pear. No. 5225 and 5226 were mahogany body and rosewood body versions and had appointments similar to the six strings of the time. These were replaced around 1935 by No. 5227, a sunburst finished, large body guitar with fancy fingerboard inlays. This would be the last of the Washburn Tenor Guitars.

10 LYON & HEALY, CHICAGO

The WASHBURN TENOR GUITAR

Originated by Lyon & Healy

The Same Fingerboard as the Tenor Banjo

The Tonal Beauty of the Guitar

Made in the Lyon & Healy Factory

The Tenor Guitar has created a sensation. Played exactly the same as the Tenor Banjo, it possesses the richness and beauty of the guitar. Every tenor banjoist will want one. It opens up to him the fascinating qualities of the Guitar without the necessity of learning to play a new instrument.

For dance orchestra work it is exquisite in waltz numbers, especially when accompanied by orchestra pianissimo—used by the most famous dance orchestras.

The Tenor Guitar is an invention of our WASHBURN experts. It is offered in the WASHBURN line in a very beautiful model, as the illustration demonstrates. The strict standards of WASHBURN construction have resulted in an instrument of the highest type.

Body—Genuine figured mahogany back and sides, beautiful satin finish; fine even grain spruce top, natural color; top edge bound with cut block wood inlaying; soundhole inlaid with lines of alternating black and white purfling; soundhole edge bound with black fiberoid; ebony heel; center of back inlaid with stripe of white holly; nickel-plated brass tailpiece with slide cover; special model bridge with ebony top.

Neck—Genuine mahogany neck; white celluloid bound ebony fingerboard; special model patent pegs with white buttons; ebony veneered headpiece; 17 German silver frets; polished bone fingerboard nut; strung with four steel strings of finest quality.

No. **5265** .... *Each $40.00*

Tenor Guitar Case

No. **6018** Black walrus grain Keratol covered fiberboard body; side opening; cowhide sewed edges; nickel-plated steel trimmings; flannel lined; leather handle.

Each *$6.25*

TONK BROS. CO., — — CHICAGO, ILLINOIS

The WASHBURN Tenor Guitars

The Tenor Guitar is an invention of our Washburn expert. It is offered in the Washburn line in very beautiful models as illustrations demonstrate. The strict standards of Washburn construction have resulted in an instrument of the highest type.

Body—Beautiful mahogany back and sides with selected spruce top, hand rubbed satin finish all over. Top and back edge bound with alternating white, black and white celluloid, stripe of narrow black and white inlay down center of back, sound hole inlaid with 3 rings.

Neck—Fine mahogany, rosewood capped veneer head piece. Ebony fingerboard inlaid with pearl position dots. Bone nut. Ebony bridge with ivorine pins. Nickel-plated geared pegs with ivorine buttons. Twenty-three-inch string length.

No. 5225 .... **$35.00**

No. 5225

The Tenor Guitar is played exactly the same as the Tenor Banjo, it possesses the richness and beauty of the Guitar. Every tenor banjoist will want one. It opens up to him the fascinating qualities of the Guitar without the necessity of learning to play a new instrument.

Body—Selected rosewood back and sides, fine grained white spruce top. Top edge inlaid with black and white inlay bound with ivorine, back edge bound with ivorine, narrow black and white inlay down center of back, 3 ring inlay around sound hole, hand rubbed satin finish throughout.

Neck—Genuine mahogany. Ebony fingerboard inlaid with fancy pearl position dots. Rosewood veneer capped head piece inlaid with pearl. Bone nut, ebony bridge inlaid with pearl on each side, with ivorine bridge pins, ivorine end pin. Geared nickel-plated pegs with ivorine buttons, twenty-three-inch string length.

No. 5226 .... **$50.00**

No. 5226

Cases to Fit "*Washburn*" Tenor Guitars

Washburn Tenor Guitars are slightly larger in size and therefore require special cases.

No. 91½ Utility style, side opening case. Stiff chipboard body covered with walrus grain Keratol, leather bound edges, flannel lining. Each ..... **$ 7.50**

No. 92 3-ply veneer shell, covered with the best quality of black Keratol, lined with fine silk plush, nickel-plated lock and key. Each **26.70**

For Cheaper Styles of Tenor Guitars, see page 106

The ornate Models 308, 309, 380 and 3150 were the earliest top-of-the-line Washburns, followed by post-WWI Models 2375 and the Style A/Deluxe 5238. The short-lived series of "Bell" guitars was the final top-of-the-line Washburn by Lyon & Healy.

An outrageously unique shaped body was the main difference between the Bell and the DeLuxe. A scalloped peghead shape was a change from Washburn's traditional squared-off style and would influence later shapes. Otherwise the Bell and the DeLuxe had similar construction; spruce tops, rosewood bodies, mahogany necks, ebony fingerboards, bridges and peghead overlays, gold tuners with pearl buttons and gold leaf designs on the faces. Price with case for Bell Guitar No. 5271 was $195 compared to $140 for the DeLuxe. No. 5270 was a mahogany version with rosewood fingerboard and bridge for $165 with case. No. 5260 was the Bell-shaped, Koa-bodied Hawaiian Harp Guitar (See p.107). They even made a Bell ukulele (see p.108) and a Bell Tiple (see p.109). Very few of these interesting boxes were made by Lyon & Healy and Tonk Bros. chose not to pursue the Bells.

Around 1927, Lyon & Healy released its Shrine Ukulele (see p.108). Joining the uke for a short time were a Shrine Tenor Guitar and a Shrine 6-string. The ukelele stayed in the line throughout the '30s, but no information could be found on the guitars. It's possible they offered a Shrine Tiple (and a Bell Tenor Guitar). All three instruments pictured here have both Washburn and Lyon & Healy stamps on the inside but no labels, serial numbers or model numbers. Like the Bells, the Shrine guitars were not pursued by Tonk Bros.

The
WASHBURN "BELL"
Guitar
Made in the Lyon & Healy Factory

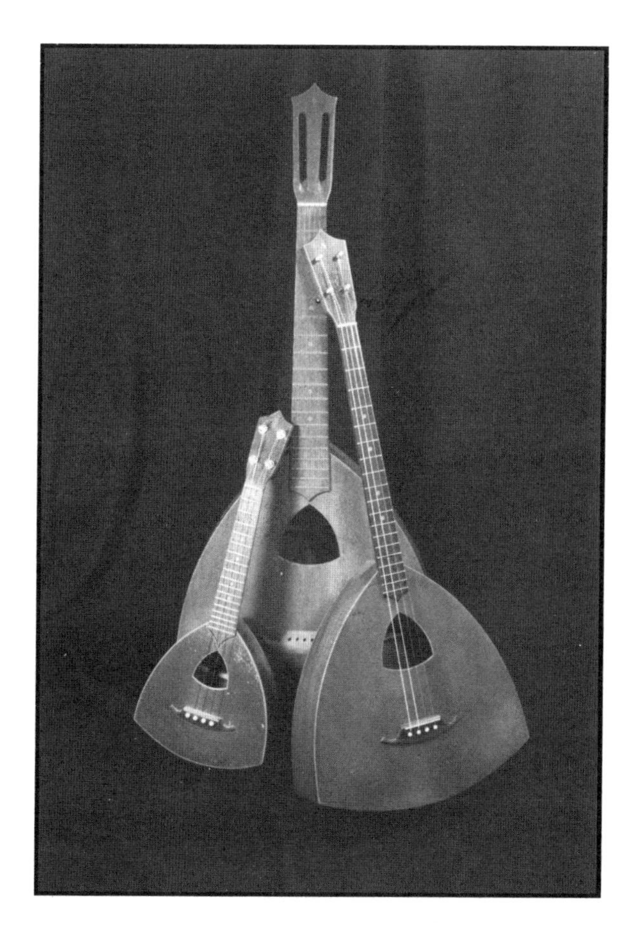

Steel-String Flattops

Tonk Bros. would add an Auditorium size No. 5234 DeLuxe around 1930, featuring a new peghead shape with "Washburn" inlaid and delicate fingerboard inlays replacing the simple dots. By 1933, the price had dropped from $150 to $100. The Guitar Cyclopedia section in the April, 1934 issue of *Musical Merchandise Review* listed for Washburn "A complete new line will be announced end of this month." [sic.] Shortly thereafter, the $45 No. 5257 Solo Model replaced the DeLuxe as the top-of-the-line flattop and the $40 No. 5256 Solo Model replaced the Aristocrat, showing the effects of the Depression.

The Washburn Solos were amongst the leaders of the bass heavy, steel string flattops of the 1930s golden era, as Martin had made less than a hundred Dreadnoughts and Gibson was just releasing its first Jumbo. With Large Auditorium-sized, X-braced bodies and 14-fret, solid peghead necks, the 15 5/8" x 19 3/8" x 5" guitars were up-to-the-minute structurally. No. 5256 had a mahogany body and for $5 more (a very smart investment), No. 5257 with a rosewood body was available. Both guitars had solid spruce tops, mahogany necks and ebony fingerboards with dot inlays. The bodies were multiple-bound and fitted with "fine tortoise celluloid guard plates." The mahogany body was discontinued by 1937 but the rosewood model, renumbered No.5246, lasted until the line was discontinued.

Two other flattops were pictured in the '35 catalog. The No. 5206 was a sunburst finished, 14 frets clear of the body version of the Classic, offering more guitar for less money. The Concert-sized Inspiration No.52_ _ featured a new peghead and raised pickguard. The small-bodied 1937 Junior model No.5240 carried on the smaller size into the late-'30s, a time when big flattops became the norm for Washburn and the rest of the American builders. The Junior was fitted with an engraved celluloid peghead overlay with "Washburn" on the diagonal between the tuning pegs and radial lines above and below the name. Similarly constructed overlays were also seen regularly on instruments made by Harmony and Kay in the '30s, '40s and '50s.

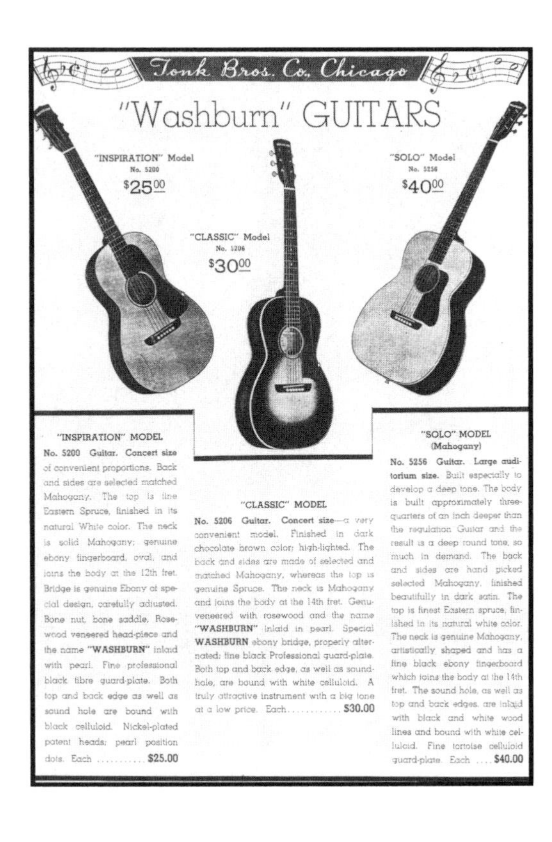

Tonk Bros. Co. Chicago

"Washburn" GUITARS

"INSPIRATION" Model $25.00

"CLASSIC" Model $30.00

"SOLO" Model $40.00

"INSPIRATION" MODEL

No. 5200 Guitar. Concert size of convenient proportions. Back and sides are selected matched Mahogany. The top is fine Eastern Spruce, finished in its natural White color. The neck is solid Mahogany; genuine ebony fingerboard, oval, and joins the body at the 12th fret. Bridge is genuine Ebony of special design, carefully adjusted. Bone nut, bone saddle. Rosewood veneered head-piece and the name **"WASHBURN"** inlaid with pearl. Fine professional black fibre guard-plate. Both top and back edge as well as sound hole are bound with black celluloid. Nickel-plated patent heads; pearl position dots. Each **$25.00**

"CLASSIC" MODEL

No. 5206 Guitar. Concert size—a very convenient model. Finished in dark chocolate brown color; high-lighted. The back and sides are made of selected and matched Mahogany, whereas the top is genuine Spruce. The neck is Mahogany and joins the body at the 14th fret. Genu- veneered with rosewood and the name **"WASHBURN"** inlaid in pearl. Special **WASHBURN** ebony bridge, properly alternated; fine black Professional guard-plate. Both top and back edge, as well as sound-hole, are bound with white celluloid. A truly attractive instrument with a big tone at a low price. Each **$30.00**

"SOLO" MODEL (Mahogany)

No. 5256 Guitar. Large auditorium size. Built especially to develop a deep tone. The body is built approximately three-quarters of an inch deeper than the regulation Guitar and the result is a deep round tone, so much in demand. The back and sides are hand picked selected Mahogany, finished beautifully in dark satin. The top is finest Eastern spruce, finished in its natural white color. The neck is genuine Mahogany, artistically shaped and has a fine black ebony fingerboard which joins the body at the 14th fret. The sound hole, as well as top and back edges, are inlaid with black and white wood lines and bound with white celluloid. Fine tortoise celluloid guard-plate. Each **$40.00**

Sometime between the '35 and '37 catalogs, a fancier version of the Solo was released with No. 5257-1/2 labels. These had the Washburn name and Deco style designs inlaid into the peghead with pearl, gold plated tuners, pearl block inlays on an ebony fingerboard and an ebony "smile" bridge. The model number changed to No. 5249 around 1937, but catalog pictures show the model, named Solo Deluxe, unchanged. The '37 catalog specified a seven-ply neck, as on No. 5257-1/2, while for '39, a "five ply Maple and Mahogany neck with buried steel truss rod for extra reinforcement" was listed. These rosewood beauties are very serious guitars.

Besides the dreadnought-shaped Large Auditorium size, Washburn offered two others, both presumably larger. The Super Auditorium and Extra Super Auditorium sizes were available in either flattop/round hole or archtop/f-hole bodies featuring the round bottom shape generally associated with archtops. The Super Auditorium archtop Collegian of '37 was joined in '39 by the Super Auditorium flattop Classic, model No. 5241. Both of these guitars are reportedly 16" wide and were fitted with the radial line peghead overlay seen on the No.5240 Junior. The Extra Super Auditorium size, reportedly 17" wide, was offered in '37 on the all new Inspiration No.5144 flattop and the Superb No.5248 archtop. The shape of the 5144 guitar looks very much like a clone of Gibson's Super Jumbo (SJ200), except that it predates it by a year! It's possible the 17" body size did, too. Unfortunately, a surviving example could not be found to measure. This would go right along with the rest of Washburn's history of being ahead of Martin and Gibson in the "bigger is better" flattop race. The neck was specified in '37 as having seven plies and by '39, five plies and a non-adjustable truss rod.

"Classic Model"
No. 5241

"Inspiration" Model
No. 5244

"Solo De Luxe" Model
No. 5249

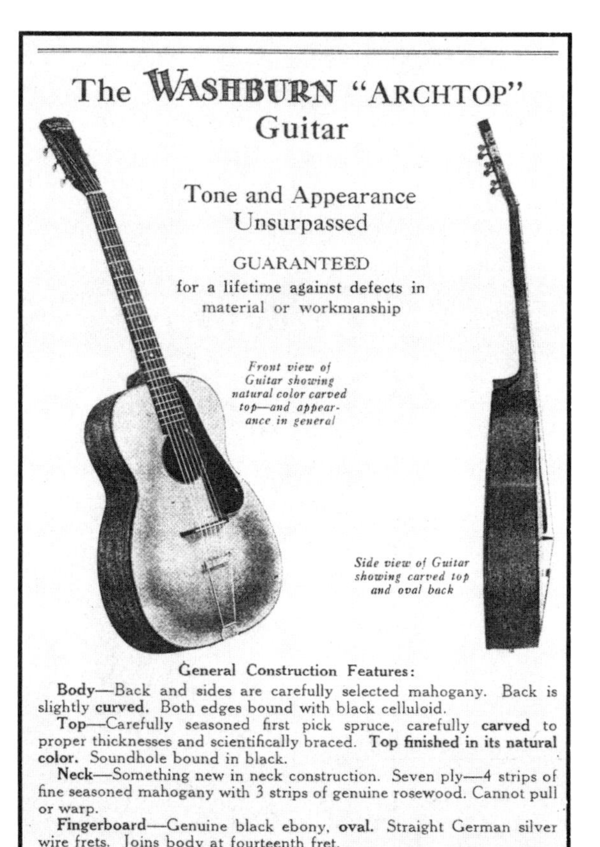

The **WASHBURN** "ARCHTOP" Guitar

Tone and Appearance Unsurpassed

GUARANTEED
for a lifetime against defects in material or workmanship

Front view of Guitar showing natural color carved top—and appearance in general

Side view of Guitar showing carved top and oval back

General Construction Features:

Body—Back and sides are carefully selected mahogany. Back is slightly **curved.** Both edges bound with black celluloid.

Top—Carefully seasoned first pick spruce, carefully **carved** to proper thicknesses and scientifically braced. **Top finished in its natural color.** Soundhole bound in black.

Neck—Something new in neck construction. Seven ply—4 strips of fine seasoned mahogany with 3 strips of genuine rosewood. Cannot pull or warp.

Fingerboard—Genuine black ebony, **oval.** Straight German silver wire frets. Joins body at fourteenth fret.

Trimmings—High grade nickel-plated patent heads. Large professional model black fibre guard plate. Genuine ebony bridge with bone saddle. Highly nickel-plated tailpiece, bone fret.

Size—Full Auditorium size, Professional model.

No. 5250..Each **$50.00**

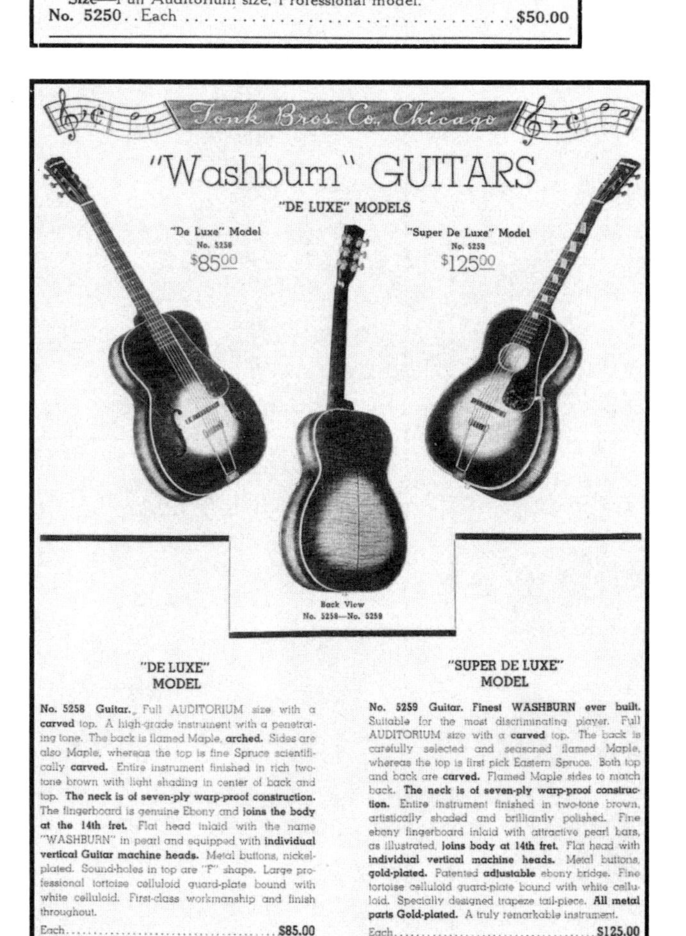

Tonk Bros. Co. Chicago

"Washburn" GUITARS

"DE LUXE" MODELS

"De Luxe" Model No. 5258 $85.00

"Super De Luxe" Model No. 5259 $125.00

Back View No. 5258—No. 5259

"DE LUXE" MODEL

No. 5258 Guitar. Full AUDITORIUM size with a **carved** top. A high-grade instrument with a penetrating tone. The back is flamed Maple, **arched.** Sides are also Maple, whereas the top is fine Spruce scientifically **carved.** Entire instrument finished in rich two-tone brown with light shading in center of back and top. **The neck is of seven-ply warp-proof construction.** The fingerboard is genuine Ebony and **joins the body at the 14th fret.** Flat head inlaid with the name "WASHBURN" in pearl and equipped with **individual vertical Guitar machine heads.** Metal buttons, nickel-plated. Sound-holes in top are "F" shape. Large professional tortoise celluloid guard-plate bound with white celluloid. First-class workmanship and finish throughout.

Each **$85.00**

"SUPER DE LUXE" MODEL

No. 5259 Guitar. Finest WASHBURN ever built. Suitable for the most discriminating player. Full AUDITORIUM size with a **carved** top. The back is carefully selected and seasoned flamed Maple, whereas the top is first pick Eastern Spruce. Both top and back are **carved.** Flamed Maple sides to match back. **The neck is of seven-ply warp-proof construction.** Entire instrument finished in two-tone brown, artistically shaded and brilliantly polished. Fine ebony fingerboard inlaid with attractive pearl bars, as illustrated, **joins body at 14th fret.** Flat head with **individual vertical machine heads.** Metal buttons, **gold-plated.** Patented **adjustable** ebony bridge. Fine tortoise celluloid guard-plate bound with white celluloid. Specially designed trapeze tail-piece. **All metal parts Gold-plated.** A truly remarkable instrument.

Each **$125.00**

The Washburn name was first put on an archtop guitar in the early '30s. No. 5250 "Archtop" Guitar featured a carved spruce top with a round soundhole, a trapeze tailpiece with floating ebony bridge, a slotted peghead, and a seven ply neck of alternating mahogany and rosewood. This construction was for strength since the neck did not have a truss rod and the guitar was designed for steel strings. An arched mahogany back completed what would soon be known as the "Collegian" model. By 1935, three more carved tops joined the line, all with solid headstocks and sunburst finishes. No. 5255 "Superb" had a round soundhole and an arched mahogany back. No. 5258 "DeLuxe" had f-holes and an arched maple back. This appears to have been Washburn's first f-hole guitar.

The name Super DeLuxe was first used on banjos and ukuleles around the time of the change from Lyon & Healy to Tonk Bros. "Super DeLuxe" No. 5259 was the first guitar to be awarded this title and Tonk Bros. called it, with slight disrespect to its predecessors, the "Finest Washburn ever built." Carved spruce top, carved flamed-maple back and sides, gold hardware and an ebony fingerboard with striking inlays put this $125 guitar in a class with Gibson's L-7 and Epiphone's Triumph, although it lacked the more modern f-holes. The cost was still less than half the price of an L-5 or Epi DeLuxe. Gibson was releasing its $400 Super 400 at this time, making the Washburn Super DeLuxe Guitar seem somewhat less than Super DeLuxe.

The orchestra guitar dominated from the mid-'30s until WWII with Gretsch, National, Rickenbacker, Vega, Regal, Kay and Harmony joining Gibson, Epiphone, custom builders D'Angelico and Stromberg and the venerable Martin company in offering professional grade archtops. Even the Larson Bros. of Chicago built some archtops, many of which have unfortunately been converted into flattops. The Bacon & Day, Slingerland, S.S. Stewart and Orpheum guitars were just a few of the "brand name" archtops that flooded the market with good to excellent quality instruments. And every jobber offered a large line of cheap to good quality archtops, totally saturating the market. American Guitar companies reportedly made 300,000 guitars in 1936, with almost 85% of them costing less than $50.

Tonk Bros. was keen to this and discontinued the $85 Deluxe and $125 Super Deluxe. The '37 catalog offered two f-hole guitars, including a revised Collegian Model No.5242 ($25) in SUPER AUDITORIUM size.

Segmented f-holes replaced the round hole on the first variation c.'36 followed by f-holes on a "Genuine spruce, finely arched" (another expression for pressed plywood) top. Dressing the guitars up was a stylish celluloid peghead overlay, as seen on the Junior and '39 Classic flattops. A carved top Extra SUPER AUDITORIUM size Superb Model No. 5248 ($57.50) was a generic late-'30s carved top/ply body guitar; decent, but nothing special, although it did continue the triple diagonal line inlays first seen on the Super Deluxe. A five-piece neck and slightly different shapes for the peghead and the f-holes were obvious changes seen in the '39 catalog. A third archtop, the SUPER AUDITORIUM sized Aristocrat Model No. 5243, was added between the Collegian and the Superb. The Aristocrat had a carved top and was fitted with better quality tuners, tailpiece and fingerboard inlays than the Collegian. Other models may have been added the last couple of years before WWII, although no mention of them could be found in the trade magazines, etc.

Up to the late-'30s, Washburns were always a distinct line, built using a completely independent set of jigs, etc. No matter who was building them, there was no counterpart available with another brand name. Some of the last models, however, were simply Regals (or possibly Harmony, Kay and/or Gibson-made) with a "Washburn By Tonk Bros." label. The word "numerous" describes the mid-line 16" archtops to come out of Chicago in the mid-to-late '30s. For example, nearly identical guitars were released under the Biltmore, Broman, Carelli and Metro brand names, none of whom operated manufacturing facilities. Regal, Harmony and Kay, all of whom made hundreds of thousands of instruments, also put their own names on similar models, including Harmony's top-of-the-line Cremona, which was considerably better than their usual models.

Following Regal's announcement in '38 to sell directly to dealers, Tonk Bros.' 1939 catalog pictured an almost identical set of guitars to the earlier models, but used updated captions. One of the big changes was to the necks, which went from seven-ply to five-ply with non-adjustable steel truss rods. This description matches up to the necks on Gibson made Recording King instruments, giving some credence to long running rumors of Gibson-made Washburns. But where are they today? Were these design changes ever implemented? The two new models suggest Gibson, although a number of other companies also come to mind. The flattop Classic had a squared off bridge instead of Washburn's usual "smile" and only had 19 frets, as on Gibson flattops of the day (excluding the Super Jumbos). Real-life examples appear to be Regal as much as anything else. It's quite possible that more is being read into the catalogs and the folklore than is really there. The names Harmony and Kay should also be considered (as well as the possibility of their involvement in some of the cheaper guitars usually associated with Gibson). Chicago's tradition of subcontracting out work goes against our ideas of quality, but apparently all of the companies were willing to build and sell parts of instruments (e.g. complete bodies) and vice versa, purchase parts of instruments when practical or necessary. These companies were businesses above all and the criss-crossing of their paths makes any definitive conclusions regarding lineage somewhat presumptuous without original documents.

Regardless of who was making what, there were scores of mid-priced guitars available before WWII and this was the market Washburn had ended up in. To offer high-end instruments would have required a factory, knowledgeable designers and builders and at least one person with a genuine interest and vision. By the time Lyon & Healy's name was again affiliated with Washburn (c.'43), the war had stopped production. It appears that rather than try to compete following the war, Tonk Bros. and Lyon & Healy chose to let the Washburn name bow out somewhat gracefully.

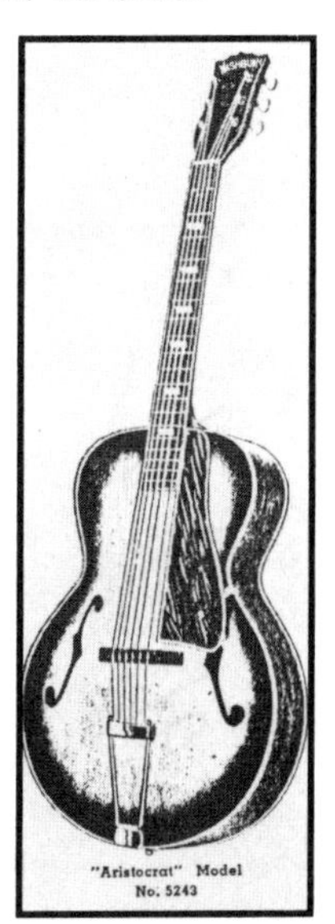

"Aristocrat" Model No. 5243

Mandolins

While the mandolin was a popular instrument when Washburn introduced their line in the 1880s, it would be almost ten years before the big mandolin craze hit. The earliest Washburn catalogs had the guitars at the front, followed by the mandolins. Starting in the late 1890s through the end of the teens, the mandolins were placed at the front, followed by the less popular guitars (the zithers were always at the back, and not because zither starts with the letter z).

There were hundreds of makers of bowl back, "potato bug" mandolins and the popular method of construction was to glue multiple strips, or ribs, side-by-side to form the shell. This required a paper or cloth lining to hold the ribs in place. George Durkee was granted his third patent with Lyon & Healy for a method of securing the ribs to wooden braces that sufficiently held the shell together. This allowed for an inner reflective surface of hardwood instead of glue-soaked paper or cloth. It also allowed the back to resonate undampened. This process must have been difficult because the factory eventually reverted to the old method.

The early line of mandolins ranged from the basic Style 71 with 9 alternating ribs of rosewood and maple to the ornate Style 80 with 35 ribs of rosewood, inlaid soundhole and pickguard and engraved tuners and tailpiece. In between were Styles 72, 73, 74, 75, and 76, all of which were somewhat plain compared to the following generations.

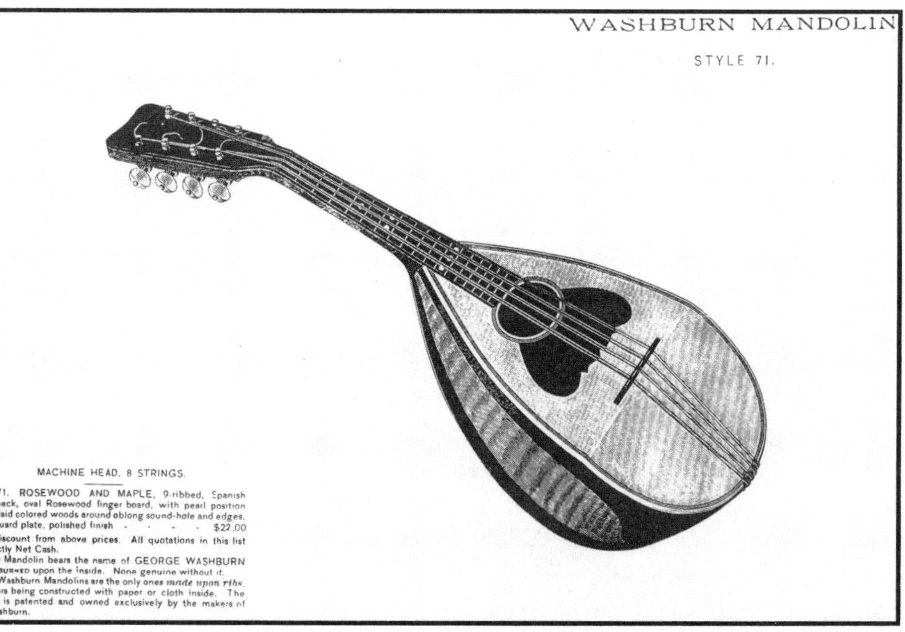

WASHBURN MANDOLIN

STYLE 71.

MACHINE HEAD, 8 STRINGS.

71. ROSEWOOD AND MAPLE, 9-ribbed, Spanish neck, oval Rosewood finger board, with pearl position nlaid colored woods around oblong sound-hole and edges, guard plate, polished finish - - - - $22.00

discount from above prices. All quotations in this list ictly Net Cash.

ry Mandolin bears the name of GEORGE WASHBURN BURNED upon the inside. None genuine without it.

Washburn Mandolins are the only ones *made upon ribs*, ers being constructed with paper or cloth inside. The s is patented and owned exclusively by the makers of ashburn.

(No Model.)

G. B. DURKEE.

MANDOLIN.

No. 368,461. Patented Aug. 16, 1887.

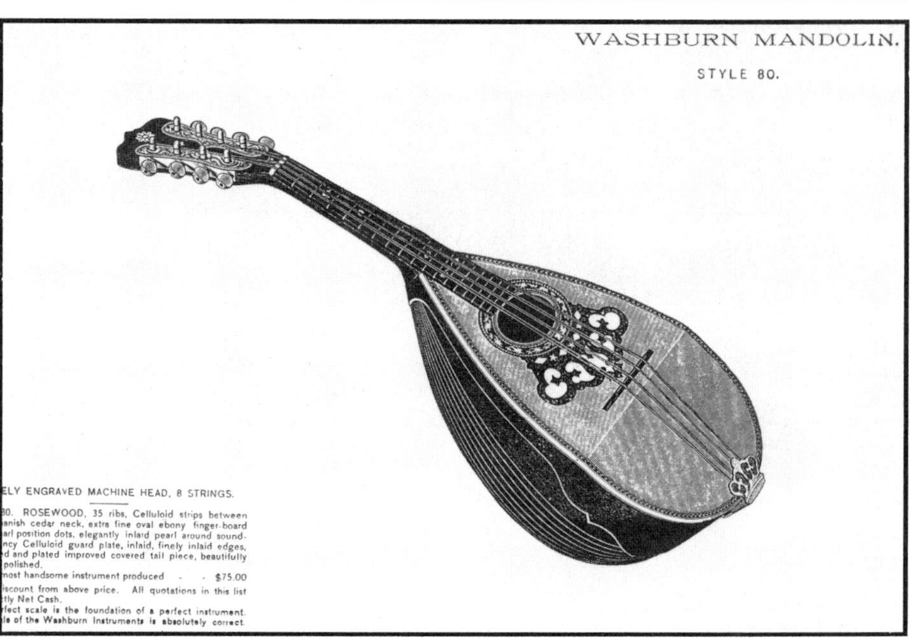

WASHBURN MANDOLIN.

STYLE 80.

ELY ENGRAVED MACHINE HEAD, 8 STRINGS.

80. ROSEWOOD, 35 ribs, Celluloid strips between anish cedar neck, extra fine oval ebony finger-board arl position dots, elegantly inlaid pearl around sound-ncy Celluloid guard plate, inlaid, finely inlaid edges, d and plated improved covered tail piece, beautifully polished.

most handsome instrument produced - - $75.00

iscount from above price. All quotations in this list tly Net Cash.

fect scale is the foundation of a perfect instrument. le of the Washburn Instruments is absolutely correct.

The whole line was dressed up in 1892 with No. 80 receiving a fully inlaid fingerboard with an exotic water bird at the end. New models included Nos. 78 and 85. No. 85 featured metal strips inlaid between the 36 rosewood ribs, a bound headstock and plenty of pearl. Gold-plated tuners and tailpiece helped justify the difference in price between the $125 No. 85 and the previously top-of-the-line No. 80 for $75. A mandola, the short-lived Style 89 joined the line as the dawn of the mandolin orchestra approached. The mandola would take the part of the viola. It's important to remember that there was no radio or recorded music at this time. Written music played a most important role in the orchestrated arrangements that were performed by large groups, or clubs, of fretted stringed instruments, and the mandola was an integral member.

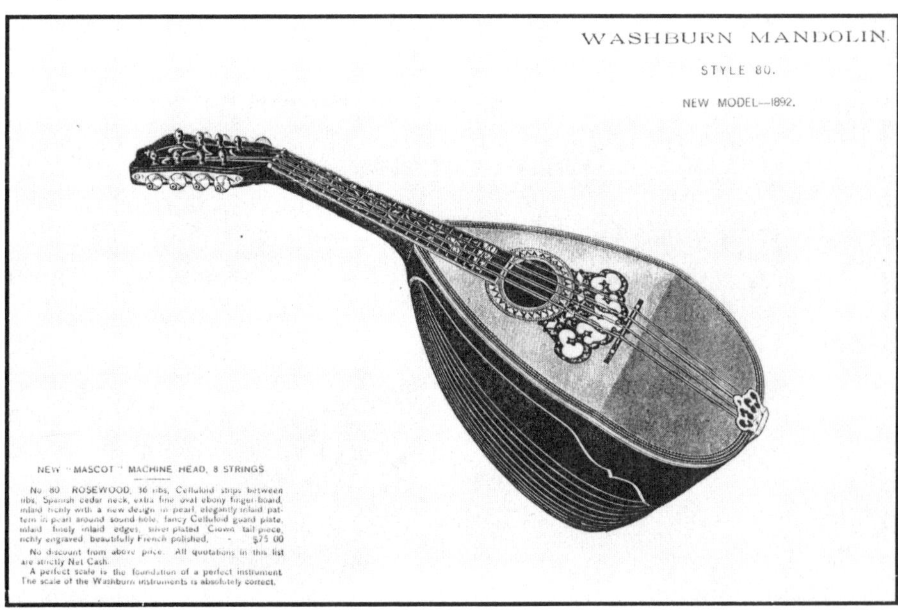

WASHBURN MANDOLIN.
STYLE 80.
NEW MODEL—1892.
NEW "MASCOT" MACHINE HEAD, 8 STRINGS
No. 80. ROSEWOOD, 36 ribs, Celluloid strips between ribs, Spanish cedar neck, extra fine oval ebony finger-board, inlaid richly with a new design in pearl, elegantly inlaid pattern in pearl around sound-hole, fancy Celluloid guard plate, inlaid finely inlaid edges, silver-plated Crown tail-piece, richly engraved, beautifully French polished, - $75 00
No discount from above price. All quotations in this list are strictly Net Cash.
A perfect scale is the foundation of a perfect instrument. The scale of the Washburn instruments is absolutely correct.

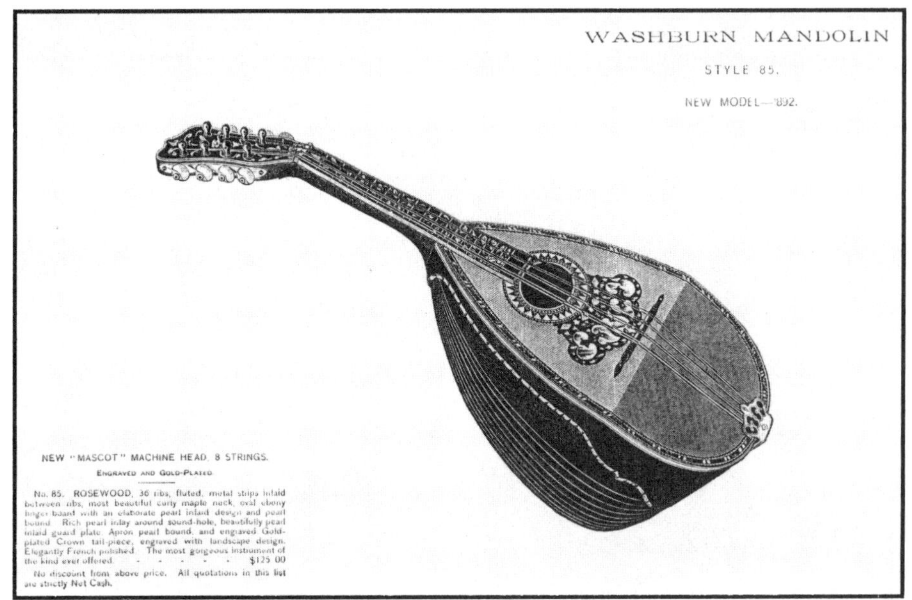

WASHBURN MANDOLIN
STYLE 85.
NEW MODEL—1892.
NEW "MASCOT" MACHINE HEAD, 8 STRINGS.
Engraved and Gold-Plated
No. 85. ROSEWOOD, 36 ribs, fluted, metal strips inlaid between ribs, most beautiful curly maple neck, oval ebony finger-board with an elaborate pearl inlaid design and pearl bound. Rich pearl inlay around sound-hole, beautifully pearl inlaid guard plate. Apron pearl bound, and engraved Gold-plated Crown tail-piece, engraved with landscape design. Elegantly French polished. The most gorgeous instrument of the kind ever offered. - - - - - $125 00
No discount from above price. All quotations in this list are strictly Net Cash.

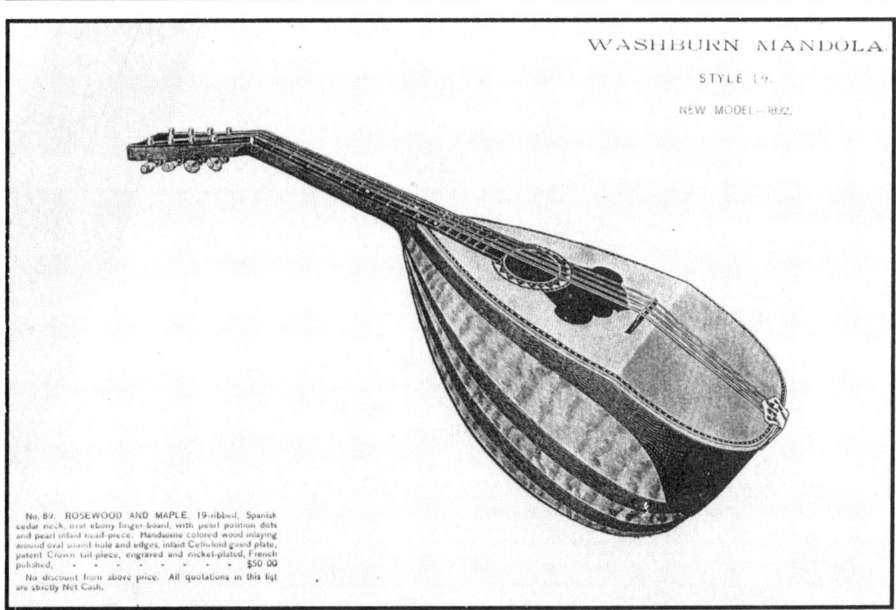

New Washburn Mandolin.

1897 MODEL.

Style 150.

EMMA CALVE.
(ABBEY & GRAU GRAND OPERA CO.)
"I have never, in all my travels, found anything that seemed to me as near perfection in the way of a Mandolin as the Washburn."

CHAS. HENLEIN.
(TEACHER AND SOLOIST, CINCINNATI, O.)
"The Washburn Mandolin I bought of you eight years ago, No. 577, is yet a perfect instrument and compares very favorably with the newer one I purchased a short time ago, No. 38,880. I can not recommend any but Washburn Guitars and Mandolins to my pupils."

DESCRIPTION.

The Washburn Special Patent Head with Etched and Nickel-plated Covering; 8 Strings.

No. 150—ROSEWOOD, 28 ribs, white celluloid inlaid between each rib; ebony veneered head-piece pearl inlaid; ebony finger-board celluloid bound, with eight engraved and inlaid pearl position marks; rich Sidney pearl, handsomely engraved and inlaid around sound-hole; fancy wood inlaid and celluloid bound edges; inlaid tortoise celluloid guard-plate with beautiful pearl ornament; finely polished, nicely etched and nickel-plated crown tail-piece, ... $50.00

No discount from above price.

An ivory or pearl plate bearing the purchaser's initials or monogram can be let into any finger-board at $2.50 extra, net.

17

At the bottom of the line, a No. 071 was added in the mid-1890s. In 1896 a new numbering scheme reflected the prices which ranged from the $15 No. 115 (formerly No. 071), to the totally new $125 No. 1125. In between were Nos. 118, 122, 130, 140, 150, 160, and 175. No. 1125 had an exquisitely inlaid butterfly as part of the pick guard and more pearl everywhere. This model was considerably fancier than the $125 top-of-the-line No. 85 that preceded it. The $75 No. 175 also had an engraved full pearl fingerboard and pearl around the border and soundhole. It too, was considerably fancier than the second-in-line $75 No. 80 it replaced. One of Lyon & Healy's claims was that their experience and established procedures allowed them to give the public more instrument for the same money as time went on. Comparisons between the two top-line models from 1892 and 1897, which stayed at $75 and $125, proved their sincerity.

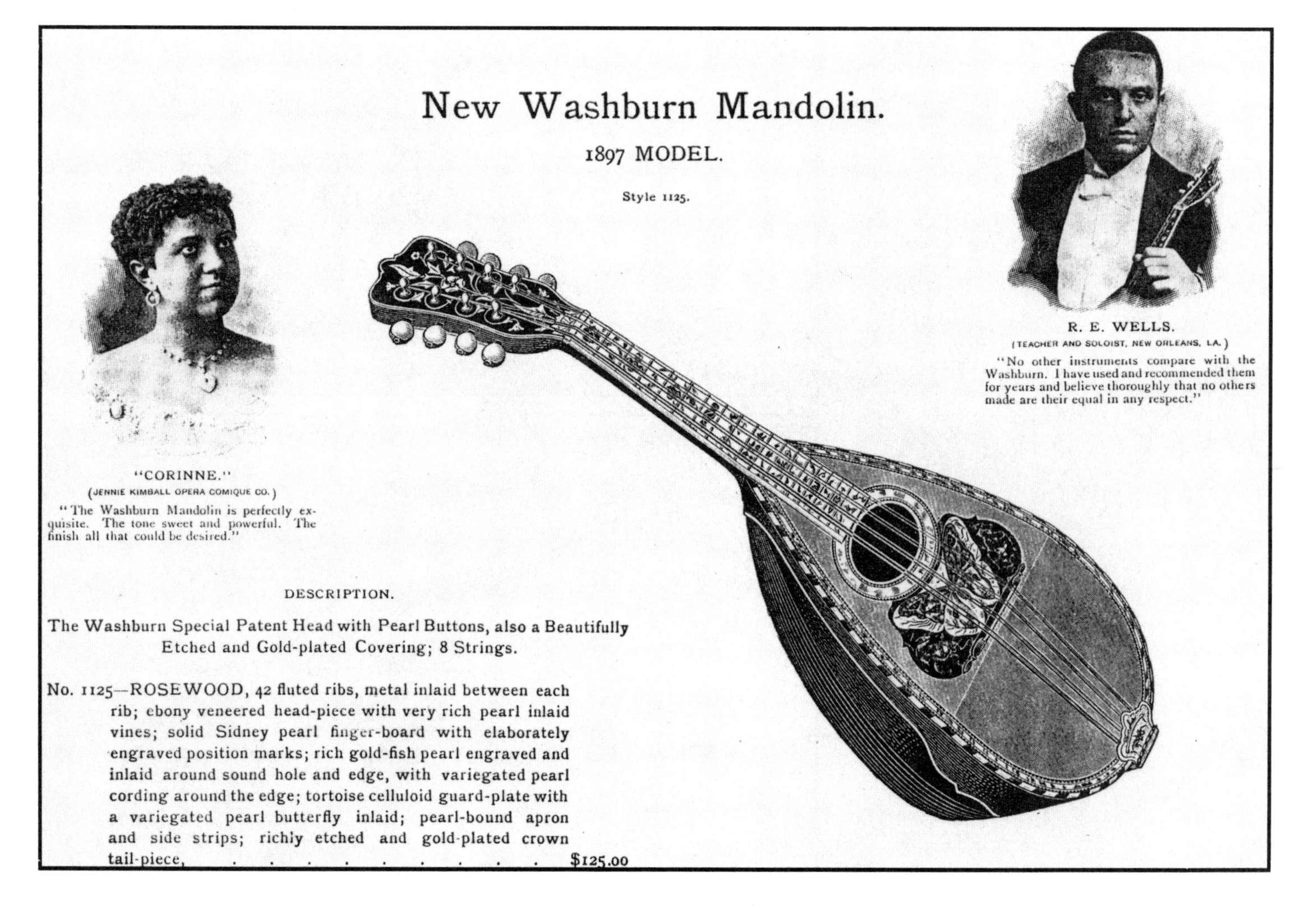

New Washburn Mandolin.

1897 MODEL.

Style 1125.

"CORINNE."
(JENNIE KIMBALL OPERA COMIQUE CO.)
"The Washburn Mandolin is perfectly exquisite. The tone sweet and powerful. The finish all that could be desired."

R. E. WELLS.
(TEACHER AND SOLOIST, NEW ORLEANS, LA.)
"No other instruments compare with the Washburn. I have used and recommended them for years and believe thoroughly that no others made are their equal in any respect."

DESCRIPTION.

The Washburn Special Patent Head with Pearl Buttons, also a Beautifully Etched and Gold-plated Covering; 8 Strings.

No. 1125—ROSEWOOD, 42 fluted ribs, metal inlaid between each rib; ebony veneered head-piece with very rich pearl inlaid vines; solid Sidney pearl finger-board with elaborately engraved position marks; rich gold-fish pearl engraved and inlaid around sound hole and edge, with variegated pearl cording around the edge; tortoise celluloid guard-plate with a variegated pearl butterfly inlaid; pearl-bound apron and side strips; richly etched and gold-plated crown tail-piece, ... $125.00

1905 saw another all-new mandolin line from Washburn. Style 215 kept the entry level at $15 and Nos. 225, 235, 250 and 275 offered increasingly fancier models ranging up to $75. Gone was the deluxe No. 1125 leaving No. 275 as the king of the bowl backs. Although not as outrageous as the 1125, the 275 did have an engraved pearl fingerboard, and forty-four ribs with thin strips of white celluloid in between. It was still at least the equivalent of Martin's $100 Style 7, their top-of-the-line at the time. No. 250 also had an engraved pearl fingerboard but only thirty-six ribs. That was still a lot of ribs. The Washburn line would remain stable through WWI with No. 1125 returning for the 1912 and 1913 catalogs, which also included a $20 No. 220 mandolin and a No. 225 mandola. Oddly enough, this was the first Washburn Mandola cataloged since 1889.

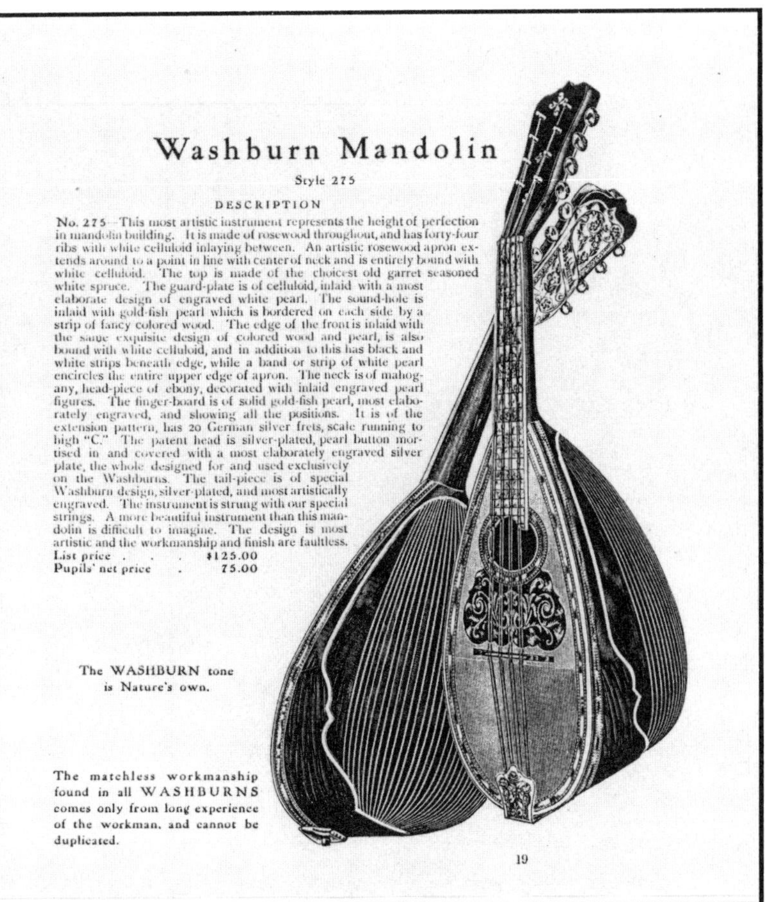

Washburn Mandolin

Style 275

DESCRIPTION

No. 275—This most artistic instrument represents the height of perfection in mandolin building. It is made of rosewood throughout, and has forty-four ribs with white celluloid inlaying between. An artistic rosewood apron extends around to a point in line with center of neck and is entirely bound with white celluloid. The top is made of the choicest old garret seasoned white spruce. The guard-plate is of celluloid, inlaid with a most elaborate design of engraved white pearl. The sound-hole is inlaid with gold-fish pearl which is bordered on each side by a strip of fancy colored wood. The edge of the front is inlaid with the same exquisite design of colored wood and pearl, is also bound with white celluloid, and in addition to this has black and white strips beneath edge, while a band or strip of white pearl encircles the entire upper edge of apron. The neck is of mahogany, head-piece of ebony, decorated with inlaid engraved pearl figures. The finger-board is of solid gold-fish pearl, most elaborately engraved, and showing all the positions. It is of the extension pattern, has 20 German silver frets, scale running to high "C." The patent head is silver-plated, pearl button mortised in and covered with a most elaborately engraved silver plate, the whole designed for and used exclusively on the Washburns. The tail-piece is of special Washburn design, silver-plated, and most artistically engraved. The instrument is strung with our special strings. A more beautiful instrument than this mandolin is difficult to imagine. The design is most artistic and the workmanship and finish are faultless.

List price $125.00
Pupils' net price . 75.00

The WASHBURN tone is Nature's own.

The matchless workmanship found in all WASHBURNS comes only from long experience of the workman, and cannot be duplicated.

19

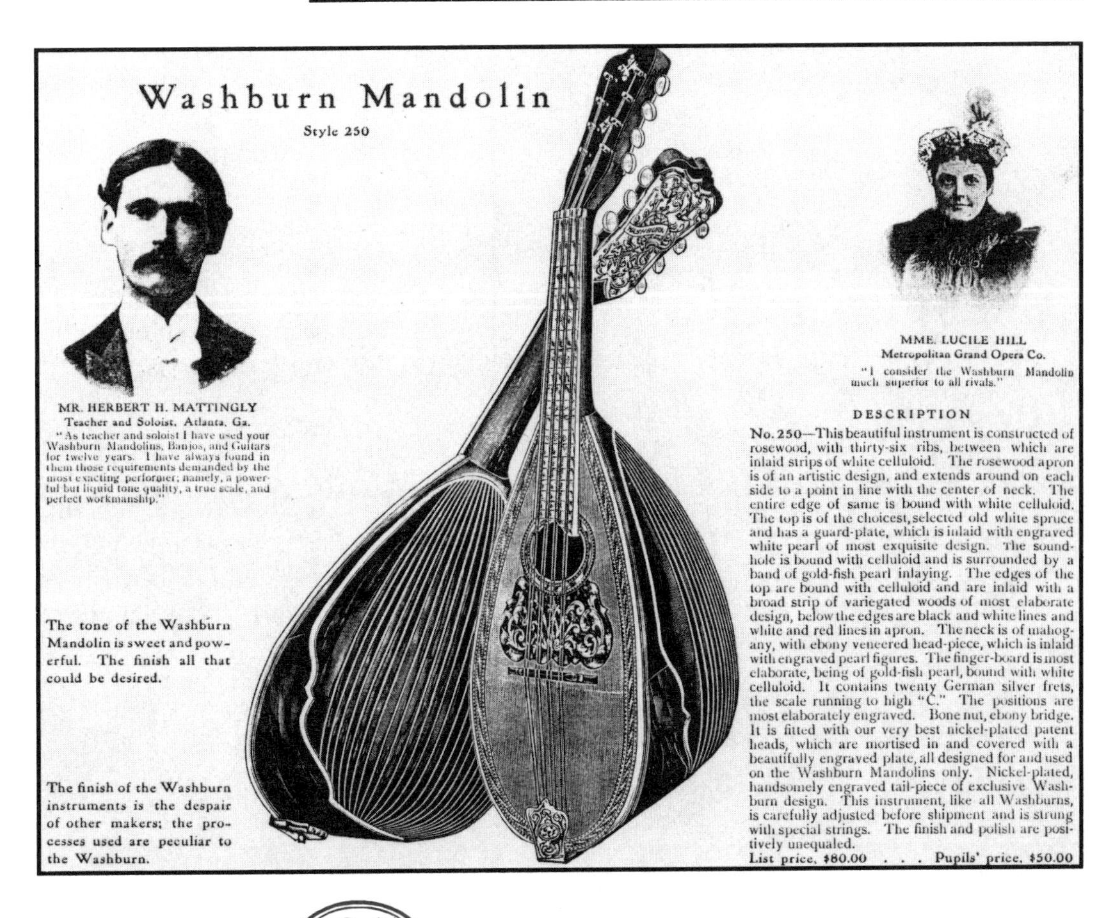

Washburn Mandolin

Style 250

MR. HERBERT H. MATTINGLY
Teacher and Soloist, Atlanta, Ga.

"As teacher and soloist I have used your Washburn Mandolins, Banjos, and Guitars for twelve years. I have always found in them those requirements demanded by the most exacting performer; namely, a powerful but liquid tone quality, a true scale, and perfect workmanship."

MME. LUCILE HILL
Metropolitan Grand Opera Co.

"I consider the Washburn Mandolin much superior to all rivals."

DESCRIPTION

No. 250—This beautiful instrument is constructed of rosewood, with thirty-six ribs, between which are inlaid strips of white celluloid. The rosewood apron is of an artistic design, and extends around on each side to a point in line with the center of neck. The entire edge of same is bound with white celluloid. The top is of the choicest, selected old white spruce and has a guard-plate, which is inlaid with engraved white pearl of most exquisite design. The sound-hole is bound with celluloid and is surrounded by a band of gold-fish pearl inlaying. The edges of the top are bound with celluloid and are inlaid with a broad strip of variegated woods of most elaborate design, below the edges are black and white lines and white and red lines in apron. The neck is of mahogany, with ebony veneered head-piece, which is inlaid with engraved pearl figures. The finger-board is most elaborate, being of gold-fish pearl, bound with white celluloid. It contains twenty German silver frets, the scale running to high "C." The positions are most elaborately engraved. Bone nut, ebony bridge. It is fitted with our very best nickel-plated patent heads, which are mortised in and covered with a beautifully engraved plate, all designed for and used on the Washburn Mandolins only. Nickel-plated, handsomely engraved tail-piece of exclusive Washburn design. This instrument, like all Washburns, is carefully adjusted before shipment and is strung with special strings. The finish and polish are positively unequaled.

List price, $80.00 . . . Pupils' price, $50.00

The tone of the Washburn Mandolin is sweet and powerful. The finish all that could be desired.

The finish of the Washburn instruments is the despair of other makers; the processes used are peculiar to the Washburn.

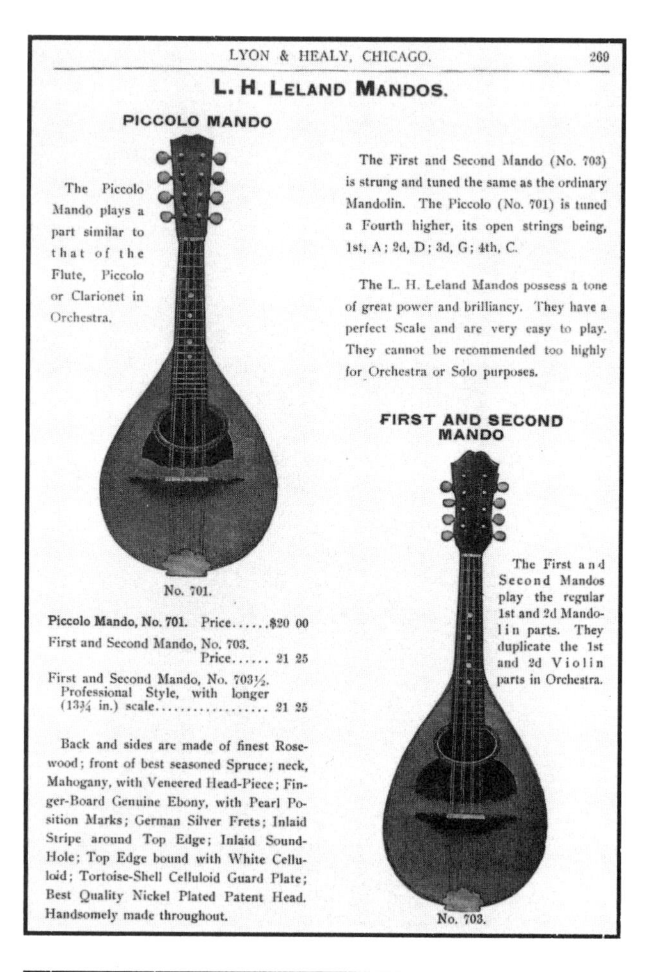

LYON & HEALY, CHICAGO. 269

L. H. LELAND MANDOS.

PICCOLO MANDO

The Piccolo Mando plays a part similar to that of the Flute, Piccolo or Clarionet in Orchestra.

The First and Second Mando (No. 703) is strung and tuned the same as the ordinary Mandolin. The Piccolo (No. 701) is tuned a Fourth higher, its open strings being, 1st, A; 2d, D; 3d, G; 4th, C.

The L. H. Leland Mandos possess a tone of great power and brilliancy. They have a perfect Scale and are very easy to play. They cannot be recommended too highly for Orchestra or Solo purposes.

No. 701.

FIRST AND SECOND MANDO

The First and Second Mandos play the regular 1st and 2d Mandolin parts. They duplicate the 1st and 2d Violin parts in Orchestra.

Piccolo Mando, No. 701. Price......$20 00
First and Second Mando, No. 703. Price...... 21 25
First and Second Mando, No. 703½. Professional Style, with longer (13¾ in.) scale.................. 21 25

Back and sides are made of finest Rosewood; front of best seasoned Spruce; neck, Mahogany, with Veneered Head-Piece; Finger-Board Genuine Ebony, with Pearl Position Marks; German Silver Frets; Inlaid Stripe around Top Edge; Inlaid Sound-Hole; Top Edge bound with White Celluloid; Tortoise-Shell Celluloid Guard Plate; Best Quality Nickel Plated Patent Head. Handsomely made throughout.

No. 703.

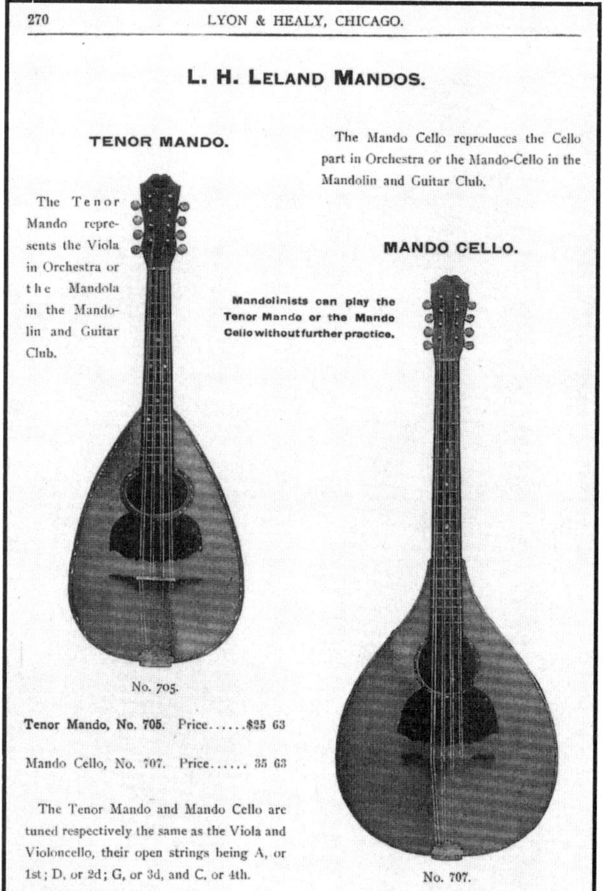

270 LYON & HEALY, CHICAGO.

L. H. LELAND MANDOS.

TENOR MANDO.

The Tenor Mando represents the Viola in Orchestra or the Mandola in the Mandolin and Guitar Club.

The Mando Cello reproduces the Cello part in Orchestra or the Mando-Cello in the Mandolin and Guitar Club.

MANDO CELLO.

Mandolinists can play the Tenor Mando or the Mando Cello without further practice.

No. 705.

Tenor Mando, No. 705. Price......$25 63

Mando Cello, No. 707. Price...... 35 63

The Tenor Mando and Mando Cello are tuned respectively the same as the Viola and Violoncello, their open strings being A, or 1st; D, or 2d; G, or 3d, and C, or 4th.

No. 707.

For a short time around 1912, Lyon & Healy marketed the L.H. Leland "Mando" Line. These were aimed directly at the popular mandolin orchestras. Gibson was enjoying great success establishing and supplying instruments for these groups with their series of thin archtops, covering the same musical range as those in a string quartet. The L.H. Leland Mando Family was designed to do the same and more. The violin part was played on the Mezzo Mando (First and Second Mando, 1913) , which, like a regular mandolin, was tuned the same as a violin (EADG high to low). The Viola part was played on the Tenor Mando, the equivalent of the long established mandola, also tuned in fifths (ADGC, high to low). The mandocello was designed to take the cello's role in the orchestra, again tuned in fifths (ADGC, high to low, one octave below the mandola). The L.H. Leland equivalent was the Baritone Mando (Mando Cello, 1913. See p.59 for the Mando-Guitar).

A number of manufacturers had made Octave Mandolas, designed to be tuned the same as a mandolin but one octave lower, between the regular mandola and the mandocello. Much discourse was printed on the merits and the shortcomings of these variations, especially concerning the inability of a small instrument to produce the lower notes. On the other hand, the case for universal notation and for players not needing to read in a number of keys was pleaded. Many members of the mandolin orchestras had only basic musical skills, but could play simple open position melodies and read in certain keys. Put enough of these players together with well-scored charts and appropriately tuned instruments and a magical transformation occurred.

Adding to the upper register of the line was the Soprano Mando (Piccolo Mando, 1913), designed to play the voice of the flute, piccolo or clarinet. The Soprano Mando, tuned in fifths (ADGC high to low), moved the fingering of the highest notes of the Mandolin down the neck five frets, making them easier to reach. The additional five fret range beyond a mandolin's highest note was available, but incredibly difficult to finger. The brighter tone of a smaller body was another possible feature of the Soprano Mando, however, its usefulness

At the other end of the scale was the Double Bass Mando (also known as the Mando Bass), a fretted version of the Upright Bass, tuned in fourths (GDAE, high to low). First seen at the Mandolinists Guild Convention in 1911, it wasn't long before both Gibson and Lyon and Healy were pushing them (the notation for writing the music was debated in the same manner as the octave mandola's). These early fretted basses were easier to play and somewhat smaller than the Upright Bass. Twenty-five years later, Regal (who was building Washburns at the time), released a fretted upright bass called the Basso-guitar. Fifteen years after that Leo Fender would unleash his revolutionary fretted electric bass, changing music history forever. His concept was not totally original, however, as Rickenbacker and Vega had offered electric basses before WWII and the idea of "Precision" fretting went back to the early part of the century.

Going back even further in the history of the bass guitar, Washburn had made a GIANT six string guitar in the 1890s that appeared to be played in the upright position. If it was indeed a playable instrument and tuned an octave below a regular guitar (as would seem necessary due to the string length) then this could be the first Bass Guitar and possibly the first fretted bass!! AND the first six string bass!!

272 LYON & HEALY, CHICAGO.

THE L. H. LELAND BASS MANDO No. 709.

A magnificent instrument, which should be in every Mandolin Orchestra. Has large, responsive tone of great beauty and carrying power.

Height, 69½ Inches.

A perfect Contra-Bass to the Mando and Mandolin family. Has the full 43-inch scale, and is tuned the same as a regular Double Bass Viol, or the four lowest strings of the Guitar.
Price $80 00

Played with a Pick or Plectrum.

Guitarists can play this instrument by considering its strings the same as the four lowest strings of the Guitar. The regular Guitar part may therefore be used for the Bass Mando without change.

Any one who can play the Double Bass Viol can also play the Double Bass Mando without further practice.

Proper Way to Hold and Play the Bass Mando.

Back and sides of Finest Maple, Mahogany finished. Top of best selected, seasoned Spruce, Ebony Finger - Board; German Silver Frets; Handsomely finished throughout.

A Guitar player can master the Bass Mando by a few minutes' practice.

The Bass Mando presents a handsome appearance, and, aside from its magnificent tone, greatly enhances the attractiveness of the Mandolin Orchestra.

THE L. H. LELAND MANDO FAMILY.
SHOWING RELATIVE SIZES.

LYON & HEALY, CHICAGO. 275

GUITAR-MANDOLINS

OUR OWN MANUFACTURE

A Mandolin with a Guitar-shaped body. It has a finger-board same as on a Mandolin, and is played in same manner; possesses a sweet, clear tone, and with its neat appearance and absolutelv correct scale, has won public favor.

No. 91.

"THE AMERICAN CONSERVATORY."

No. 81. Beautiful Imitation Rosewood Back and Sides, Hand Polished, Spruce Top, Celluloid Guard Plate, Inlaid Edge and Sound-Hole, Imitation Mahogany Neck, Rosewood Finger-Board with Pearl Position Marks, Our Own Make Machine Head, Nickel Covered Shell Pattern Tail-Piece...... Each $6 50

Twelve-string mandolins were put out under the "Columbus," "American Conservatory" and "College Line" names from the turn of the century until the 1920s, featuring four groups of three strings each, tuned the same as the 8-string mandolin. These instruments shared the bowl back body of the regular mandolin.

Another early variation of the mandolin was the Guitar Mandolin, also known as the Mandolinetto. Like a miniature guitar body, these instruments had a flat spruce top with an oval soundhole. The back and sides were rosewood. The scale length and tuning were the same as the mandolin, the difference being the way it sat in one's lap. Lyon & Healy offered their own Mandolin-Guitar from the turn of the century through WWI, by which time the bent top/flatback and archtop/arched back mandolins had established themselves as the instruments of choice. The 12-string mandolins and the Guitar Mandolins were not available after WWI (see p.96 and 100 for Banjo Mandolins).

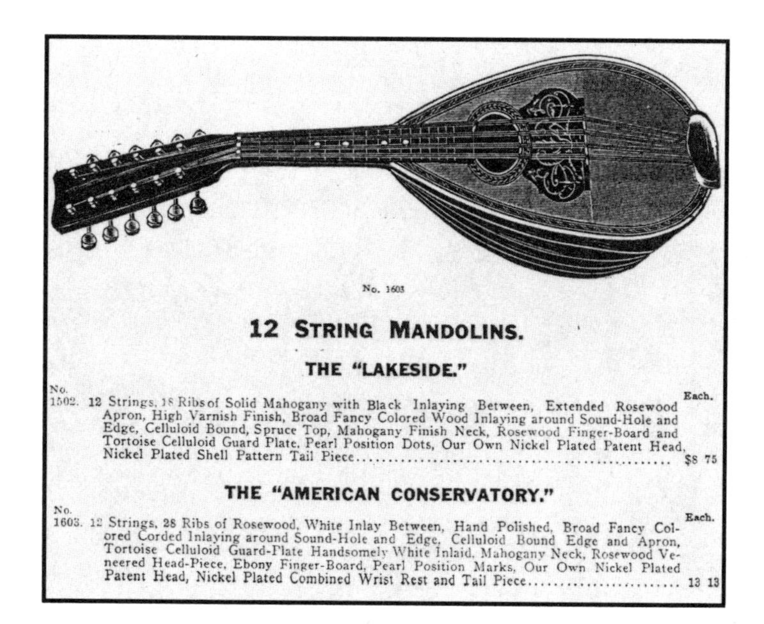

No. 1603

12 STRING MANDOLINS.

THE "LAKESIDE."

No. 1502. 12 Strings, 18 Ribs of Solid Mahogany with Black Inlaying Between, Extended Rosewood Apron, High Varnish Finish, Broad Fancy Colored Wood Inlaying around Sound-Hole and Edge, Celluloid Bound, Spruce Top, Mahogany Finish Neck, Rosewood Finger-Board and Tortoise Celluloid Guard Plate, Pearl Position Dots, Our Own Nickel Plated Patent Head, Nickel Plated Shell Pattern Tail Piece........ Each. $8 75

THE "AMERICAN CONSERVATORY."

No. 1603. 12 Strings, 28 Ribs of Rosewood, White Inlay Between, Hand Polished, Broad Fancy Colored Corded Inlaying around Sound-Hole and Edge, Celluloid Bound Edge and Apron, Tortoise Celluloid Guard-Plate Handsomely White Inlaid, Mahogany Neck, Rosewood Veneered Head-Piece, Ebony Finger-Board, Pearl Position Marks, Our Own Nickel Plated Patent Head, Nickel Plated Combined Wrist Rest and Tail Piece........ Each. 13 13

Washburn introduced a new line of Mandolins in 1915 including the bent top, "Flat-back" Styles 1425, 1430 and 1435. Through at least 1920, both bowlback and flatback mandolins were available, but the hard-to-hold Neapolitan models' days were numbered. Models 2627, 2632, 2643, 2662, and 2683, again having the last two digits represent the price, would be the last of the bowl backs, which were waning in popularity as Gibson's thin archtop design became the standard. Washburn, Martin, and a host of others would make their last "taterbugs" in the early-'20s. Following WWI, there were two different body shapes for the flatbacks, a pear-shaped version and a similar one with two decorative "points" near the neck joint. No. 2424 had a pear-shaped mahogany body and a rosewood fingerboard, No. 2434 a rosewood body with the points and an ebony fingerboard; No. 2442 was described as a somewhat fancier model with pearl inlays in the peghead and fingerboard. None of these could begin to compare with the early bowlbacks as to the degree of decoration. A Mandola, No. 1642 was added to the line but the mandolin orchestra was on its way out by this time and the bent top/flatback mandola would be phased out in the mid-'20s following a short run.

LYON & HEALY, CHICAGO 10

New Washburn Flat-Back Mandolin

Graceful in proportions and outline; tone of unusual sweetness and carrying power; bound to win its way into public favor.

No. 2424. Selected mahogany back, sides and neck, fine spruce top, both top and back edges bound with black, top edge binding supplemented with a strip of black and white purfling, sound-hole similarly bound and inlaid with four strips of black and white purfling, tortoise celluloid guard plate, rosewood extension fingerboard, inlaid pearl position dots, bone nut, rosewood veneered headpiece, ebony compensating bridge, mortised in and covered patent head, nickel-plated tailpiece. Each....................................$35.00

No. 2434. Selected rosewood back and sides, top and back edges bound with 3-ply white and black celluloid, sound-hole edged and inlaid with 5-ply white and black celluloid, tortoise celluloid guard-plate, mahogany neck with ebony topped heel, rosewood veneered head, ebony extension fingerboard, 20 Liberty silver frets. 4 pearl position dots, bone nut, 5 small white position dots inlaid in edge of fingerboard, ebony compensating bridge with bone saddle, full plate covered Washburn patent head and covered tailpiece finely nickel plated.
Price, each $51.00

No. 2442. Especially selected rosewood back and sides, and finest quality spruce top; both top and back edges are bound with black and white celluloid, marquetry inlaying in upper edge of top and around sound-hole; white and black celluloid edge in fingerboard, rosewood veneered head and white and black celluloid binding, fancy pearl inlaying in head and 10 fancy pearl position dots inlaid in ebony fingerboard, compensating bridge with ivory saddle, engraved covered patent head of fine quality, nickel-plated tailpiece, extension fingerboard, 20 Liberty silver frets.
Price, each $63.00

No. 2434

No. 2424

New Model Washburn Flat-Back Mandola

More graceful in its sweeping lines, more convenient to handle, with a tone carrying power for which the Washburn line of instruments are celebrated.

No. 1642. Finest grade of selected rosewood back and sides, eastern mountain spruce top of even grain, alternate black and white strips of thin celluloid inlay around both top and back edges, then bound with black celluloid, sound-hole encircled and bound on edge with similar trimmings, tortoise celluloid guard-plate of new and large design, mahogany neck with rosewood veneered headpiece, ebonized extension fingerboard with four inlaid position dots and bound with white celluloid, fine quality patent heads mortised in head and covered on back with nickeled plate, ebony bridge, nickel-plated tailpiece with detachable cover—the whole presenting a highly finished and perfectly adjusted instrument.

Each $63.00

No. 1642

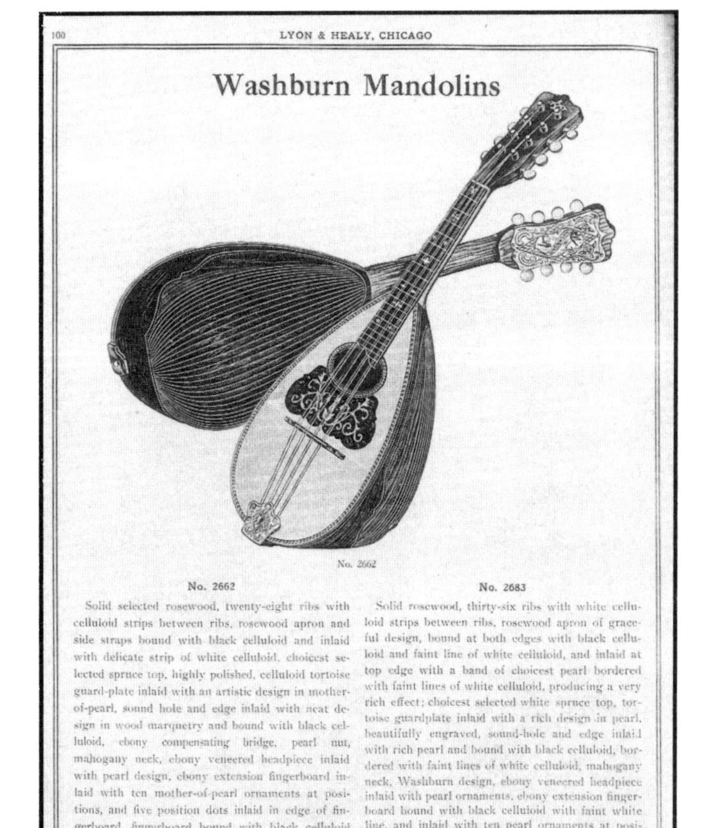

100 LYON & HEALY, CHICAGO

Washburn Mandolins

No. 2662

No. 2662

Solid selected rosewood, twenty-eight ribs with celluloid strips between ribs, rosewood apron and side straps bound with black celluloid and inlaid with delicate strip of white celluloid, choicest selected spruce top, highly polished, celluloid tortoise guard-plate inlaid with an artistic design in mother-of-pearl, sound hole and edge inlaid with neat design in wood marquetry and bound with black celluloid, ebony compensating bridge, pearl nut, mahogany neck, ebony veneered headpiece inlaid with pearl design, ebony extension fingerboard inlaid with ten mother-of-pearl ornaments at positions, and five position dots inlaid in edge of fingerboard, fingerboard bound with black celluloid and ornamented with faint line of white celluloid, Liberty silver frets, silver-plated full plate Washburn patent heads, engraved silver-plated tailpiece, Washburn design, strung with best quality Damascus steel strings. Price....................$93.00

No. 2683

Solid rosewood, thirty-six ribs with white celluloid strips between ribs, rosewood apron of graceful design, bound at both edges with black celluloid and faint line of white celluloid, and inlaid at top edge with a band of choicest pearl bordered with faint lines of white celluloid, producing a very rich effect; choicest selected white spruce top, tortoise guardplate inlaid with a rich design in pearl, beautifully engraved, sound-hole and edge inlaid with rich pearl and bound with black celluloid, bordered with faint lines of white celluloid, mahogany neck, Washburn design, ebony veneered headpiece inlaid with pearl ornaments, ebony extension fingerboard bound with black celluloid with faint white line, and inlaid with ten pearl ornaments at positions, also five position dots inlaid in edge of fingerboard, ebony bridge with pearl saddle, pearl nut, full plate silver-plated engraved patent head with pearl buttons, engraved silver-plated tailpiece, Washburn design, strung with Damascus steel strings. Price $124.50

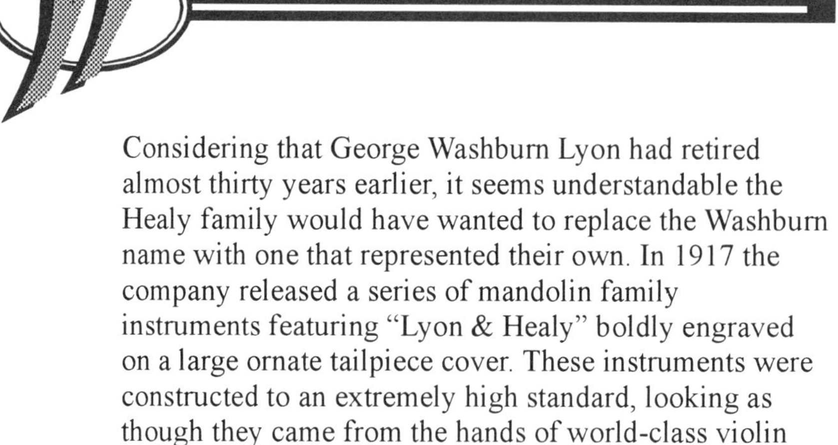

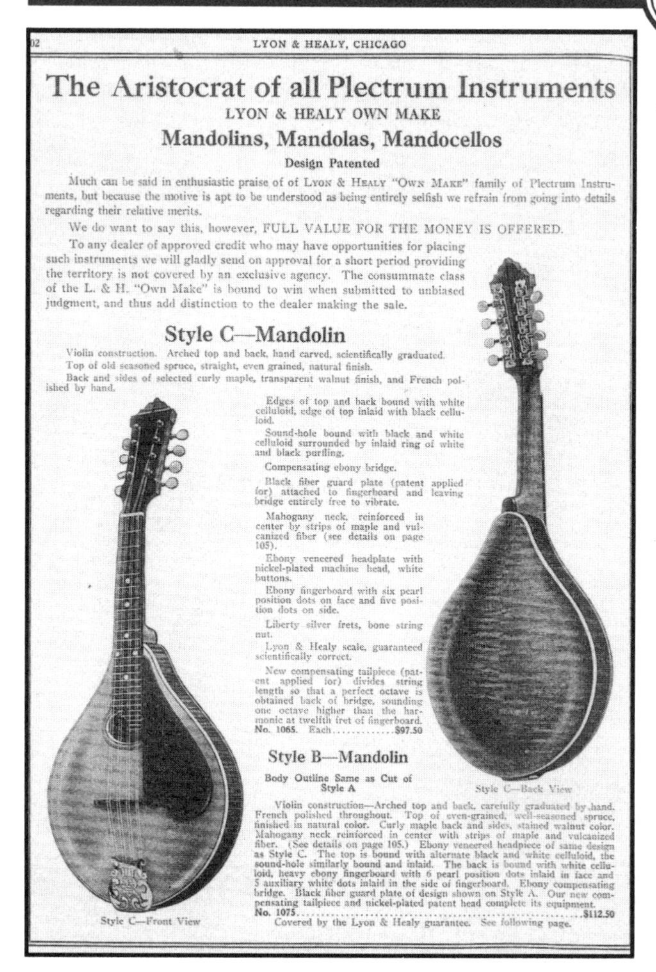

02 LYON & HEALY, CHICAGO

The Aristocrat of all Plectrum Instruments

LYON & HEALY OWN MAKE

Mandolins, Mandolas, Mandocellos

Design Patented

Much can be said in enthusiastic praise of of LYON & HEALY "OWN MAKE" family of Plectrum Instruments, but because the motive is apt to be understood as being entirely selfish we refrain from going into details regarding their relative merits.

We do want to say this, however, FULL VALUE FOR THE MONEY IS OFFERED.

To any dealer of approved credit who may have opportunities for placing such instruments we will gladly send on approval for a short period providing the territory is not covered by an exclusive agency. The consummate class of the L. & H. "Own Make" is bound to win when submitted to unbiased judgment, and thus add distinction to the dealer making the sale.

Style C—Mandolin

Violin construction. Arched top and back, hand carved, scientifically graduated.

Top of old seasoned spruce, straight, even grained, natural finish.

Back and sides of selected curly maple, transparent walnut finish, and French polished by hand.

Edges of top and back bound with white celluloid, edge of top inlaid with black celluloid.

Sound-hole bound with black and white celluloid surrounded by inlaid ring of white and black purfling.

Compensating ebony bridge.

Black fiber guard plate (patent applied for) attached to fingerboard and leaving bridge entirely free to vibrate.

Mahogany neck, reinforced in center by strips of maple and vulcanized fiber (see details on page 105).

Ebony veneered headplate with nickel-plated machine head, white buttons.

Ebony fingerboard with six pearl position dots on face and five position dots on side.

Liberty silver frets, bone string nut.

Lyon & Healy scale, guaranteed scientifically correct.

New compensating tailpiece (patent applied for) divides string length so that a perfect octave is obtained back of bridge, sounding one octave higher than the harmonic at twelfth fret of fingerboard.

No. 1065. Each.............$97.50

Style B—Mandolin

Body Outline Same as Cut of Style A

Violin construction—Arched top and back, carefully graduated by hand. French polished throughout. Top of even-grained, well-seasoned spruce, finished in natural color. Curly maple back and sides, stained walnut color. Mahogany neck reinforced in center with strips of maple and vulcanized fiber. (See details on page 105.) Ebony veneered headpiece of same design as Style C. The top is bound with alternate black and white celluloid, the sound-hole similarly bound and inlaid. The back is bound with white celluloid, heavy ebony fingerboard with 6 pearl position dots inlaid in face and 5 auxiliary white dots inlaid in the side of fingerboard. Ebony compensating bridge. Black fiber guard plate of design shown on Style A. Our new compensating tailpiece and nickel-plated patent head complete its equipment.

No. 1075...$112.50

Covered by the Lyon & Healy guarantee. See following page.

Style C—Front View

Style C—Back View

LYON & HEALY, CHICAGO 103

The Aristocrat of all Plectrum Instruments

LYON & HEALY OWN MAKE

Mandolins, Mandolas, Mandocellos

Design Patented

Style A—Mandolin

Violin construction. Arched top and back, hand carved, scientifically graduated.

Top of selected old spruce of fine, straight, even grain, natural finish.

Back and sides of handsome curly maple, transparent, walnut finish, and French polished by hand.

Edges of top and back bound with black and white celluloid.

Sound-hole bound with black and white celluloid and surrounded by ring of black and white celluloid.

Compensating ebony bridge.

Black fibre guard plate (patent applied for) attached to fingerboard and corner post, in no way interfering with free vibration of bridge and top.

Mahogany neck reinforced in center with strips of maple and vulcanized fibre. (See details of construction on page 105.)

Artistic scroll head.

Specially designed Lyon & Healy improved non-slip machine heads with hard rubber headplate and black buttons.

Ebony fingerboard bound on edges with black celluloid.

Six pearl position dots on face and five on side of fingerboard.

Liberty silver frets, bone string nut, new Liberty silver covered compensating tailpiece (patent applied for) so dividing string length that a perfect octave is obtained back of bridge, sounding one octave higher than the harmonic at twelfth fret of fingerboard.

No. 1100. Each............$150.00

Style A—Back View

Lyon & Healy Guaranty

Every Lyon & Healy Own Make Mandolin, Mandola and Mandocello bears our unlimited written guarantee. This guarantees not only against defective workmanship and material, but means that we will protect the first-hand purchaser for all time by making good, f. o. b. our factory, any checking of top, back or sides, warping of neck, fingerboard, or other shortcomings, barring ordinary wear and tear, not due to accident or abuse.

Style A—Front View

Considering that George Washburn Lyon had retired almost thirty years earlier, it seems understandable the Healy family would have wanted to replace the Washburn name with one that represented their own. In 1917 the company released a series of mandolin family instruments featuring "Lyon & Healy" boldly engraved on a large ornate tailpiece cover. These instruments were constructed to an extremely high standard, looking as though they came from the hands of world-class violin makers, which is very possible. The Lyon & Healy "Own Make" Mandolins, Mandolas and Mandocellos have long been considered some of the finest instruments ever made, by any manufacturer, in design, finish and tone.

Three mandolins were available, with the top model, Style A, being considered the best mandolin of all time by many orchestra players up through today. The Style A featured a hand carved top of best quality spruce with an oval soundhole. The back was carved from highly figured maple and the outline of the body was embellished by two symmetrically placed "points." These set off two mirror imaged spirals carved into the "artistic scroll peghead." The gears to the tuners were set into the headstock from the front, concealed by a black coverplate. The backside of the headstock was carved into a graceful volute. A reinforced mahogany neck incorporated laminates of maple and "vulcanized fibre" for strength.

A small telescoping rod was built into the side of all but the earliest mandolins and could be pulled out to stabilize the instrument on the player's leg. A black "fibre" pickguard matched the peghead cover (these look like ebony), complementing the ebony bridge and 24-fret extension fingerboard. Black tuner buttons and black binding on the body, neck and soundhole completed the theme of this incredible instrument. The neck joined the body between the 10th and 11th fret frets and was the 13-3/4" scale length popularized by Gibson, instead of the traditional 13". The tailpiece, designed expressly for these instruments, featured a string clamp to allow the section of string behind the bridge to vibrate cleanly, exactly two octaves above the open string.

Two other similar models featured a very stylish, Deco-inspired, stairstep headstock instead of the scroll, with exposed tuners mounting from the rear. The Style B, featured the same body as the Style A, while the Style C's body was a plain pear shape. All three are regarded as orchestra quality.

Two other Style A instruments were available, a mandola and a mandocello, identical except for the size, to the mandolin. This trio has been considered somewhat of an orchestra player's Holy Grail since its release, although the mandolin craze was on its way out when the Style A's were manufactured. Like Gibson's 1920's mandolins and late-1930's banjos, the craft and design of the best instruments came after their popularity had diminished, but before the instruments' musical resurgences, making all of the models mentioned hard to come by today (Better bring TWO Gold Cards if you want a Lyon & Healy/Washburn Mandocello!). While the mandola and mandocello were offered until Tonk Bros. took over the line in '28, apparently very few were built. Described in the mid-'20s catalogs as matching the new asymetrical-bodied mandolins (see following page). It's doubtful the change in body shape actually occured on the mandolas and mandocellos.

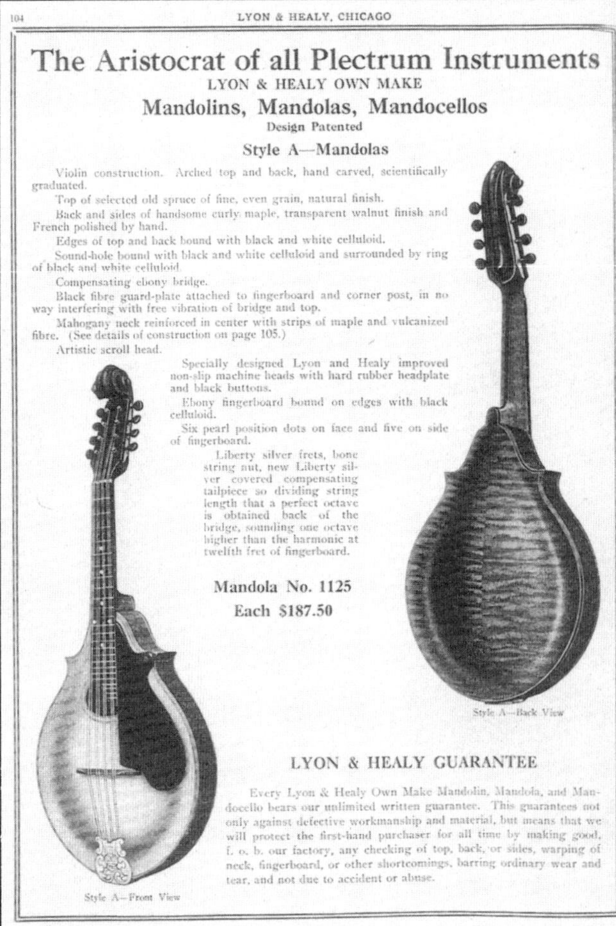

104 LYON & HEALY, CHICAGO

The Aristocrat of all Plectrum Instruments

LYON & HEALY OWN MAKE

Mandolins, Mandolas, Mandocellos

Design Patented

Style A—Mandolas

Violin construction. Arched top and back, hand carved, scientifically graduated.

Top of selected old spruce of fine, even grain, natural finish.

Back and sides of handsome curly maple, transparent walnut finish and French polished by hand.

Edges of top and back bound with black and white celluloid.

Sound-hole bound with black and white celluloid and surrounded by ring of black and white celluloid.

Compensating ebony bridge.

Black fibre guard-plate attached to fingerboard and corner post, in no way interfering with free vibration of bridge and top.

Mahogany neck reinforced in center with strips of maple and vulcanized fibre. (See details of construction on page 105.)

Artistic scroll head.

Specially designed Lyon and Healy improved non-slip machine heads with hard rubber headplate and black buttons.

Ebony fingerboard bound on edges with black celluloid.

Six pearl position dots on face and five on side of fingerboard.

Liberty silver frets, bone string nut, new Liberty silver covered compensating tailpiece so dividing string length that a perfect octave is obtained back of the bridge, sounding one octave higher than the harmonic at twelfth fret of fingerboard.

Mandola No. 1125

Each $187.50

Style A—Front View

Style A—Back View

LYON & HEALY GUARANTEE

Every Lyon & Healy Own Make Mandolin, Mandola, and Mandocello bears our unlimited written guarantee. This guarantees not only against defective workmanship and material, but means that we will protect the first-hand purchaser for all time by making good, f. o. b. our factory, any checking of top, back, or sides, warping of neck, fingerboard, or other shortcomings, barring ordinary wear and tear, and not due to accident or abuse.

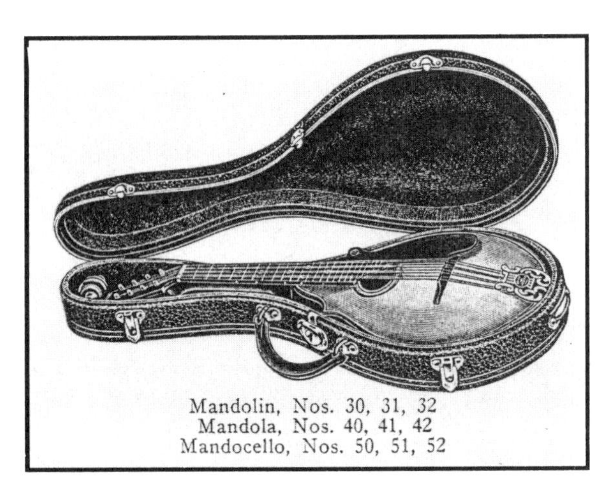

Mandolin, Nos. 30, 31, 32
Mandola, Nos. 40, 41, 42
Mandocello, Nos. 50, 51, 52

LYON & HEALY, CHICAGO 105

The Aristocrat of all Plectrum Instruments

LYON & HEALY OWN MAKE

Mandolins, Mandolas, Mandocellos

Design Patented

Style A—Mandocello

Violin construction. Arched top and back, hand carved, scientifically graduated.

Top of selected old spruce of fine, even grain, natural finish.

Back and sides of handsome curly maple, transparent walnut finish and French polished by hand.

Edges of top and back bound with black and white celluloid.

Soundhole bound with black and white celluloid and surrounded by ring of black and white celluloid.

Compensating ebony bridge.

Black fibre guard plate (patent applied for) attached to fingerboard and corner post, in no way interfering with free vibration of bridge and top.

Mahogany neck reinforced in center with strips of maple and vulcanized fibre.

Artistic scroll head.

Specially designed Lyon & Healy improved non-slip machine heads with hard rubber head plate and black buttons.

Ebony fingerboard bound on edges with black celluloid.

Six pearl position dots on face and five on side of fingerboard.

Liberty silver frets, bone string nut, new Liberty silver covered compensating tail piece (patent applied for) so dividing string length that a perfect octave is obtained back of bridge, sounding one octave higher than the harmonic at twelfth fret of fingerboard.

Mandocello No. 1150

Each $225.00

See foregoing pages for copy of Lyon & Healy guarantee

Style A—Front view

Style A—Back view

Full length view of neck.

In these creations of the mandolin builder's art, the trade and public is offered the only perfect trio of the Mando family ever devised.

These illustrations show the construction of neck used in the Lyon & Healy Own Make mandolin. The fibre strip in the center precludes the possibility of the neck warping or giving in any way. This is the most rigid and dependable neck ever built.

End view of neck where joined to body.

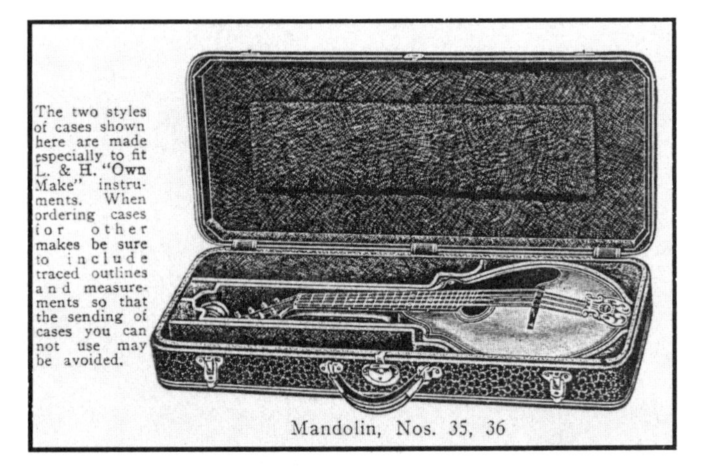

The two styles of cases shown here are made especially to fit L. & H. "Own Make" instruments. When ordering cases for other makes be sure to include traced outlines and measurements so that the sending of cases you can not use may be avoided.

Mandolin, Nos. 35, 36

During the early '20s, the Washburn name was added to the top-of-the-line Style A Mandolin. Around this time the scale length was shortened to 13", with the neck joining the body at the 9th fret. The "point" on the treble side was dropped lower on the body to facilitate playing in the upper registers. This gave the body an asymmetrical shape. A Style A Professional model was available with an "extended" extension fingerboard going to G# instead of E.

Although the Lyon & Healy tailpiece would remain on the instrument, even through the Tonk Bros. era, the Style A's model name was soon changed to the Washburn "Deluxe" No. 5283. The original Lyon & Healy Own Make label was changed to Washburn by Lyon & Healy and then, following the sale to Tonk Brothers, a new label with Washburn by Tonk Bros. was used. Although made in limited numbers, the Lyon & Healy/Washburn Style A/Washburn Deluxe was available almost unchanged for twenty years before it faded with the rest of the Washburn line.

A variation of the Style C became standard in the early '20s with a different headstock shape, the 9th fret neck-to-body joint and a 13" scale length. Some of these were marketed by Ditson with a label bearing both the Lyon & Healy and Ditson names. Replacing the Washburn Style C of the early-'20s was the Washburn "Aristocrat" No. 5282 in the mid-'20s, lasting into the mid-'30s before being discontinued. The short-lived Style B, nearly identical to the first Style A, was offered unchanged as a Washburn model in the '23 catalog before being discontinued. Apparently the last B's had the asymetrical body and this was the model chosen for reissue as the "Country Mandolin" in the '70s.

12 LYON & HEALY, CHICAGO

The
WASHBURN "DELUXE"
Mandolin

IT remained for Lyon & Healy, who brought the Lyon & Healy Harp to perfection and made it the world's standard of harp quality, to perform the same duty for another instrument—the mandolin.

Today the WASHBURN Mandolin is known for its unique and distinguishing features. It is a musician's instrument, not one belonging to the theoretical manufacturer. In workmanship, appearance and in playing qualities, it represents the best which scientific skill and professional musical knowledge can offer.

It is unique in model, in principle, and in construction—a radical departure from the "tinny toned" instruments of a few years ago. Advanced ideas and features are represented. Among these is the violin form of construction, with the straight span preceding the arch, inside the edge of both back and front, which gives the violin its marvelous strength and vibrating power, and which is precisely duplicated in the WASHBURN Mandolins. These features are explained in detail on the following page.

There is in the WASHBURN tone a sweetness, power, and a far-carrying quality that delights the player. There is an instant response to the slightest touch on the strings. Under prolonged playing, the tone retains its vibrant fullness and vigor. Then again, when a passage calls for even execution, the tone flows smooth and mellow under the pick.

The design of the instrument is such that playing is easy. The reaches of the fingerboard are quickly accomplished. There is an easy feel to the fingerboard. The rigid neck insures absolute perfection of scale in all keys. The fretting is accurate to one one-thousandth of an inch. Patent heads, bridge, neck, soundboard, heelplate—all have been considered with an eye to strength, beauty and utility.

The WASHBURN "De Luxe"
Mandolin

As a jewel, cunningly mounted, gains fresh beauty and evokes greater appeal, so the WASHBURN "*DeLuxe*" with its refinements and additional embellishments creates in the musician new enthusiasm. Here is the instrument for the concert artist who knows the value of appearances and for the amateur who takes the greatest pride and interest in his art and in his instrument. For richness of appearance and for finished beauty this style is unrivalled.

Specifications

Body—Top carved from ¾-inch fine grain quarter sawed spruce, natural color, graduated in thickness; golden brown curly maple sides; carved golden brown figured maple back; top and back edges of body inlaid with white and black fiberoid; oval sound hole bound with white and black fiberoid. Highly polished.

Neck—Thirteen-inch scale; polished mahogany neck reinforced with vulcanized fibre; artistic hand carved scroll head; ebony extension fingerboard bound with black celluloid; 6 pearl position dots; 24 nickel silver frets; ebony bridge and polished bone fingerboard nut.

Trimmings—Specially made and improved patent heads covered with hard black rubber head plate; black celluloid buttons; patent vulcanized fibre guard plate; patent tailpiece with artistic nickel silver cover.

Case—Black seal grain Keratol covered 3-ply wood body; side opening; silk plush lined; nickel-plated brass trimmings, lock and clasps; steel valance; two compartments for accessories; leather handle.

No. 5283 *Complete with case* *$140.00*

WASHBURN "De Luxe" Mandola

No. 5300 Same specifications as WASHBURN "*De Luxe*" Mandolin ....*Complete with case* *$175.00*

WASHBURN "De Luxe" Mandocello

No. 5310 Same specifications as WASHBURN "*De Luxe*" Mandolin ....*Complete with case* *$200.00*

25,000 Feet for 1,000 Washburn Feet

From a selection of 25,000 feet of choice spruce and maple, a stringed instrument expert selects not more than 1,000 feet of lumber fit to be used in the manufacture of WASHBURN Mandolins. For three and four, and even five years, this perfect wood is aged and seasoned in scientifically constructed steam kilns before it meets with our exacting requirements. This is one of the unusual features embodied in the construction of the perfect mandolin.

Beautifully finished wood is a matter of pride among the men who have spent the better part of their lives in the WASHBURN factory.

The beauty and strength of this excellent workmanship is further enhanced by artistic celluloid trimmings, genuine ebony fingerboards, pearl position dots and nickel silver frets.

Excluding the asymetrical Deluxe, the pear-shaped body became the standard Washburn mandolin for the '20s and '30s. The "two pointed pear" was last seen on the early-'20s Styles D (maple) and F (mahogany). Styles E (rosewood) and G (mahogany), both pear-shaped, would become the Inspiration No.5280 and the Classic No. 5281 in the mid '20s, still with flat backs and bent tops. The Deluxe tailpiece and the arched top and back, carved from solid pieces of spruce and curly maple, helped set the Aristocrat No. 5282 (Style C) apart from the far more affordable Inspiration and Classic models. The mandolin line was virtually unchanged following the Tonk Bros. takeover, and would stay the same until the mid '30s, when the carved top Aristocrat was dropped and the scale length was changed from 13" to 14" on the flatbacks. Longer scale lengths had been popularized by Gibson for years and Tonk Bros. followed their lead. The Inspiration was otherwise about the same, but the Classic was given a maple body and a sunburst finish. Still in the line was the Deluxe No. 5283 before WWII ended production of all the Washburns.

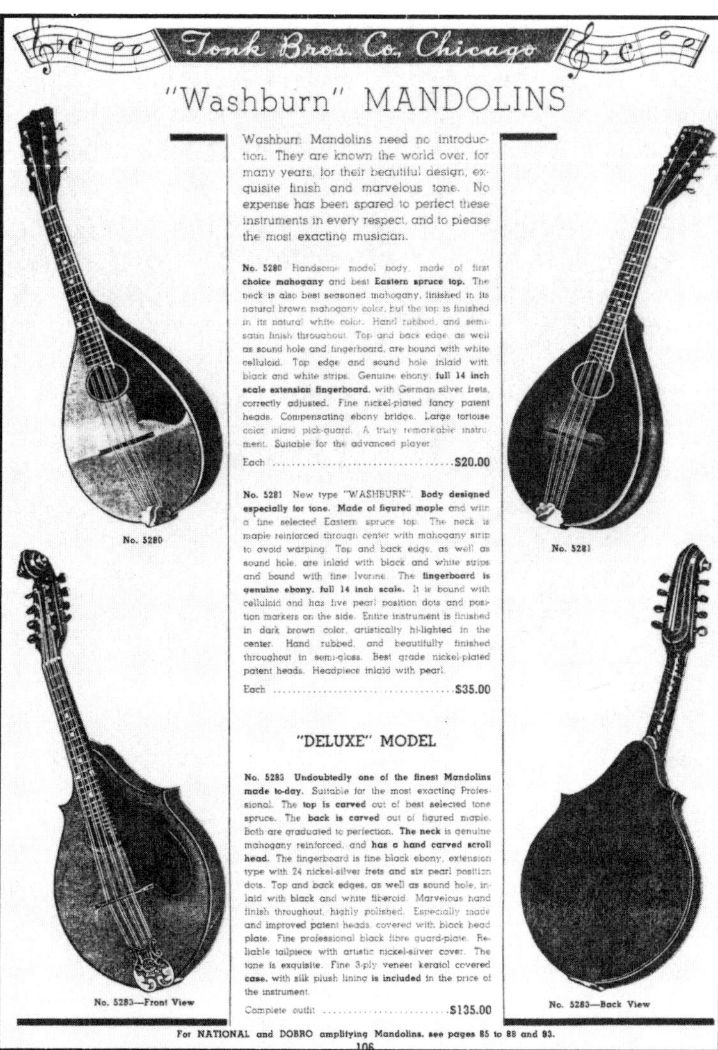

Tonk Bros. Co. Chicago

"Washburn" MANDOLINS

Washburn Mandolins need no introduction. They are known the world over, for many years, for their beautiful design, exquisite finish and marvelous tone. No expense has been spared to perfect these instruments in every respect, and to please the most exacting musician.

No. 5280 Handsome model body, made of first **choice mahogany** and best **Eastern spruce top.** The neck is also best seasoned mahogany, finished in its natural brown mahogany color, but the top is finished in its natural white color. Hand rubbed, and semi-satin finish throughout. Top and back edge, as well as sound hole and fingerboard, are bound with white celluloid. Top edge and sound hole inlaid with black and white strips. Genuine ebony, **full 14 inch scale extension fingerboard,** with German silver frets, correctly adjusted. Fine nickel-plated fancy patent heads. Compensating ebony bridge. Large tortoise color inlaid pick-guard. A truly remarkable instrument. Suitable for the advanced player.

Each **$20.00**

No. 5281 New type "WASHBURN". **Body designed especially for tone. Made of figured maple** and with a fine selected Eastern spruce top. The neck is maple reinforced through center with mahogany strip to avoid warping. Top and back edge, as well as sound hole, are inlaid with black and white strips and bound with fine Ivorine. The **fingerboard is genuine ebony, full 14 inch scale.** It is bound with celluloid and has five pearl position dots and position markers on the side. Entire instrument is finished in dark brown color, artistically hi-lighted in the center. Hand rubbed, and beautifully finished throughout in semi-gloss. Best grade nickel-plated patent heads. Headpiece inlaid with pearl.

Each **$35.00**

No. 5280

No. 5281

"DELUXE" MODEL

No. 5283 Undoubtedly one of the finest Mandolins made to-day. Suitable for the most exacting Professional. The **top is carved** out of best selected tone spruce. The **back is carved** out of figured maple. Both are graduated to perfection. **The neck** is genuine mahogany reinforced, and **has a hand carved scroll head.** The fingerboard is fine black ebony, extension type with 24 nickel-silver frets and six pearl position dots. Top and back edges, as well as sound hole, inlaid with black and white fiberoid. Marvelous hand finish throughout, highly polished. Especially made and improved patent heads, covered with black head plate. Fine professional black fibre guard-plate. Reliable tailpiece with artistic nickel-silver cover. The tone is exquisite. Fine 3-ply veneer keratol covered **case,** with silk plush lining **is included** in the price of the instrument.

Complete outfit **$135.00**

No. 5283—Front View

No. 5283—Back View

For NATIONAL and DOBRO amplifying Mandolins, see pages 85 to 88 and 93.

106

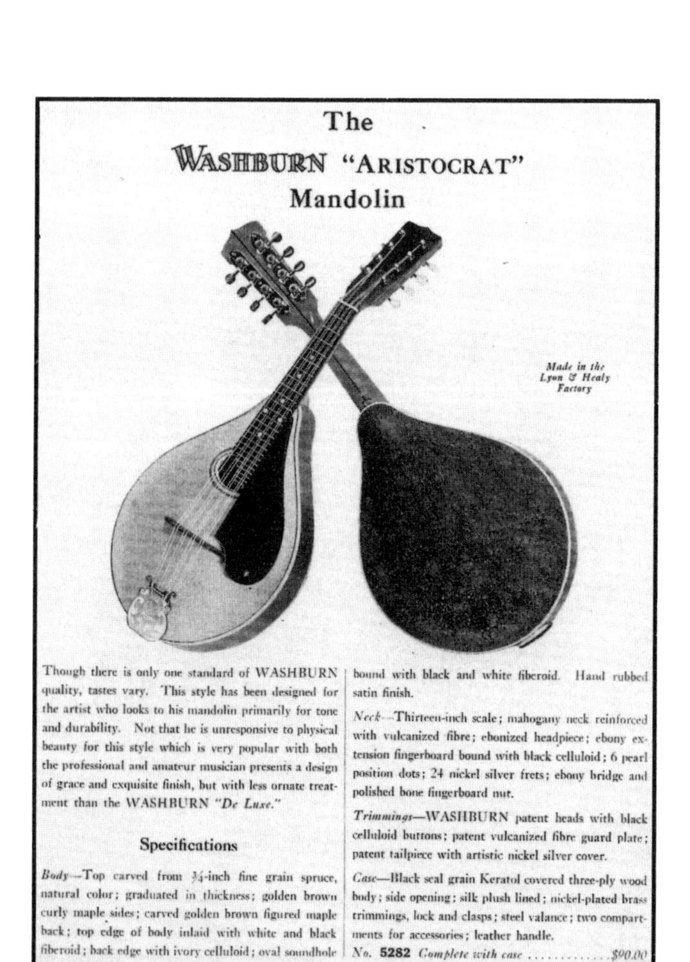

The

WASHBURN "ARISTOCRAT"

Mandolin

Made in the Lyon & Healy Factory

Though there is only one standard of WASHBURN quality, tastes vary. This style has been designed for the artist who looks to his mandolin primarily for tone and durability. Not that he is unresponsive to physical beauty for this style which is very popular with both the professional and amateur musician presents a design of grace and exquisite finish, but with less ornate treatment than the WASHBURN *"De Luxe."*

Specifications

Body—Top carved from ¾-inch fine grain spruce, natural color; graduated in thickness; golden brown curly maple sides; carved golden brown figured maple back; top edge of body inlaid with white and black fiberoid; back edge with ivory celluloid; oval soundhole bound with black and white fiberoid. Hand rubbed satin finish.

Neck—Thirteen-inch scale; mahogany neck reinforced with vulcanized fibre; ebonized headpiece; ebony extension fingerboard bound with black celluloid; 6 pearl position dots; 24 nickel silver frets; ebony bridge and polished bone fingerboard nut.

Trimmings—WASHBURN patent heads with black celluloid buttons; patent vulcanized fibre guard plate; patent tailpiece with artistic nickel silver cover.

Case—Black seal grain Keratol covered three-ply wood body; side opening; silk plush lined; nickel-plated brass trimmings, lock and clasps; steel valance; two compartments for accessories; leather handle.

No. **5282** *Complete with case* *$90.00*

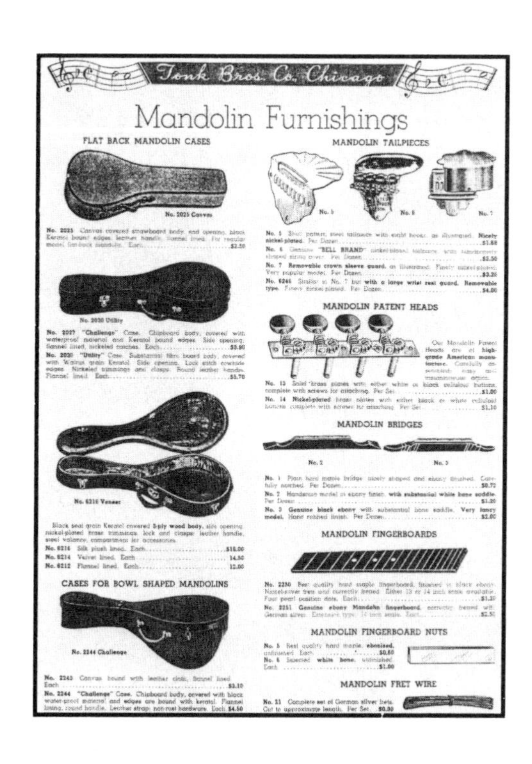

Tonk Bros. Co. Chicago

Mandolin Furnishings

FLAT BACK MANDOLIN CASES

No. 2025 Canvas

No. 2025 Canvas covered strawboard body, end opening, black Keratol bound edges, leather handle, flannel lined. For regular model flat-back mandolin. Each $2.50

No. 2030 Utility

No. 2027 "Challenge" Case. Chipboard body, covered with waterproof material and Keratol bound **edges**. Side opening, flannel lined, nickeled catches. Each $3.90

No. 2030 "Utility" Case. Substantial fibre board body, covered with Walrus grain Keratol. Side opening. Lock stitch cowhide edges. Nickeled trimmings and clasps. Round leather handle. Flannel lined. Each $5.70

No. 6216 Veneer

Black seal grain Keratol covered **3-ply wood body,** side opening, nickel-plated brass trimmings, lock and clasps; leather handle, steel valance, compartment for accessories.

No. 6216 Silk plush lined. Each $16.00

No. 6214 Velvet lined. Each 14.50

No. 6212 Flannel lined. Each 12.00

CASES FOR BOWL SHAPED MANDOLINS

No. 2244 Challenge

No. 2243 Canvas bound with leather cloth, flannel lined. Each $3.10

No. 2244 "Challenge" Case. Chipboard body, covered with black water-proof material and **edges** are bound with keratol. Flannel lining, round handle. Leather strap; non-rust hardware. Each $4.50

MANDOLIN TAILPIECES

No. 5 No. 6 No. 7

No. 5 Shell pattern, steel tailpiece with eight hooks, as illustrated. **Nicely nickel-plated.** Per Dozen $1.68

No. 6 Genuine **"BELL BRAND"** nickel-plated tailpiece, with handsomely shaped string cover. Per Dozen $2.50

No. 7 Removable crown sleeve guard, as illustrated. Finely nickel-plated. Very popular model. Per Dozen $3.20

No. 6246 Similar to No. 7 but **with a large wrist rest guard. Removable type.** Finely nickel-plated. Per Dozen $4.00

MANDOLIN PATENT HEADS

Our Mandolin Patent Heads are of **high-grade American manufacture.** Carefully assembled; easy and [illegible] action.

No. 13 Solid brass plates with either white or black celluloid buttons, complete with **screws** for attaching. Per Set $1.00

No. 14 Nickel-plated brass plates with either black or white celluloid buttons complete with screws for attaching. Per Set $1.10

MANDOLIN BRIDGES

No. 2 No. 3

No. 1 Plain hard maple bridge, nicely shaped and ebony finished. Carefully notched. Per Dozen $0.72

No. 2 Handsome model in ebony finish, **with substantial white bone saddle.** Per Dozen $1.20

No. 3 Genuine black ebony with substantial bone saddle. **Very fancy model.** Hand rubbed finish. Per Dozen $2.00

MANDOLIN FINGERBOARDS

No. 2250 Best quality hard maple fingerboard, finished in black ebony. Nickel-silver frets and correctly fretted. Either 13 or 14 inch scale available. Four pearl position dots. Each $1.25

No. 2251 Genuine ebony Mandolin fingerboard, correctly fretted with German silver. Extension type, 14 inch scale. Each $2.50

MANDOLIN FINGERBOARD NUTS

No. 5 Best quality hard maple, **ebonized,** unfinished. Each $0.60

No. 6 Selected **white bone,** unfinished. Each $1.00

MANDOLIN FRET WIRE

No. 11 Complete set of German silver frets. Cut to approximate length. Per Set $0.30

Zithers

Before Washburn made banjos, harps, mandolas, violins, mandocellos, pianos, ukuleles, or tiples, they were building zithers, the origins of which trace back to the ancient lyre. At $200 in 1889 for the top-of-the-line Style 56, compared to $100 for the Model 308 guitar and $75 for the Model 80 Mandolin, the Zithers were Washburns big-ticket items, with half of the eight models offered costing $100 or more.

Zithers usually had between twenty and thirty "open" strings that were plucked or picked and an additional five-string fretted fingerboard (a sixth string was optional). These frets were quite high. The body was hollow with a round soundhole and constructed of "richly grained" woods. Brazilian rosewood was stock for styles 51, 52, and 53 (the lowest Model, No. 50, used maple). Styles 54, 55 and 56 offered a variety of fine woods, with decoration obviously taking precedence over tone. "Elegant French walnut, fancy pattern mahogany or any richly figured wood, as desired."

Breaking with Washburn's usual numbering system was the Style 58 "Oriental" Harp Zither, which cost slightly less than Style 56. The "Oriental" referred to the design, with oval soundhole and scalloped edges. Like Styles 55 and 56, 58 was a "Harp" zither, having a "column" to support and brace the neck, allowing the body to be gracefully scooped into, exposing a section of the strings in a harp-like fashion. Style 56 had gold-plated tuning pins and "patent head" which was engraved as well. Although not specified, the tuner buttons were probably pearl, as was common on deluxe models. Pearl inlays abounded on the borders, and around the soundhole with dots, stars, flowers, birds, etc. being inlaid into the top. "An Elaborate Instrument in Every Particular."

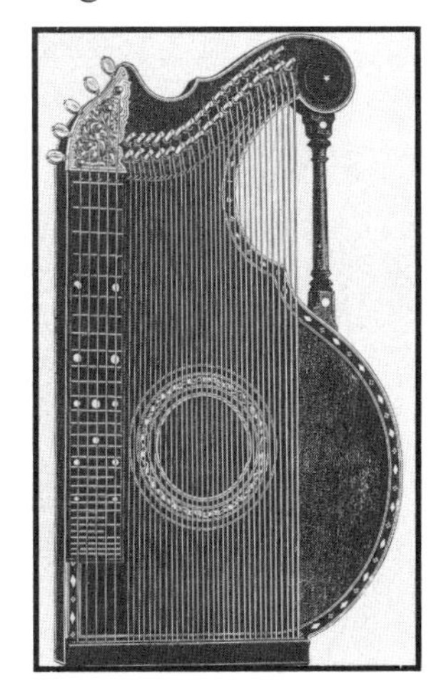

"Why!—do you play?"
"Only when I can get a Washburn."
No Home is Complete Without a New 1897 Model
Washburn Guitar, Mandolin Banjo or Zither

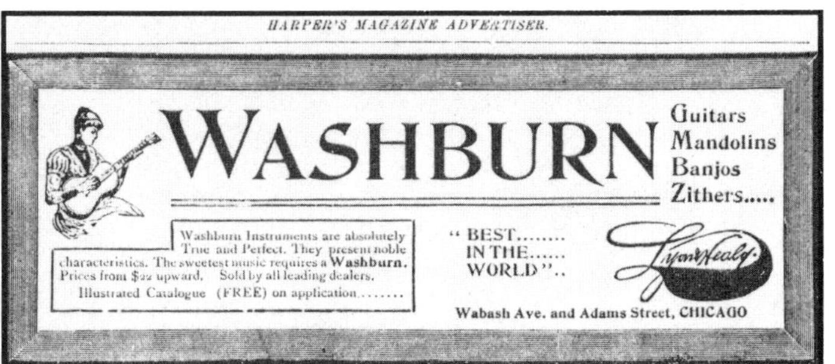

Designed for bass or accompaniment, the Style 62 "Elegie" or "Song" zither was offered for a short time. This was a longer scale length instrument, strung with heavy strings.

In 1892, Styles 151, 152, 161, 162, 171, and 172 replaced the 1889 line. Gone were the ornate models with the $75 Style 172 being the deluxe version. The economic conditions may have had something to do with this drastic change in policy but it was becoming clear that the zither was fading in popularity.

The 1897 models cost $25 for the Style 125 and $35 for the Style 135 and that was it! "Concert Size and finer Washburn Zithers made to order" was the postscript. A concert size Style 145 was added in 1906 and the 125 and 135 became the 130 and 140. The model numbers reflected the price, therefore, the change in numbers. A picture of the old 125 was printed in the catalog, still showing the 125 model number. The company was not upgrading these models, just raising the prices. By WWI the prices were $52.50 and $75 and, following the war, Models 160, 175 and 190 were offered as the last Washburn zithers. The inherent design of the instrument limited advanced technique and the invention of the auto harp and the popularity of the other fretted instruments brought about the public, and not Washburn, retiring the Zither.

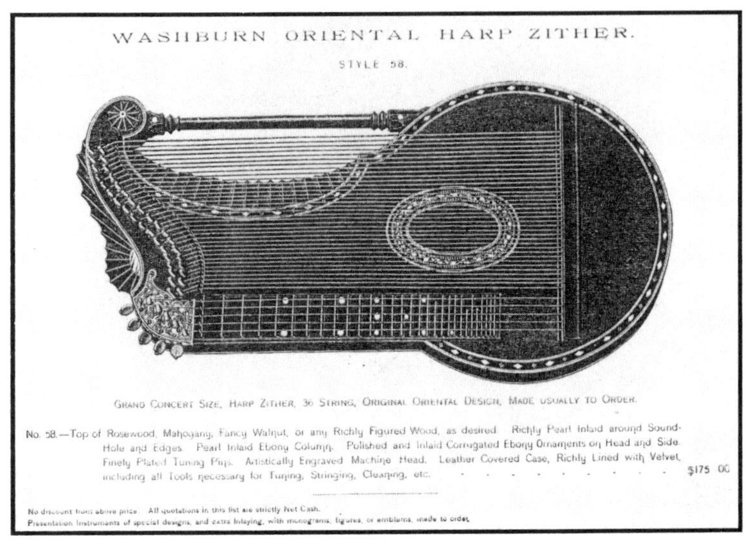

WASHBURN ORIENTAL HARP ZITHER.
STYLE 58.
GRAND CONCERT SIZE, HARP ZITHER, 36 STRING, ORIGINAL ORIENTAL DESIGN, MADE USUALLY TO ORDER.
No. 58.—Top of Rosewood, Mahogany, Fancy Walnut, or any Richly Figured Wood, as desired. Richly Pearl Inlaid around Sound-Hole and Edges. Pearl Inlaid Ebony Column. Polished and Inlaid Corrugated Ebony Ornaments on Head and Side. Finely Plated Tuning Pins. Artistically Engraved Machine Head. Leather Covered Case, Richly Lined with Velvet, including all Tools necessary for Tuning, Stringing, Cleaning, etc. $175 00
No discount from above price. All quotations in this list are strictly Net Cash.
Presentation Instruments of special designs, and extra Inlaying, with monograms, figures, or emblems, made to order.

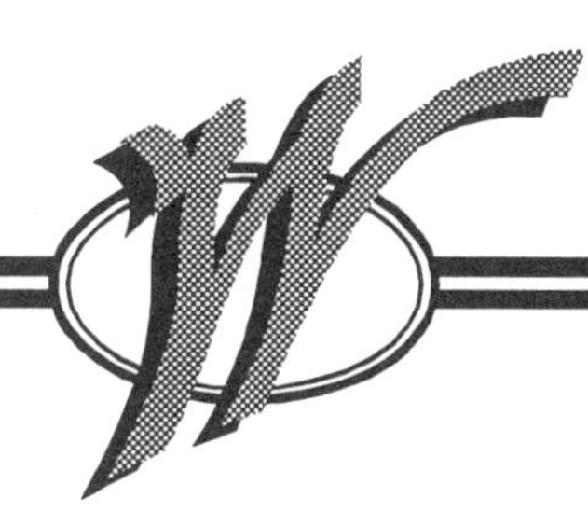

Banjos

The Washburn line was slow in adding the banjo, which was still evolving from the primitive gut string, fretless models popularized in the first half of the 1800s. Lyon & Healy sold fretless banjos with five, six and seven strings and were agents for the Dobson Silver Bell fretted banjos in the early 1880s. These models had slotted pegheads and the elongated heel common to early banjos. Shortly after opening their factory, Lyon & Healy began making its own banjos and was granted a patent in 1887 for a tailpiece designed by shop foreman George Durkee and future Lyon & Healy President C.N. Post. Prices started at $2 for a wood shelled, fretless 5-string with a tacked on head. The non-tunable "tackhead" construction was common on homemade and inexpensive banjos in the 1800s. For $2.50, a tunable head with four brackets could be had. Prices and the number of brackets went up accordingly, with as many as fifty brackets crammed together around an 11" shell.

No. 1091.

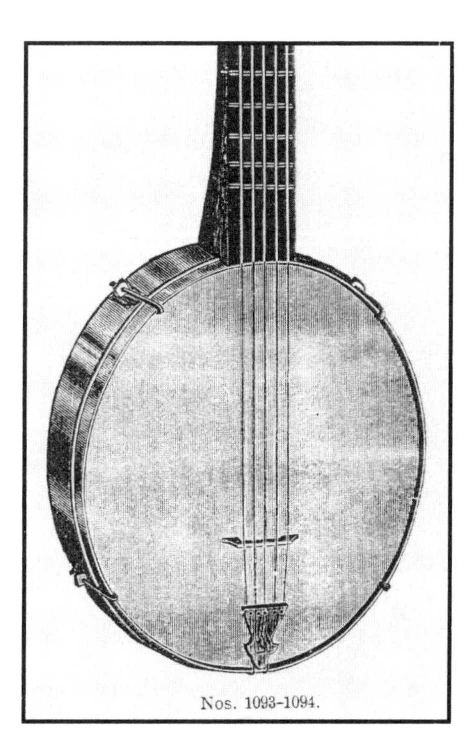

Nos. 1093-1094.

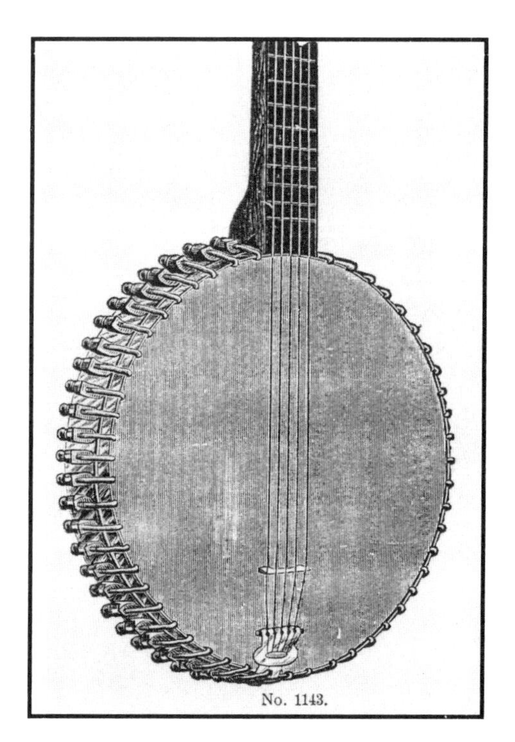

No. 1143.

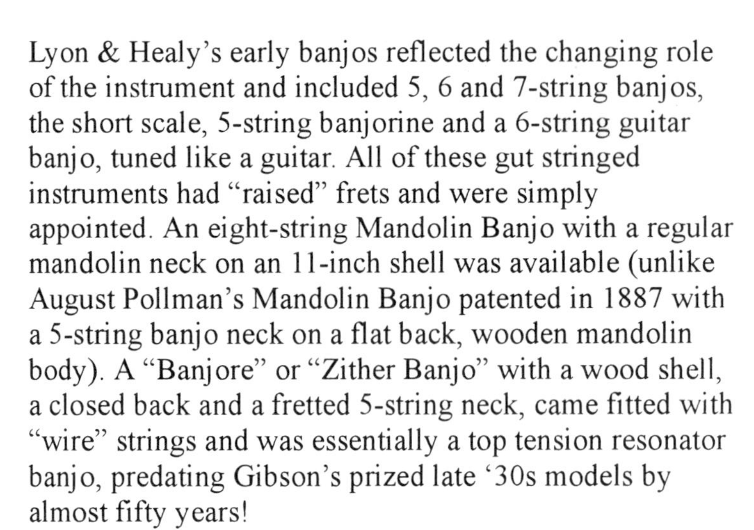

Lyon & Healy's early banjos reflected the changing role of the instrument and included 5, 6 and 7-string banjos, the short scale, 5-string banjorine and a 6-string guitar banjo, tuned like a guitar. All of these gut stringed instruments had "raised" frets and were simply appointed. An eight-string Mandolin Banjo with a regular mandolin neck on an 11-inch shell was available (unlike August Pollman's Mandolin Banjo patented in 1887 with a 5-string banjo neck on a flat back, wooden mandolin body). A "Banjore" or "Zither Banjo" with a wood shell, a closed back and a fretted 5-string neck, came fitted with "wire" strings and was essentially a top tension resonator banjo, predating Gibson's prized late '30s models by almost fifty years!

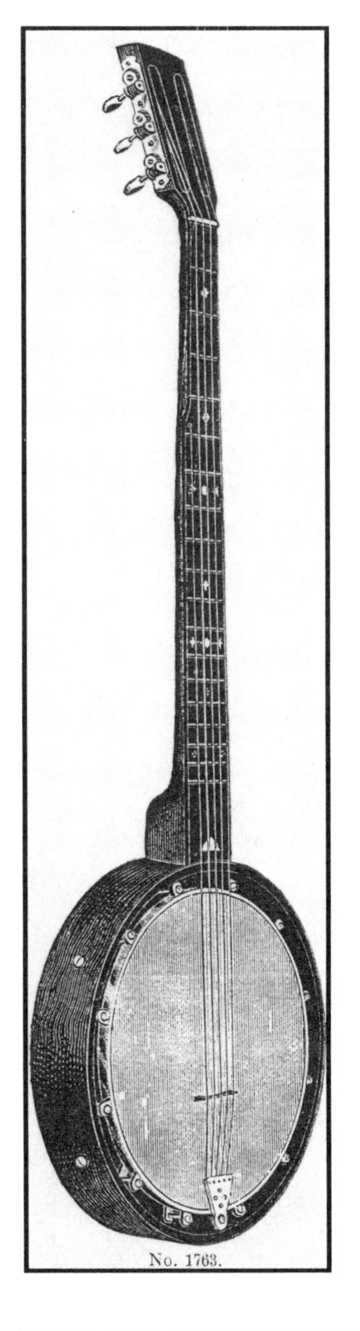

No. 1763.

SPECIAL NET PRICE LIST

BANJOS,

GUITAR AND MANDOLIN BANJOS, BANJORINES,

Banjo Cases and Strings,

Tambourines,

BONES,

Castanets and Instruction Books

ALL PRICES QUOTED HEREIN ARE NET CASH.

To insure prompt attention, the money should accompany all orders.

These goods can be sent C. O. D., subject to examination, only when a sufficient sum is remitted with the order to insure express charges both ways.

Prices quoted include all packing charges and free delivery to any transportation company in the city.

LYON & HEALY,

IMPORTERS AND MANUFACTURERS,

State and Monroe Streets,

CHICAGO.

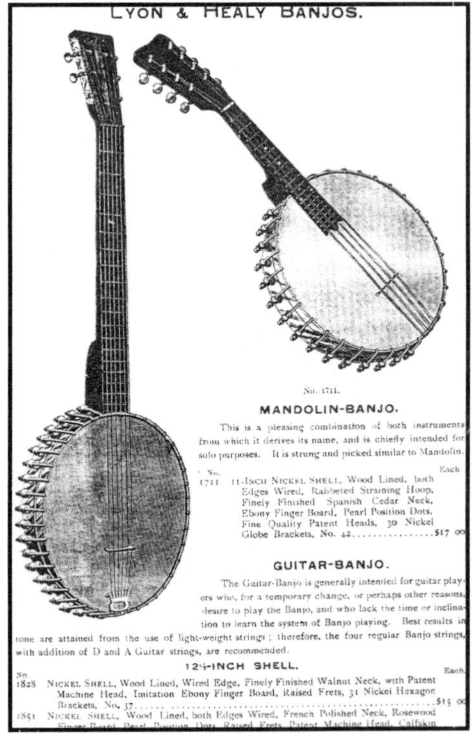

LYON & HEALY BANJOS.

No. 1711.

MANDOLIN-BANJO.

This is a pleasing combination of both instruments from which it derives its name, and is chiefly intended for solo purposes. It is strung and picked similar to Mandolin.

No.		Each
1711	11-INCH NICKEL SHELL, Wood Lined, both Edges Wired, Rabbeted Straining Hoop, Finely Finished Spanish Cedar Neck, Ebony Finger Board, Pearl Position Dots, Fine Quality Patent Heads, 30 Nickel Globe Brackets, No. 42	$17 00

GUITAR-BANJO.

The Guitar-Banjo is generally intended for guitar players who, for a temporary change, or perhaps other reasons, desire to play the Banjo, and who lack the time or inclination to learn the system of Banjo playing. Best results in tone are attained from the use of light-weight strings; therefore, the four regular Banjo strings, with addition of D and A Guitar strings, are recommended.

12½-INCH SHELL.

No.		Each
1828	NICKEL SHELL, Wood Lined, Wired Edge, Finely Finished Walnut Neck, with Patent Machine Head, Imitation Ebony Finger Board, Raised Frets, 31 Nickel Hexagon Brackets, No. 37	$15 00
1851	NICKEL SHELL, Wood Lined, both Edges Wired, French Polished Neck, Rosewood [illegible]	

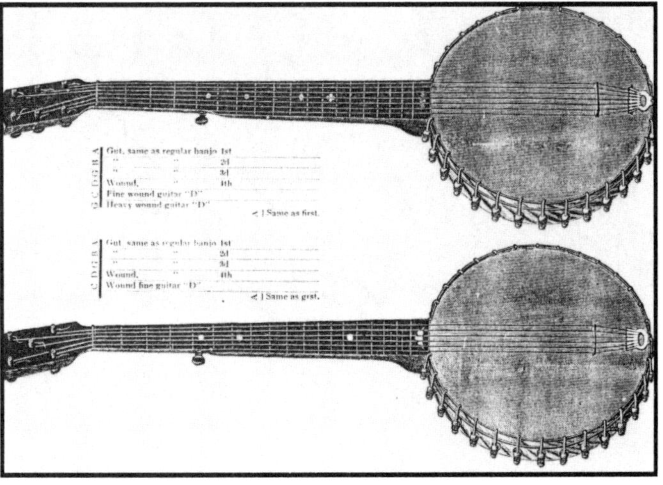

LYON & HEALY BANJORINE.

This instrument is intended for use with one or more Banjos as a leading instrument. When the Banjorine is played in Key of E, the regular Banjo should be tuned in A.

No.		Each.
1865.	12-INCH GERMAN SILVER SHELL, Wood Lined, Finished in Black Inside, both Edges Wired, Plain Strainer Hoop, Birch Neck, Ebony Finger Board, with Pearl Position Dots and Raised Frets, Black Pegs, 25 Nickel Plated Hexagon Brackets ....$	12 50
1866.	12½ INCH GERMAN SILVER SHELL, Wood Lined, Rosewood Veneered Inside, both Edges Wired, Rabbeted Strainer Hoop, French Polished Birch Neck with Metal Stay Piece, Heavy Ebony Finger Board, Position Ornaments and Raised Frets, Imitation Ivory Pegs, 31 Nickel Globe Brackets, No. 42, with Safety Nuts......$	20 00

BANJORINE.

13

The Lyon & Healy-made "Professional" line of banjos from the early 1890s offered a wide variety of shell sizes, starting with the 7 and 9-inch Ladies sizes. Standard and Large size 10, 11, 12 and 13-inch shells rounded out the line. Prices ranged from $14 to $26 for the somewhat plain instruments. The 10 and 11-inch models were available with elaborate fingerboard inlays, carved tuning pegs capped with amethyst colored glass, an intricately engraved shell and "Lyon & Healy" on a plaque at the end of the fingerboard. Prices were $38 and $40. A simpler version of the 12-inch shell was the "Semi-Professional" model for $17. The "Star" models were a short-lived experiment having the neck connected to the rim, with no dowel stick across the shell.

After making guitars for close to ten years it was announced that Washburn would be offering banjos designed to be "the very best that can be produced."

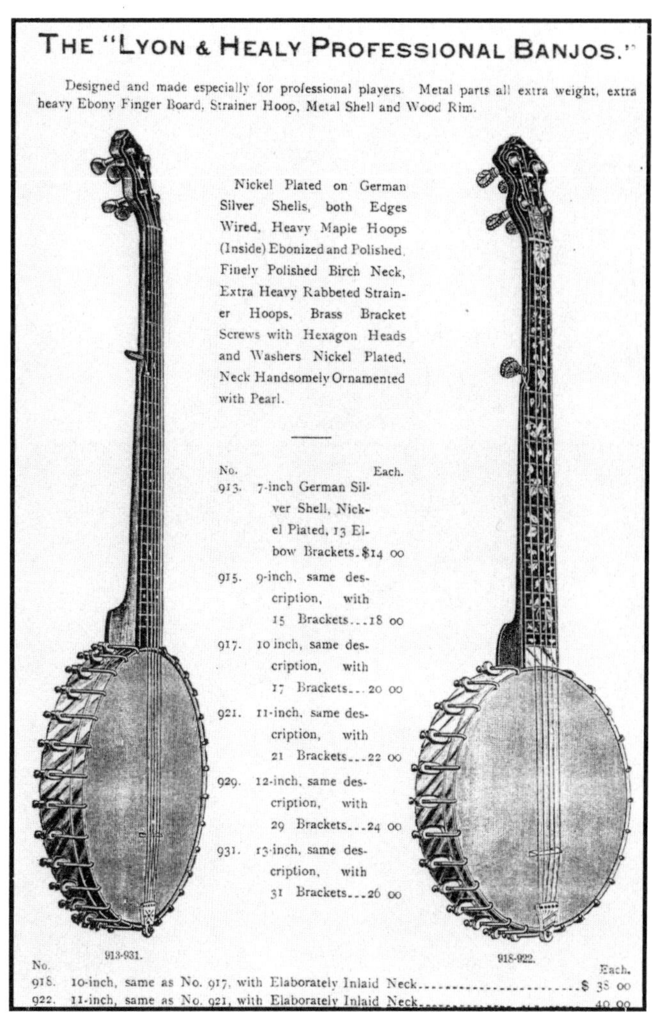

THE "LYON & HEALY PROFESSIONAL BANJOS."

Designed and made especially for professional players. Metal parts all extra weight, extra heavy Ebony Finger Board, Strainer Hoop, Metal Shell and Wood Rim.

Nickel Plated on German Silver Shells, both Edges Wired, Heavy Maple Hoops (Inside) Ebonized and Polished, Finely Polished Birch Neck, Extra Heavy Rabbeted Strainer Hoops, Brass Bracket Screws with Hexagon Heads and Washers Nickel Plated, Neck Handsomely Ornamented with Pearl.

No.		Each.
913.	7-inch German Silver Shell, Nickel Plated, 13 Elbow Brackets.	$14 00
915.	9-inch, same description, with 15 Brackets...	18 00
917.	10 inch, same description, with 17 Brackets...	20 00
921.	11-inch, same description, with 21 Brackets...	22 00
929.	12-inch, same description, with 29 Brackets...	24 00
931.	13-inch, same description, with 31 Brackets...	26 00

913-931.

918-922.

No.		Each.
918.	10-inch, same as No. 917, with Elaborately Inlaid Neck	$ 38 00
922.	11-inch, same as No. 921, with Elaborately Inlaid Neck	40 00

LYON & HEALY BANJOS.

ANNOUNCEMENT.

WASHBURN BANJOS.

The name Washburn in connection with Musical Instruments assures the very best that can be produced, and the Banjos of this celebrated line are worthy of the appelation.

The material entering into their construction is the finest that money can buy, and in elegance of design, perfection of workmanship, purity and volume of tone, they are peerless.

In placing these upon the market we can truthfully say they are the crowning effort of our many years of experience in Banjo making.

A handsome souvenir containing descriptions of Washburn Guitars, Mandolins, Zithers and Banjos, together with portraits of famous artists, will be mailed free upon application.

No. 1165.

"SEMI-PROFESSIONAL"

12-INCH.

German Silver Shells, Wood Lined, Rosewood Veneered inside, both edges wired, Rabbetted Strainer Hoops, French Polished Birch Necks with Metal Stay Pieces, Rosewood Finger Board, Pearl Position Ornaments, Raised Frets and Celluloid Imitation Ivory Pegs, finest quality Calf Heads.

No.		Each.
1165	12-inch Shell, 19-inch Neck, 31 Nickel Globe Brackets, No. 42, with Safety Nuts....	$17 00

The title page of the 1892 Washburn catalog mentioned guitars, mandolins and zithers but not banjos. Inside, however, were four pages of banjos, including plain and fancy Banjorines, plain 5-string models with 7, 9, 10, 11, and 12 inch shells and 5-string models featuring elaborately inlaid fingerboards and 10, 11 and 12-inch engraved shells.

Also available "made-to-order" were similar models with additional detail work such as a carved heel, carved ivory pegs and gold-plated trimmings. These magnificent instruments would be the most ornate open-back banjos Washburn would catalog. The ebony fingerboard was inlaid with pearl leaves and a non-tarnishing gold-colored metal (10K?) for the vine. The heel cap was also inlaid with pearl. The catalog listed these top models as "Washburn Presentation Banjos" even though they were standard in their appointments, unlike the usual custom-spec Presentation models.

WASHBURN BANJORINES.

STYLES 452 TO 462.

LATEST IMPROVED.

NICKEL-PLATED on German silver shells, both edges wired, heavy shell inside, shaded and polished. Beautifully made neck, French Polished, with heavy ebony finger-board, inlaid pearl position dots and ornaments. Carved walrus tusk pegs, new and improved "new departure" strainer hoop, adjustable tail-piece, Imperial brackets, hexagon-head bracket screws, handsome washers inside hoop. All metal parts finely nickel-plated.

No. 452. 12-Inch Shell, 30 Brackets, - - $35 00

No. 462. 12-Inch Shell, same description as above, with elaborately pearl inlaid finger-board and head-piece. - - - - 45 00

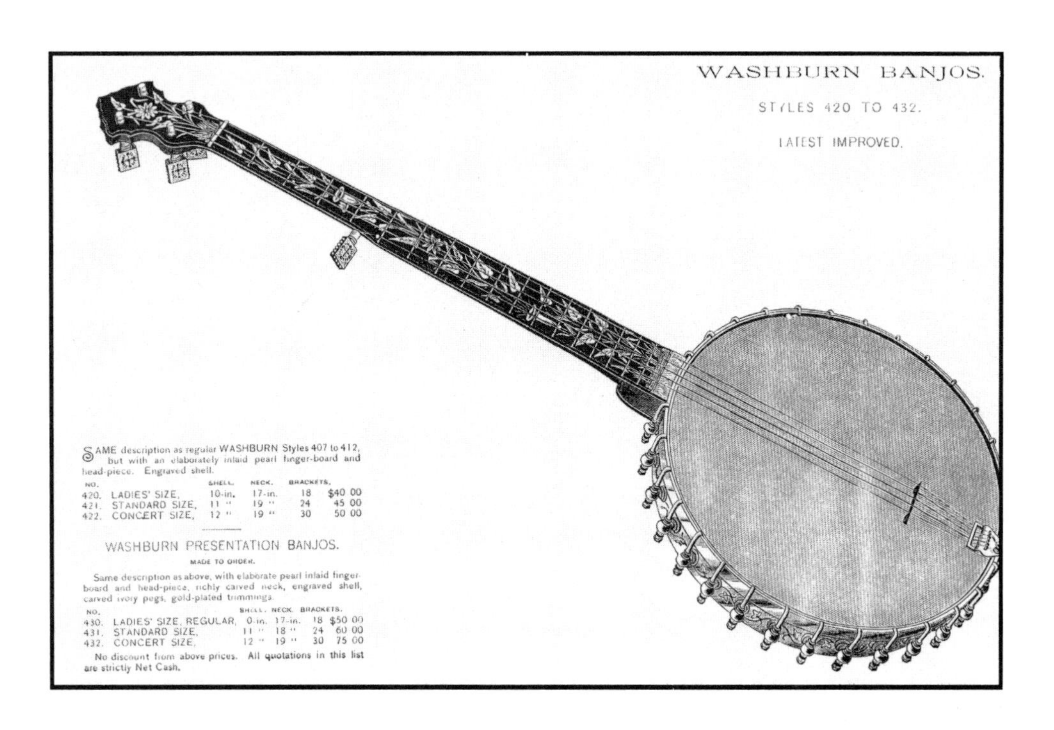

WASHBURN BANJOS.

STYLES 420 TO 432.

LATEST IMPROVED.

SAME description as regular WASHBURN Styles 407 to 412, but with an elaborately inlaid pearl finger-board and head-piece. Engraved shell.

NO.		SHELL.	NECK.	BRACKETS.	
420.	LADIES' SIZE,	10-in.	17-in.	18	$40 00
421.	STANDARD SIZE,	11 "	19 "	24	45 00
422.	CONCERT SIZE,	12 "	19 "	30	50 00

WASHBURN PRESENTATION BANJOS.

MADE TO ORDER.

Same description as above, with elaborate pearl inlaid finger-board and head-piece, richly carved neck, engraved shell, carved ivory pegs, gold-plated trimmings.

NO.		SHELL.	NECK.	BRACKETS.	
430.	LADIES' SIZE, REGULAR,	0-in.	17-in.	18	$50 00
431.	STANDARD SIZE,	11 "	18 "	24	60 00
432.	CONCERT SIZE,	12 "	19 "	30	75 00

No discount from above prices. All quotations in this list are strictly Net Cash.

By 1897, the Washburn banjo line had been trimmed down to nothing but 5-strings, in 10-1/2 and 11" shells. Gone were the fully inlaid fingerboards. This is not to say the top of the line No. 1050 was at all plain, with its engraved shell, carved heel and tasteful inlays. And for anyone depending on inlaid position markers, the fingerboard was certainly easier to navigate than the vine pattern version it replaced. The popular duo "Mays & Hunter" were important endorsers of the 1050.

These new models, Nos. 1015, 1030, 1050, 1120 and 1135, would run basically unchanged from the late 1890s until WWI, with some slight cosmetic changes the last few years. The model numbers and the prices, from $15 to $50, remained stable for almost twenty years, a remarkable feat, even for the time. The Cole banjo makers of Boston are often associated with these models and one of the last versions appears very similar to the Cole Eclipse model.

Just before WWI a tone ring was added, referred to as a "combination patent truss." This "air conditioned" method used "spikes" or "stilts" to isolate the head from the edge of the rim and was standard equipment until the early '20s (other banjo makers used ball bearings and/or springs to accomplish a similar function).

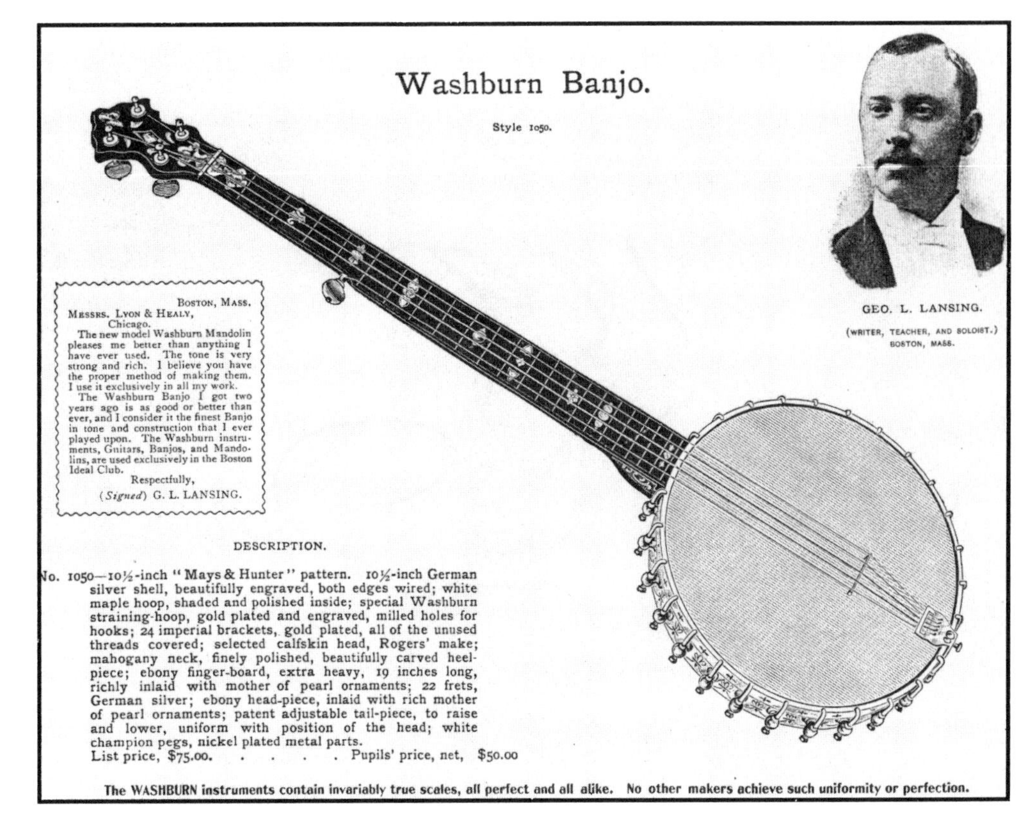

Washburn Banjo.

Style 1050.

GEO. L. LANSING.

(WRITER, TEACHER, AND SOLOIST.)
BOSTON, MASS.

BOSTON, MASS.
MESSRS. LYON & HEALY,
Chicago.
The new model Washburn Mandolin pleases me better than anything I have ever used. The tone is very strong and rich. I believe you have the proper method of making them. I use it exclusively in all my work.
The Washburn Banjo I got two years ago is as good or better than ever, and I consider it the finest Banjo in tone and construction that I ever played upon. The Washburn instruments, Guitars, Banjos, and Mandolins, are used exclusively in the Boston Ideal Club.
Respectfully,
(*Signed*) G. L. LANSING.

DESCRIPTION.

No. 1050—10½-inch "Mays & Hunter" pattern. 10½-inch German silver shell, beautifully engraved, both edges wired; white maple hoop, shaded and polished inside; special Washburn straining-hoop, gold plated and engraved, milled holes for hooks; 24 imperial brackets, gold plated, all of the unused threads covered; selected calfskin head, Rogers' make; mahogany neck, finely polished, beautifully carved heel-piece; ebony finger-board, extra heavy, 19 inches long, richly inlaid with mother of pearl ornaments; 22 frets, German silver; ebony head-piece, inlaid with rich mother of pearl ornaments; patent adjustable tail-piece, to raise and lower, uniform with position of the head; white champion pegs, nickel plated metal parts.
List price, $75.00. . . . . . Pupils' price, net, $50.00

The WASHBURN instruments contain invariably true scales, all perfect and all alike. No other makers achieve such uniformity or perfection.

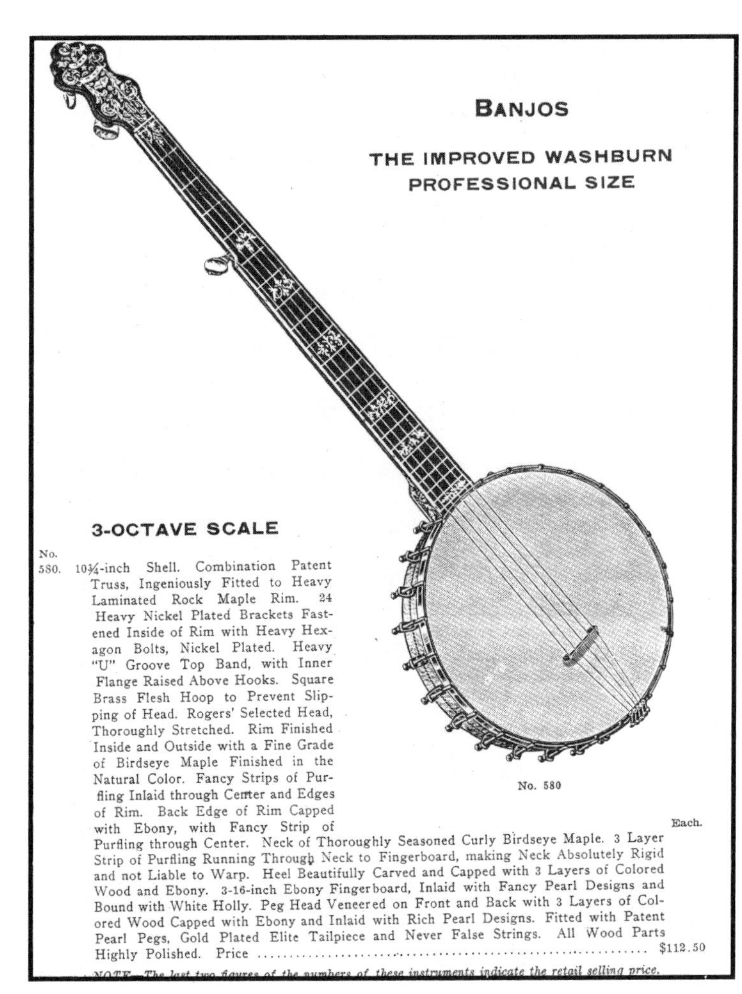

BANJOS

THE IMPROVED WASHBURN PROFESSIONAL SIZE

3-OCTAVE SCALE

No. 580. 10¾-inch Shell. Combination Patent Truss, Ingeniously Fitted to Heavy Laminated Rock Maple Rim. 24 Heavy Nickel Plated Brackets Fastened Inside of Rim with Heavy Hexagon Bolts, Nickel Plated. Heavy "U" Groove Top Band, with Inner Flange Raised Above Hooks. Square Brass Flesh Hoop to Prevent Slipping of Head. Rogers' Selected Head, Thoroughly Stretched. Rim Finished Inside and Outside with a Fine Grade of Birdseye Maple Finished in the Natural Color. Fancy Strips of Purfling Inlaid through Center and Edges of Rim. Back Edge of Rim Capped with Ebony, with Fancy Strip of Purfling through Center. Neck of Thoroughly Seasoned Curly Birdseye Maple. 3 Layer Strip of Purfling Running Through Neck to Fingerboard, making Neck Absolutely Rigid and not Liable to Warp. Heel Beautifully Carved and Capped with 3 Layers of Colored Wood and Ebony. 3-16-inch Ebony Fingerboard, Inlaid with Fancy Pearl Designs and Bound with White Holly. Peg Head Veneered on Front and Back with 3 Layers of Colored Wood Capped with Ebony and Inlaid with Rich Pearl Designs. Fitted with Patent Pearl Pegs, Gold Plated Elite Tailpiece and Never False Strings. All Wood Parts Highly Polished. Price .... Each. $112.50

No. 580

NOTE—The last two figures of the numbers of these instruments indicate the retail selling price.

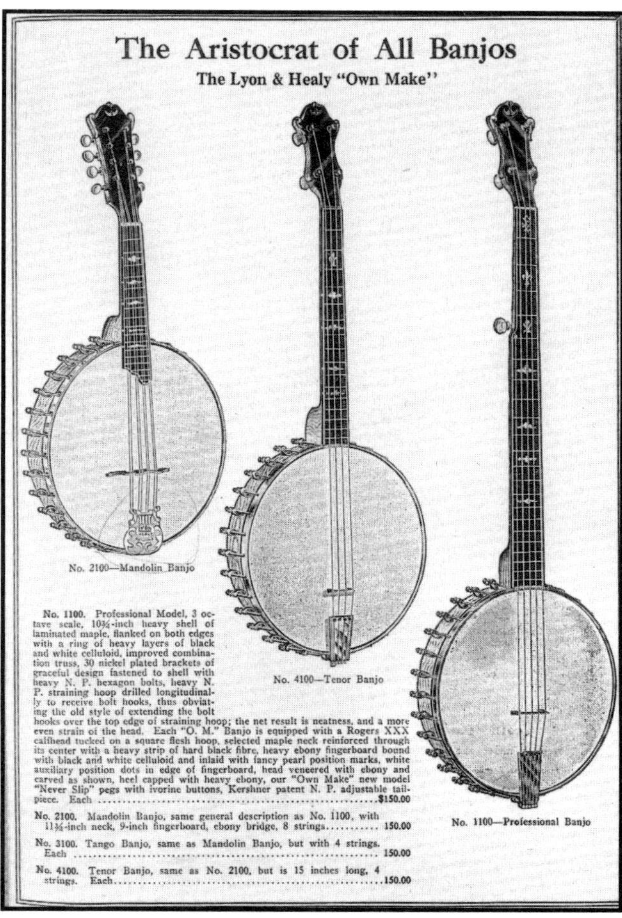

The Aristocrat of All Banjos

The Lyon & Healy "Own Make"

No. 2100—Mandolin Banjo

No. 4100—Tenor Banjo

No. 1100—Professional Banjo

No. 1100. Professional Model, 3 octave scale, 10¾-inch heavy shell of laminated maple, flanked on both edges with a ring of heavy layers of black and white celluloid, improved combination truss, 30 nickel plated brackets of graceful design fastened to shell with heavy N. P. hexagon bolts, heavy N. P. straining hoop drilled longitudinally to receive bolt hooks, thus obviating the old style of extending the bolt hooks over the top edge of straining hoop; the net result is neatness, and a more even strain of the head. Each "O. M." Banjo is equipped with a Rogers XXX calfhead tucked on a square flesh hoop, selected maple neck reinforced through its center with a heavy strip of hard black fibre, heavy ebony fingerboard bound with black and white celluloid and inlaid with fancy pearl position marks, white auxiliary position dots in edge of fingerboard, head veneered with ebony and carved as shown, heel capped with heavy ebony, our "Own Make" new model "Never Slip" pegs with ivorine buttons, Kershner patent N. P. adjustable tailpiece. Each $150.00

No. 2100. Mandolin Banjo, same general description as No. 1100, with 11¾-inch neck, 9-inch fingerboard, ebony bridge, 8 strings.......... 150.00

No. 3100. Tango Banjo, same as Mandolin Banjo, but with 4 strings. Each 150.00

No. 4100. Tenor Banjo, same as No. 2100, but is 15 inches long, 4 strings. Each.................... 150.00

Following WWI, prices skyrocketed to from $28 for the dot-inlaid entry level No. 1528, to $110 for the top-of-the-line No. 15110 with multi-colored binding and intricate inlay work. Gold-plated "geared" tuning pegs and a multiple-ply veneer on the backside of the peghead and the heel set the neck off. Replacing the old style engraved metal shells was a bird's-eye maple shell, inlaid on the outside, the inside and the bottom edge. Nearly as fancy as the models of thirty years before, but in a noticeably more modern style, these were still old-fashioned instruments and some of the last Washburn open-back 5-string banjos.

Lyon & Healy "Own Make" models were also offered, featuring a Mandolin Banjo, the Tango Banjo and a Tenor Banjo as well as a 5-string, open-back model. These were part of the short-lived experiment of "Own Make" instruments that included the Style A Mandolin Family. Costing nearly as much as the top-of-the-line Washburns ($100 for the top Lyon & Healy banjo, $110 for Washburn's), it's possible these were an attempt to replace Washburn as Lyon & Healy's top grade (see p.90).

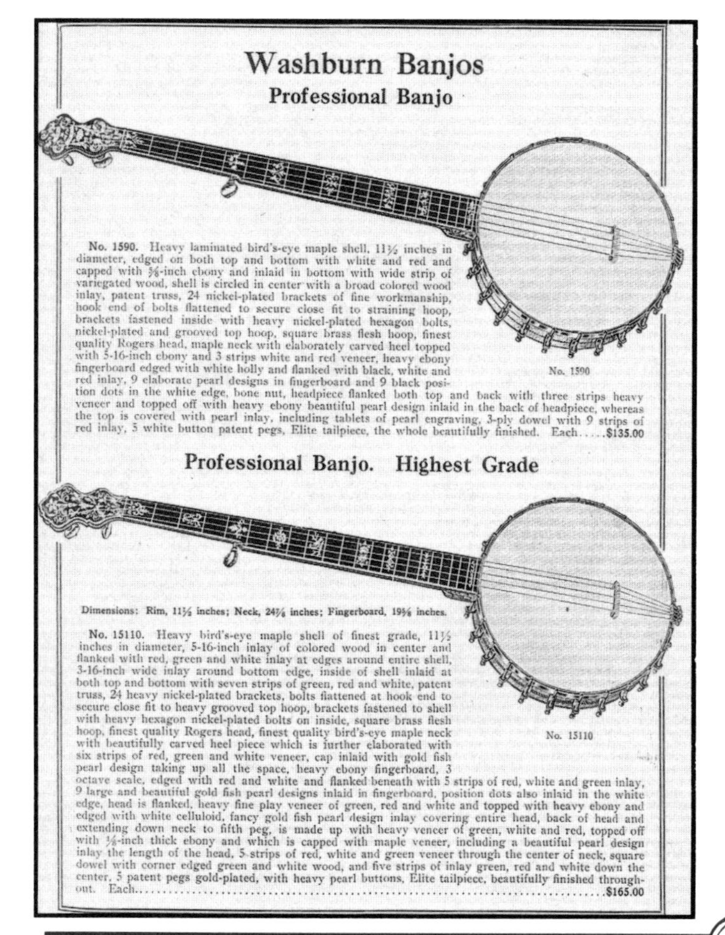

Washburn Banjos

Professional Banjo

No. 1590. Heavy laminated bird's-eye maple shell, 11½ inches in diameter, edged on both top and bottom with white and red and capped with ⅝-inch ebony and inlaid in bottom with wide strip of variegated wood, shell is circled in center with a broad colored wood inlay, patent truss, 24 nickel-plated brackets of fine workmanship, hook end of bolts flattened to secure close fit to straining hoop, brackets fastened inside with heavy nickel-plated hexagon bolts, nickel-plated and grooved top hoop, square brass flesh hoop, finest quality Rogers head, maple neck with elaborately carved heel topped with 5-16-inch ebony and 3 strips white and red veneer, heavy ebony fingerboard edged with white holly and flanked with black, white and red inlay, 9 elaborate pearl designs in fingerboard and 9 black position dots in the white edge, bone nut, headpiece flanked both top and back with three strips heavy veneer and topped off with heavy ebony beautiful pearl design inlaid in the back of headpiece, whereas the top is covered with pearl inlay, including tablets of pearl engraving, 3-ply dowel with 9 strips of red inlay, 5 white button patent pegs, Elite tailpiece, the whole beautifully finished. Each.....$135.00

No. 1590

Professional Banjo. Highest Grade

Dimensions: Rim, 11½ inches; Neck, 24⅞ inches; Fingerboard, 19⅝ inches.

No. 15110. Heavy bird's-eye maple shell of finest grade, 11½ inches in diameter, 5-16-inch inlay of colored wood in center and flanked with red, green and white inlay at edges around entire shell, 3-16-inch wide inlay around bottom edge, inside of shell inlaid at both top and bottom with seven strips of green, red and white, patent truss, 24 heavy nickel-plated brackets, bolts flattened at hook end to secure close fit to heavy grooved top hoop, brackets fastened to shell with heavy hexagon nickel-plated bolts on inside, square brass flesh hoop, finest quality Rogers head, finest quality bird's-eye maple neck with beautifully carved heel piece which is further elaborated with six strips of red, green and white veneer, cap inlaid with gold fish pearl design taking up all the space, heavy ebony fingerboard, 3 octave scale, edged with red and white and flanked beneath with 5 strips of red, white and green inlay, 9 large and beautiful gold fish pearl designs inlaid in fingerboard, position dots also inlaid in the white edge, head is flanked, heavy fine play veneer of green, red and white and topped with heavy ebony and edged with white celluloid, fancy gold fish pearl design inlay covering entire head, back of head and extending down neck to fifth peg, is made up with heavy veneer of green, white and red, topped off with ⅛-inch thick ebony and which is capped with maple veneer, including a beautiful pearl design inlay the length of the head, 5 strips of red, white and green veneer through the center of neck, square dowel with corner edged green and white wood, and five strips of inlay green, red and white down the center, 5 patent pegs gold-plated, with heavy pearl buttons, Elite tailpiece, beautifully finished throughout. Each....................$165.00

No. 15110

Following twenty years of offering only the 5-string, it was time for the Washburn banjo line to expand. The mandolin orchestra was fading in popularity, being replaced by the sound of the banjo. Washburn offered eight grades of "Professional" banjos, their term for 5-strings. The top three grades were only available as Professional models, but the lower five were also available (at the same price) as Mandolin Banjos, Tango Banjos (same as mandolin but only four strings) and Tenor Banjos. These were all open-back models with identical appointments to their 5-string counterparts. The Tango Banjo was basically a Banjorine without the fifth string and the Tenor Banjo was basically a longer-necked version of the Tango Banjo. Of the three, only the Tenor Banjo really caught on, but within a few years after its introduction it became "the" banjo of choice, leaving the 5-string for "old-timers." The chordal approach to playing the Tenor Banjo was completely different from the melodic approach generally used for the 5-string, and it became all the rage in the Roaring Twenties. (See Tenor guitars, p.76). Another popular instrument of the time was the ukulele which lent itself to the new Ukulele Banjos. Like the Mandolin Banjo, these were almost novelty items, being so similar to their wood bodied namesakes, and were only offered for a

The New Washburn Ukulele Banjos

The wonderful popularity of the Ukulele Banjo furnished the incentive to improve on those already in the market, and in the Washburns here described the evidence will be found that our expectations have been fully realized.

For a big, yet sweet tone and for ultra classiness in getup and finish the Washburn Ukulele Banjo is unrivalled.

Every detail is a finished product in which quiet elegance is proclaimed.

Made in the Lyon & Healy factories is sufficient guarantee of superior workmanship and finish.

No.		Each
3.	Shell of laminated maple, 7 inches in diameter, veneered on side and top with nyssawood, 8 machine cut elbow brackets on inside of shell fastened with nickel plated hexagon bolts and washers, 8 slot head machine screws for tightening head, die cast metal straining hoop, fine calfskin head, nyssawood neck, scroll sawed headpiece, rosewood pegs, 4 black position dots, nickel plated tail piece, strung with fine gut strings	$27.00
2.	Shell of laminated maple, 7 inches in diameter, capped with a ring of rosewood, maple neck with scroll sawed head with rosewood capping, rosewood fingerboard with inlaid frets, 4 white position dots inlaid in side of fingerboard, 8 machine-cut elbow brackets fastened on inside of shell with hexagon bolts, slothead machine screws for tightening head, die cast white metal straining hoop, Rogers calfskin head, nickel plated tailpiece, black button patent friction pegs, strung with fine grade gut strings	33.75
1.	Shell of laminated maple, 7 inches in diameter, veneered with fine grade mahogany on outside top and bottom edges, bound with white celluloid on both edges, maple neck with mahogany veneered scroll sawed head, rosewood capped heel, rosewood fingerboard, with inlaid frets and bone nut, 4 pearl position dots, 4 auxiliary dots in the side of fingerboard, 8 machine-cut elbow brackets fastened on inside of shell with hexagon bolts, slot-head machine screws for tightening head, die cast white metal straining hoop, white button patent friction pegs with nickel plated metal parts, nickel plated tailpiece, strung with fine grade gut strings.	42.00

No. 3

No. 1

Lyon & Healy Own Make Banjo "Trijo" Banjo

Three Banjos in One

Ukulele Banjo - Tango Banjo - Piccolo Banjo

Maximum tone combined with individuality and sweetness.

No.		Each
545.	Heavy laminated rock maple shell with both edges capped with black celluloid, natural color finish, improved combination patent truss construction, 14 finely finished elbow brackets heavily nickel plated, each bracket has a boss which is set in the side of shell, thus adding to the security and rigidity of adjustment, relieving at the same time the strain on bracket bolts. Heavily nickel plated hooks with closed end ball nuts, heavy brass straining hoop drilled to receive hook ends of bolts, as shown in cut; XXX Rogers calfskin head, nickel plated Kershner tailpiece, finest quality seasoned maple neck, head heavily veneered and carved as shown, heel capped with rosewood ⅛ inch thick, rosewood fingerboard with 4 position dots inlaid in the upper side when instrument is held in playing position, bone nut, L. & H. own make patent pegs with ivorine buttons. Strung as a ukulele unless otherwise ordered	$67.50

This instrument can be supplied as a mandolin banjo by adding a set of patent heads. Is made to order only.

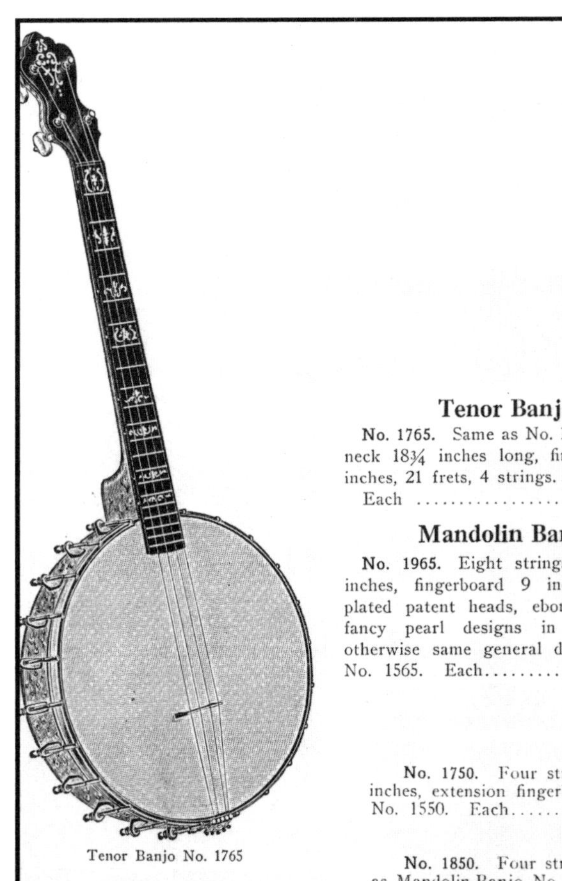

Tenor Banjo No. 1765

Professional Banjo

No. 1550. Wood shell, neck 24⅞ inches, fingerboard 19⅝ inches, 3-octav scale, 11½-inch shell, combination patent truss, heavily laminated birch rim 22 heavy nickel-plated brackets fastened on inside of rim with heavy hexagon bolts, nickel-plated; heavy rabbeted top hoop nickel-plated; square brass flesh hoop, rim finished in natural color, with top and bottom edges ebonized; Rogers head, birch neck with ebony strip through center, making neck absolutely rigid; 3-16-inch ebony fingerboard, inlaid at positions with beautiful pearl designs; Liberty silver frets; peg head and heel veneered with ebony; fancy pearl inlay in peg head; fitted with patent pegs, Elite tailpiece, neck cam, holding neck rigid in rim; all wood parts highly polished. Each.....$75.00

Tenor Banjo

No. 1765. Same as No. 1565 but with neck 18¾ inches long, fingerboard 15 inches, 21 frets, 4 strings.
Each $97.50

Mandolin Banjo

No. 1965. Eight strings, neck 11¾ inches, fingerboard 9 inches, nickel-plated patent heads, ebony bridge, 5 fancy pearl designs in fingerboard, otherwise same general description as No. 1565. Each...............$97.50

Mandolin Banjo

No. 1950. Eight strings, nickel-plated patent head, 11½-inch shell, neck 11¾ inches, extension ebony fingerboard, 9 inches, Liberty silver frets, otherwise same as No. 1550. Each........$75.00

Tenor Banjo

No. 1750. Four strings, patent pegs, 11½-inch shell, neck 18¾ inches, extension fingerboard, 15 inches, 21 frets, otherwise same as No. 1550. Each..$75.00

Tango Banjo

No. 1850. Four strings, patent head, otherwise same description as Mandolin-Banjo No. 1550. Each..........................$75.00

The two final figures of stock number of Washburn Instruments represents the retail price. For example, Banjo No. 1542 retails at $42.00; No. 1950 at $50.00.

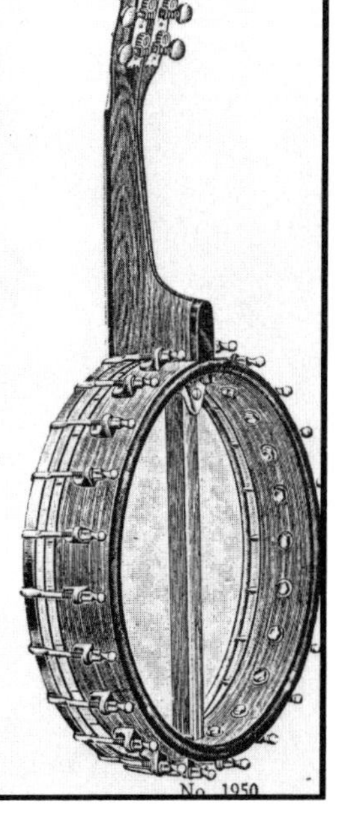

No. 1950

An ad from 1923 described a new solid brass "Air Cushion Tone Chamber" which replaced the "Patent Truss" tone ring and practically enveloped the top half of the shell. Referred to as the "Air Cushioned Resonator" in the '23 catalog, it obviously had nothing to do with a banjo resonator, which would soon show up on the Washburn models of the mid-'20s. With the new tone ring, the head was mated to the edge of the rim with only the thin sheet of brass between the head and the wood. At the top of the line was, like the guitars and banjos of the time, a Style A (Available on special order, the $300 A "Special" featured gold-plating and fancier pearl work). Styles B and C also incorporated the tone ring, followed by the D and E models at the lower end of the line. All five styles had open backs and were available as Regular, Tenor or Plectrum models. Banjo mandolins were still offered as Styles C, D and E.

Exclusive Features
of WASHBURN BANJOS

The WASHBURN Resonator
and Tone Amplifier

The Tone Amplifier is the metal ring attached to the resonator, as illustrated. It is made of bell-brass and has a distinct effect upon the tone as may be noticed when the banjo is played with it removed. This amplifier is not attached by chance or for mere decorative effect. It has been scientifically designed for a distinct purpose and is one of the reasons why the tone of the WASHBURN is unmatched.

The resonator is made of *five-ply laminated* wood. It therefore cannot warp. Here, too, the wonderful effect it has upon the tone of the banjo is noticed when the instrument is played with the resonator removed. This is without doubt the greatest step forward in banjo resonator construction.

Things were changing in the world of banjos and six styles of Tenor Banjos were soon available, featuring the popular new "resonator" design. Models included the Dansant No. 5177 ($110, also available as Plectrum No. 5152 or Regulation No. 5102), the Classic No. 5179 ($130), the Syncopator No. 5181 ($160, also available as Plectrum No. 5156 or Regulation No. 5106), the Aristocrat No. 5183 ($210), the Aristocrat Special No. 5185 ($260) and the DeLuxe No. 5187 ($350). The banjos were fitted with a new version of the "Kerschner Unique tailpiece" which allowed the string tension on the bridge to be adjusted. Lyon & Healy claimed these were designed, patented and manufactured for their banjos, and that they were a great improvement over earlier models. The finely crafted wood resonators, which became standard on most banjos in the '20s, were inlaid around the borders with multi-colored trim. The heyday of the banjo had arrived and Washburn was ready with a varied line of up-to-date instruments. The open-back banjo family lived on through the mid-'20s at the bottom of the Washburn line as the Inspiration models. The Tenor Nos. 5175 (10-3/4" shell) and 5176 (12" shell) were standard with the Plectrum No. 5150, Regulation (5-string) No. 5100, Mandolin No. 5125 and Guitar No. 5115 banjos available at the same price ($60).

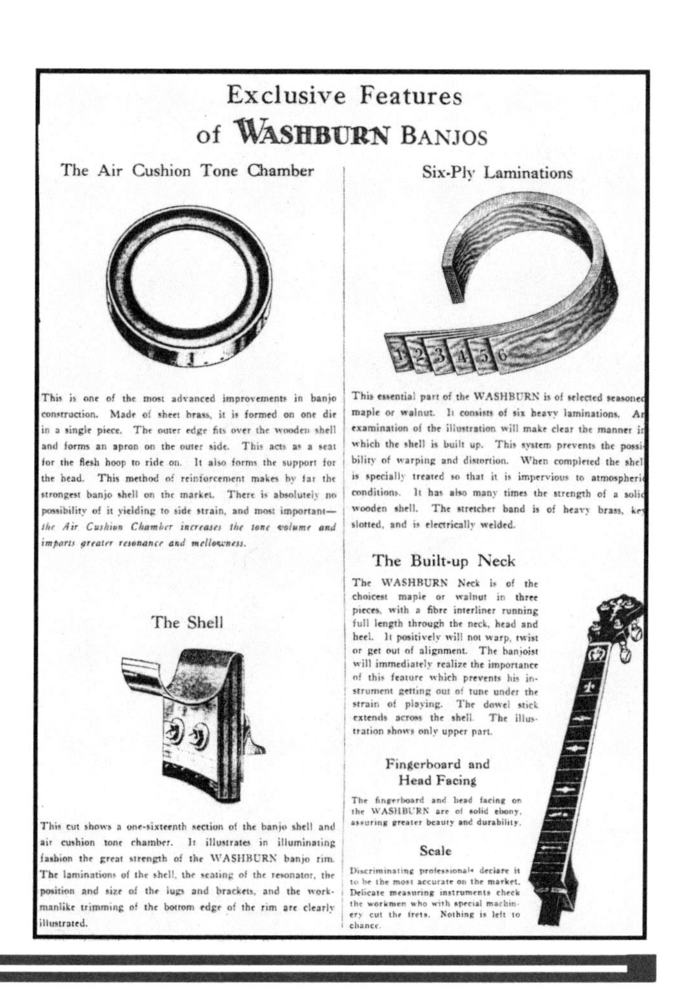

Exclusive Features
of WASHBURN BANJOS

The Air Cushion Tone Chamber

This is one of the most advanced improvements in banjo construction. Made of sheet brass, it is formed on one die in a single piece. The outer edge fits over the wooden shell and forms an apron on the outer side. This acts as a seat for the flesh hoop to ride on. It also forms the support for the head. This method of reinforcement makes by far the strongest banjo shell on the market. There is absolutely no possibility of it yielding to side strain, and most important—*the Air Cushion Chamber increases the tone volume and imparts greater resonance and mellowness.*

The Shell

This cut shows a one-sixteenth section of the banjo shell and air cushion tone chamber. It illustrates in illuminating fashion the great strength of the WASHBURN banjo rim. The laminations of the shell, the seating of the resonator, the position and size of the lugs and brackets, and the workmanlike trimming of the bottom edge of the rim are clearly illustrated.

Six-Ply Laminations

This essential part of the WASHBURN is of selected seasone maple or walnut. It consists of six heavy laminations. A examination of the illustration will make clear the manner i which the shell is built up. This system prevents the possi bility of warping and distortion. When completed the shel is specially treated so that it is impervious to atmospheri conditions. It has also many times the strength of a soli wooden shell. The stretcher band is of heavy brass, ke slotted, and is electrically welded.

The Built-up Neck

The WASHBURN Neck is of the choicest maple or walnut in three pieces, with a fibre interliner running full length through the neck, head and heel. It positively will not warp, twist or get out of alignment. The banjoist will immediately realize the importance of this feature which prevents his instrument getting out of tune under the strain of playing. The dowel stick extends across the shell. The illustration shows only upper part.

Fingerboard and
Head Facing

The fingerboard and head facing on the WASHBURN are of solid ebony, assuring greater beauty and durability.

Scale

Discriminating professionals declare it to be the most accurate on the market. Delicate measuring instruments check the workmen who with special machinery cut the frets. Nothing is left to chance.

Regarding Tonk Bros.' acquisition of Washburn and the subsequent dealings with J.R. Stewart and Regal, things are not perfectly clear today concerning who made what, when and where. An article from 1927 on Rex Schepp and his new $700 Washburn banjo (which was played on early Vitaphone talkies) showed a fancy but typical mid-'20s Lyon & Healy instrument. "Made in the Lyon & Healy Factory" accompanied all the new resonator instruments in the Washburn banjo catalog of c.'26-'27. The Tonk Bros. catalog of 1928 showed basically the same model names and numbers as Lyon & Healy used, but with newly decorated instruments.

It seems the banjo production went straight to Regal in 1928. The top-of-the-line DeLuxe No. 5187 became the Super DeLuxe No. 5187 and the Aristocrat Special No. 5185 became the DeLuxe No. 5185. The backs of the resonators were inlaid with wood marquetry scenes of a tree overlooking a rolling field. The giveaway "Regal Made" feature on these instruments is the peghead ornamentation of a wandering minstrel, inlaid using multiple shades of pearl. This is one of THE most stunning peghead decorations ever to grace a musical instrument and it was a standard feature on the top three models of banjos through at least the late-'30s. The minstrel became a Regal trade mark, showing up on some of the beautiful big-bodied jazz guitars bearing the company's name in the 1930s (see p.37).

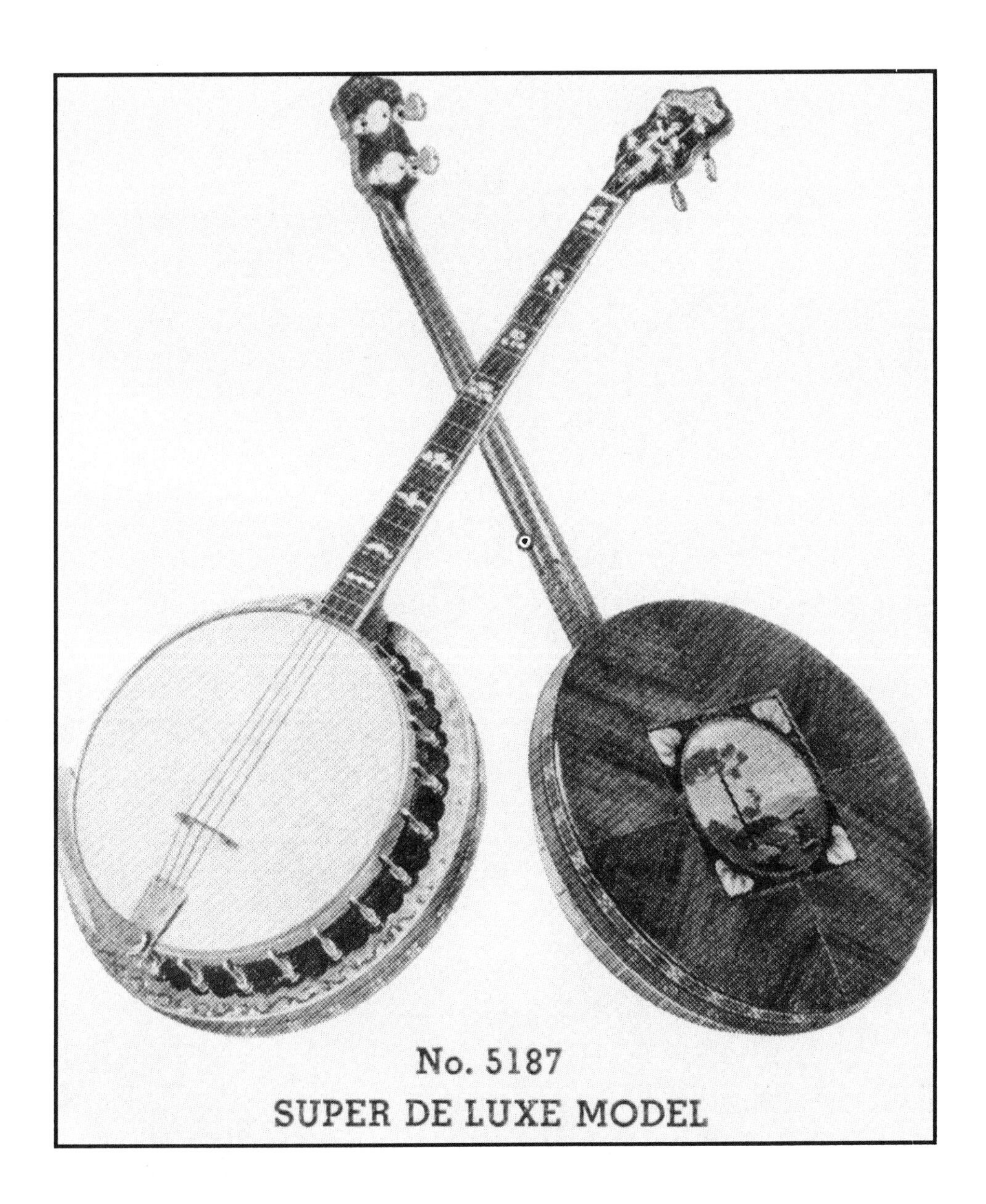

No. 5187
SUPER DE LUXE MODEL

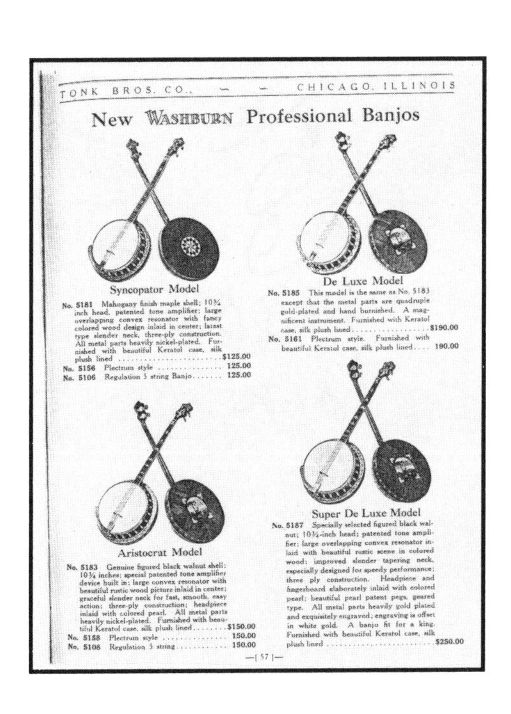

TONK BROS. CO. — — CHICAGO, ILLINOIS

New WASHBURN Professional Banjos

Syncopator Model

No. 5181 Mahogany finish maple shell; 10¾ inch head, patented tone amplifier; large overlapping convex resonator with fancy colored wood design inlaid in center; latest type slender neck, three-ply construction. All metal parts heavily nickel-plated. Furnished with beautiful Keratol case, silk plush lined $125.00
No. 5156 Plectrum style 125.00
No. 5106 Regulation 5 string Banjo 125.00

De Luxe Model

No. 5185 This model is the same as No. 5183 except that the metal parts are quadruple gold-plated and hand burnished. A magnificent instrument. Furnished with Keratol case, silk plush lined $190.00
No. 5161 Plectrum style. Furnished with beautiful Keratol case, silk plush lined 190.00

Aristocrat Model

No. 5183 Genuine figured black walnut shell; 10¾ inches; special patented tone amplifier device built in; large convex resonator with beautiful rustic wood picture inlaid in center; graceful slender neck for fast, smooth, easy action; three-ply construction; headpiece inlaid with colored pearl. All metal parts heavily nickel-plated. Furnished with beautiful Keratol case, silk plush lined $150.00
No. 5158 Plectrum style 150.00
No. 5108 Regulation 5 string 150.00

Super De Luxe Model

No. 5187 Specially selected figured black walnut; 10¾-inch head; patented tone amplifier; large overlapping convex resonator inlaid with beautiful rustic scene in colored wood; improved slender tapering neck, especially designed for speedy performance; three ply construction. Headpiece and fingerboard elaborately inlaid with colored pearl; beautiful pearl patent pegs, geared type. All metal parts heavily gold plated and exquisitely engraved; engraving is offset in white gold. A banjo fit for a king. Furnished with beautiful Keratol case, silk plush lined $250.00

—[57]—

Violins

No instrument can compare to the violin in terms of fanatical appreciation of quality instruments by its players. Subsequently, no instrument commands the price of a great violin, many of which were built centuries ago. Lyon & Healy started a long relationship with the violin by first retailing new instruments. This would be an important part of their business for over 100 years. In the late 1800s, the violin department had reached a level of expertise that allowed them to begin dealing in rare old instruments as well, competing with dealers in New York, Boston and Europe.

By the turn of the century, Lyon & Healy were by far the largest dealer of old violins in the country and probably the world. They published a stock list of over 500 classic instruments, ranging in price from \$35 to \$5,000, an extreme amount of money at the time. Jay C. Freeman was head of the old violin department and regularly traveled to Europe and around the U.S. buying and selling high-end violins. He would travel with a shipping crate of instruments for players to examine and test. He would also host the many famous artists that stopped at Lyon & Healy when visiting Chicago, including some who made special buying trips. Another key figure in the violin department was John. R. Dubbs, who started in 1891 and would eventually head the department, working there fifty years. Lyon & Healy's repair shop had the finest reputation and people sent violins from all over the country to be repaired there. In-house experts offered appraisals of instruments for a small fee and included a certificate of authenticity with every old violin sold. They guaranteed you were buying what they said you were, a classy touch . . .

OF MUSICAL GOODS. 23

GENUINE OLD VIOLINS

To those who are desirous of securing a genuine old violin, whether at \$35.00 or at \$5,000.00, we would say that as we are the largest violin dealers in this country our collection of rare old master-pieces is very complete and so extensive as not to permit of description in this catalogue. We publish a very handsome souvenir catalogue containing descriptions of upwards of 500 rare instruments, which we will be pleased to send free on application. In conjunction thereto we publish a concise yet very complete historical sketch of violin building from its inception about the middle of the 16th century to the present time. The biographical sketches of the different violin makers will not only be of interest but will be of absolute advantage to every violinist or violin teacher to have in his library. Upon the receipt of ten two cent stamps we will forward this book postpaid to any address. Our violins are sent out in the very finest possible playing order. We guarantee the authenticity of each instrument. We issue a handsome certificate to that effect with each violin sold. We sell for cash, or if good references are furnished, ¼ cash, balance divided into equal monthly payments of \$5.00 per month, 6 per cent. interest. When the amount is large, monthly payments are extended a period of two years, at 6 per cent, per annum, the whole amount to be fully paid in two years.

The Restoration of Old Violins

This might very justly be classed with the fine arts. It is an art entirely distinct from that of the violin-builder. As a rule violin makers, devoting their efforts to the construction of violins, are poor repairers. At the same time a skilled repairer is nearly always a good violin-maker.

A first-class repairer must first of all have an intimate knowledge of old violins—information which not one violin-maker in a hundred possesses. In fact, very few can identify with certainty Italian, French, and German violins. This is owing solely to the lack of opportunity of handling constantly good specimens of the various schools, and thus becoming acquainted with their distinctive characteristics. Not understanding the differences in the violins themselves, how then can a violin-maker understand the differences in the qualities of tone which distinguish one type of violin from another? To go a step farther, how is he to know what his aim should be when he begins to repair a violin of whose tonal posibilities he is ignorant, because he is unable to designate the violin itself? It follows, as a matter of course, therefore, that he is working in the dark. *He* will be satisfied with the tone he secures, no matter how bad it may be, because he has no comprehension of the quality of tone that belongs rightfully to the instrument. Supposing him to have been handling a fine Brescian violin, in sound condition, which normally would possess the most mellow, soulful tone imaginable, and owing to his unskillful treatment, his stiff bas-bar, his scraping (so called regraduation), etc., it comes out with a shrill, hard uneven sound, like a cheap new violin, he would still be content. *He* repaired it, and if it has no tone it is not *his* fault, but that of the instrument itself—such is the invariable declaration. Many fine old master-pieces, worth large sums, are ruined, rendered worthless, through ignorant treatment. Now and then, however, if too much wood has not been taken out from the top or back, they can be redeemed by a skillful repairer.

But the trouble is there are so few skilled repairers and so many of the other kind. We are, however, fortunate in having a thorough organization. Connected with our old violin department is our violin repair shop, where not only all our own choice instruments receive proper adjustment, but others which are sent us from all parts of the country. Our work is of one kind only, that of the most artistic nature possible. Our prices are as low as is consistent with such work.

We will cheerfully furnish estimates free on all instruments sent us for that purpose. The cost of properly repairing an old violin, which has been laid away for many years so that it requires entire regluing, linings, blocks, bas-bar, post, new neck, finger-board, pegs, bridge, tail-piece, etc., ranges from \$20.00 to \$50.00. The work usually requires about six weeks' time.

The prices for minor repairs range as follows

New bridge set.......50c and	\$0.75
New sound-post	.75
New bas-bar (including post and bridge)	8.00
New finger-board	3.00
New neck grafted into old scroll	8.00
New entire neck, scroll and neck	6.00
New set of pegs	1.50
Regluing top and back from \$1.00 to	5.00
Regluing cracks from 75c upwards.	

Revarnish entire, from \$7.00 to	\$25.00
Re-edging top or back, from 8.00 to	15.00
Re-enforcing top or back, with patch, from \$3.00 to	15.00
Rehairing bow	.75
Pure silver wrapping	1.00
Other silver wrapping	.50
Leather wrapping	.35
New ivory tip	1.00
New frog, from \$1.50 to	5.00

Certificates and Expert Opinion of Old Violins

We are in daily receipt of applications from persons asking our expert opinion and certificate for violins in their possession. Inasmuch as all this requires knowledge of a very special kind, and it is necessary that much study and attention be given each instrument, unless for good and sufficient reasons, we shall hereafter charge a fee of five dollars for each violin examined. Violins sent to us will receive prompt and careful consideration.

See form of certificate attached.

Rare Old Violins

For over thirty years our collection of Rare Violins has been recognized as the leading one in this country. This is due to the exquisite care with which every old violin is bought and adjusted by our Violin Expert.

An old violin well bought is a joy forever, injudiciously bought it is a source of loss and dissatisfaction. Please remember only a small percentage of old violins are good—in other words, it does not follow that because it is old that a violin is necessarily good

Mr. Dealer, every violinist in your town is a prospective buyer for a good old violin—get after him, cultivate the quality idea in his mind. Eventually you will land a profitable sale.

We have a stock of several hundred Old Vionns at all times. Each is covered by our guarantee and is fairly priced—so as to give the buyer good value and allow a profit for you and a small one for us. Prices range from \$100.00 to \$20,000.00. We take old violins in exchange at a fair valuation by us.

We sell either for cash, or when desired by responsible purchasers, for 20 per cent cash, balance in 24 monthly payments, with interest.

Mr. Dealer, your list of customers includes many violinists. Explain the joy which comes from the use of a fine old violin. Write what is required and let us send you a specially selected list from available stock—together with a letter to you with full descriptions and advice on closing a sale.

Send for Catalog.

Department G,
LYON & HEALY.

Rare Old Violins

No. 2176	*Antonius Stradivarius*, Cremona, 1697. Red varnish; magnificent state of preservation; large broad model; grand tone. Price	\$8500.00
No. 2206	Giovanni Paolo Maggini, Brescia, about 1620. The celebrated Maggini of the Hawley Collection	4000.00
No. 2160	Sanctus Serafino, Venice, about 1725. Flawless specimen of this great artist's work	3750.00
No. 2143	Lorenzo Guadagnini, 1743. Red varnish; a violin for an artist. Price	2500.00
No. 2223	Joseph Guarnerius del Jesu, Cremona, 1729. Orange red varnish; small pattern, beautiful tone. Price	2500.00
No. 1878	Gio. Paolo Maggini, Brescia, about 1610. Brown varnish. Fine example of this great maker's work. Price	2000.00
No. 1847	Andreas Guarnerius, Cremona. Magnificent specimen; brownish red varnish. Price	1800.00
No. 2142	Jacobus Stainer, Absom, 1661. Beautiful wood; translucent varnish; Amatise model; exquisite tone	1500.00
No. 2178	Bernardus Calconius, Genoa, 1762. Excellent artist's solo violin. Italian quality of tone	900.00
No. 2285	Joannes Antonius Rocca, Turin, 1845. Broad Stradivarius model. Exceptional solo instrument	850.00
No. 2286	Giovanni Grancino, Milan, 1703. Amber varnish. Broad tone. Splendid specimen	850.00
No. 2207	Antonius and Hieronymus Amati. Magnificent tone. Amber varnish	800.00
No. 2147	Petrus and Francesque Mantagazza, Milan, 1711. Perfection of workmanship and finish	850.00
No. 2064	Andreas Castagneri, Paris, 1741. A high-class instrument for all-round use	800.00
No. 2057	Nicolas Lupot, Paris, 1804. Perfect specimen. Great carrying capacity	850.00
No. 2053	Nicolas Lupot, Paris, 1824. Lupot's finest work	800.00
No. 1859	Gasparo da Salo, Brescia, about 1580	800.00
No. 2216	Francois Pique, Paris, 1800. Magnificent, large toned instrument	750.00
No. 2243	Thos. Balestrieri, 1763. Excellent solo violin	750.00
No. 2062	Jos. Guadagnini, 1790. Small model, beautiful orange brown varnish. An ideal violin	850.00
No. 2157	Nicolas Lupot, Paris, 1792. Broad Stradivari model, two-piece back	650.00
No. 1575	Ferdinandus Gagliano, Naples, 1757. Guarnerius model. Splendid concert instrument	750.00
No. 1783	Anselmo Bellosius, Venice, 17—. Small model. Orange varnish. Musician's violin	600.00
No. 2070	Francisco Pressenda, Turin, 1840. Finely preserved specimen of Pressenda's best work	600.00
No. 1730	Pietro and Francisco Mantagazza, Milano, about 1750. Robust tone. Perfect state of preservation	500.00
No. 2035	Andraeus Castagneri, Paris, 1730. Extraordinary brilliance and power	500.00

Lyon & Healy also employed buyers to look for classic instruments in Europe, which was a long established market. The French were replicating the famous name violins of the 17th & 18th century as early as 1840 and a high degree of knowledge concerning details and value was prevalent amongst dealers & players. This market pre-dated the vintage guitar market of today by more than a hundred years and close examination of the two shows distinct parallels concerning pricing and inflation of values, availability, forgeries and reproductions, rumors and boastful claims, and in general, a raised awareness of the exceptional.

Lyon & Healy approached rare violins with a fervor, going to great lengths and expense to acquire, and then offer for sale, the *creme de la creme*. The company took a great deal of pride in their previous sales of fine violins at outrageous prices. Again this behavior parallels that of many of today's dealers of vintage guitars, implying these traits are possibly inherent in humans and not the effect of contemporary influences. Some examples to ponder; 1698 Stradivarius for $6,500 in 1906, 1697 Stradivarius for $8,500 and 1620 Maggini for $4,000 in 1908. Fine old bows were also dealt by Lyon & Healy, with desirable examples by Francois Tourte costing between $165 and $350 in 1906. To get an idea of $350 in 1906, look at the top of the line Washburn guitar for that year, the Model 380 with full pearl fingerboard and trim. You could buy four of them for the price of a bow!! Or you could buy 125 of them for the price of a Strad . . .

Lyon & Healy bought a collection of 12 fine violins from the estate of the late R.D. Hawley of Hartford, CT. So fine was this collection that a book was published describing and picturing the instruments. Another large collection was bought from Ralph Granger of San Diego. By 1916 Lyon & Healy would boast of selling more than a half-dozen "Strads" for $10,000 or more, including the 1711 "Healy Stradivarius." Another high profile sale was a 1737 Guarnerius from the Hawley collection to H.J. Havemeyer. (These were early examples of previous or current owner's names being attached to old instruments, as if their owning them had anything to do with the musical quality or "value" of the instruments. For a musician who has gained fame through his or her work to be associated with an instrument would surely make the builder proud, as both dedicated their lives to their art. To share one's name with a great violin (or guitar) merely through its acquisition is a dishonor to the builder and his hard-earned good name.) It's interesting to note that almost all of the high ticket violins neither sound nor play the way they were originally designed, being equipped with metal strings instead of gut and in the name of playability, new necks of longer scale between the body and the scroll! And you wouldn't buy that '30s flattop because its neck had been reset . . .

The Washburn name was put on a series of violins for a short time just before World War I. Fourteen models, all in the style of Stradivari and Guarneri ranged in price from $18.75 to $125. These were made at the Lyon & Healy factory and by using Washburn's good name, offered dealers instruments not available to anyone except Washburn dealers. These dealers were under contract to maintain prices, and not include gratis items such as books, strings, cases, etc. Teachers were the only customers entitled to a discount. Today many of the Lyon & Healy-made violins are highly respected and offer serious instruments to those unable to afford five, six and seven figure pricetags.

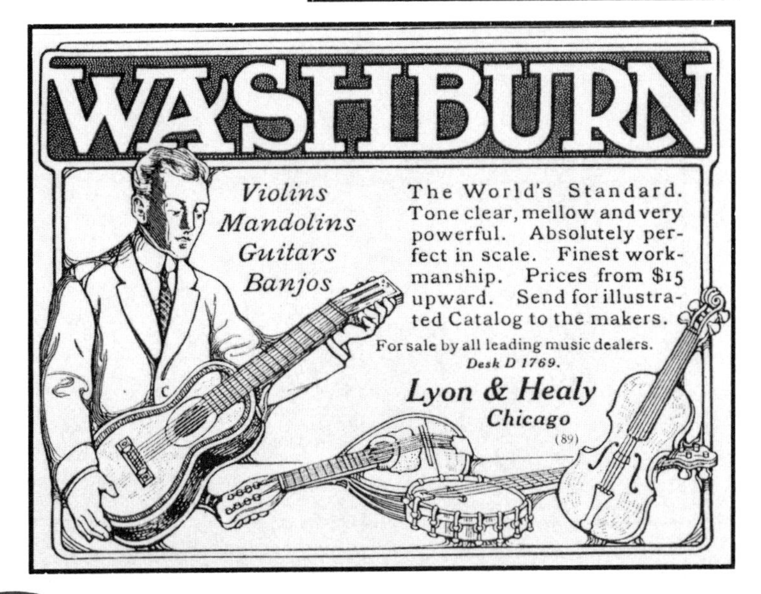

Pianos

Lyon and Healy sold more pianos than anyone at the turn of the century and carried all the major brands. They offered their own Lyon & Healy-make pianos for years and for a time between the turn of the century and WWI, the Washburn name was put on a series of upright pianos made in the Chicago Lyon & Healy Piano Factory. Early Models included the A7, A9, A11 and A12. Later models were identified with single letters A, B, C etc. They were designed to be dependable, well constructed pianos for average Americans. Washburn Pianos were a step up from the many cheap brands that flourished as America tried to put a piano in every home (160,000 manufactured and sold annually at the turn of the century). They were in no way, however, an attempt to compete with the grand piano. This was the first time the Washburn name was used on a less than world class line of instruments. Apparently this happened shortly following the death of Patrick Healy, who was obviously prouder of the name than those who immediately followed him.

Hawaiian Guitars

Following WWI, Hawaiian Music became extremely popular in America. In response, Lyon & Healy offered a number of steel string guitars with high nuts, for playing "slack key" style. A steel bar, open tunings, high action and exotic woods set the Hawaiian Guitars apart from regular guitars. A 9-string flattop and a guitar with an early adjustable height bridge were available by 1920 and one Washburn, made of flamed mahogany with black binding, No. 5235, topped the line. Thin, white trim highlighted the binding. Ebony fingerboard, ebony bridge and black tuner buttons added to the contrast between the flamed mahogany and the black trim.

A Bell-shaped Hawaiian Harp Guitar, Model 5260, was a companion to the Model 5270 Bell guitar but featured beautiful flamed Koa for the body (see p.54). The green binding was a match to the Shrine series and, equally whimsical, the round neck with standard heel construction joined the body at the third fret! Actually, the instrument was unfretted, so the short, round neck, which would have been great for open chords and open position runs, represented a lot of unnecessary work on the manufacturing end. Perhaps this was to avoid infringing on the established Weissenborn neck design. Standard-shaped Hawaiian guitars were available throughout the '20s in mahogany, rosewood and Koa under the Washburn, Lyon & Healy and "Camp 2-in-1" names. Tonk Bros. handled the Weissenborn line before their acquisition of Washburn and shortly thereafter began to offer the National and Dobro lines as well. The Washburn Hawaiian guitars were quickly phased out, joining the bowlback mandolins, zithers, and open back banjos.

Hawaiian Style Guitars

For Playing With Steel

9-String Hawaiian Guitar No. 1201

No.		Each
411.	"Jupiter." Adjusted for Hawaiian style playing. Standard size, imitation Koa wood finish throughout, sound hole bound with white celluloid, ebonized fingerboard and bridge, 3 position dots, good quality patent heads and tail piece, strung with steel strings	$12.75
415.	Standard size. birch back and sides, finished a very fine imitation of mahogany, spruce top, two-ring wood inlaying around sound hole, front and back edges bound with white celluloid, top edge inlaid with wood stripe inside celluloid binding, inlaid stripe in black, ebonized fingerboard, pearl position dots, patent compensating bridge whereby strings can be raised or lowered at will, nicely finished	16.00

No.		Each
1201.	Hawaiian "9 string" guitar. Made of birch, top, back and sides finished in imitation of Koa wood, ebonized fingerboard, cherry finished neck, 3 position dots in fingerboard, good quality patent heads, nickel-plated tail piece, strung with steel strings	$17.88
571.	The Lakeside. Enlarged model, birch top, sides and back finished in imitation of Koa wood, corded wood binding around sound hole, top and back edges similarly bound, cherry finished neck, ebonized bridge and fingerboard, inlaid position dots, good quality patent heads	15.75

Hawaiian Style Washburn Guitar

In the making of a Washburn Brand Hawaiian Guitar we serve that class of trade which demands a strictly first quality instrument in its integral completeness. The model, tone and finish present a whole so perfectly blended as to satisfy the most critical player.

No. 2535. Concert size, six strings. Highest grade of choicest flamed mahogany. Top, back and sound hole bound with black celluloid with a faint line of white celluloid, producing a decidedly neat, artistic effect. Top edge inlaid with alternating black and white celluloid strips. Sound hole decorated with a three-ring inlaying of white and black celluloid. Top and back edge of sides inlaid with a hair-line of white celluloid. Inlaid strip in back. Mahogany neck. Ebony bridge, bone saddle. Ebony fingerboard bound with black celluloid with a faint line of white celluloid. Rosewood veneered head piece. Bone nut. Best quality patent head. Each $52.50

No. 571

N. B.—These guitars can be converted into the regular by simply cutting the fingerboard nut down to proper height.

For Washburn Ukuleles and Taropatch see page 137.

No. 2535

Ukuleles, Taropatches

The Ukulele or "the bouncing flea," was a big part of the Hawaiian sound, with its sweet but cutting voice. Lyon & Healy offered the Hawaiian-made originals of Jonah Kumalae and Leonardo Nunes as well as two new flamed mahogany Washburns. Model 2621 was constructed of solid mahogany, while the slightly fancier Model 2723 had a Koa wood fingerboard and bridge. A Washburn Taropatch was offered in the early days of the Uke. This instrument had eight strings instead of the usual four, giving it somewhat more volume. The fingerings were the same on the Ukulele and the Taropatch. Five Washburn Ukes were listed in the '23 catalog, Styles 700, 701, 702, 703 and 704. 703 and 704 had curly Koa bodies, with gold leaf vine patterns on the top of the 704.

Later Lyon & Healy-era Washburn Ukulele models included the Junior, Inspiration and Collegian models, all relatively plain, the Solo and Superb with the gold leaf vine pattern on the top and two models of Super DeLuxe Ukes. The flamed Koa Model 5320 Super Deluxe was finished around the top and back edges and soundhole with a thin border of pearl, and had fancy inlays on a bound ebony fingerboard. A bound and pearl inlaid headstock, a fancy back stripe and an ebony and ivorine heel cap made this an amazing piece of work, somewhat comparable to Martin's top-of-the-line 5K Uke.

One of a number of mid-'20s Washburns with exaggerated shapes was the Shrine Model Ukulele. These mid-priced models had quasi-balalaika shaped triangular bodies bound with green plastic and matching triangular shaped form-fit cases. Model 5330 was made of mahogany with an ebony fingerboard, fitted with green plastic dot inlays, saddle and nut. Model 5331 was made of birch and cost a third less. A 6-string guitar and a Tenor Guitar were short-lived variations, featuring the triangular body and green trim. A very short-lived variation of the Bell Guitar was the Bell Ukulele No. 5325, made entirely of mahogany. A fancier version is rumored to have also been available. The Shrine Model and the rest of the ukulele line lasted at least into the late-'30s before fading out along with the Washburn guitars (see p.101 for Ukulele Banjos).

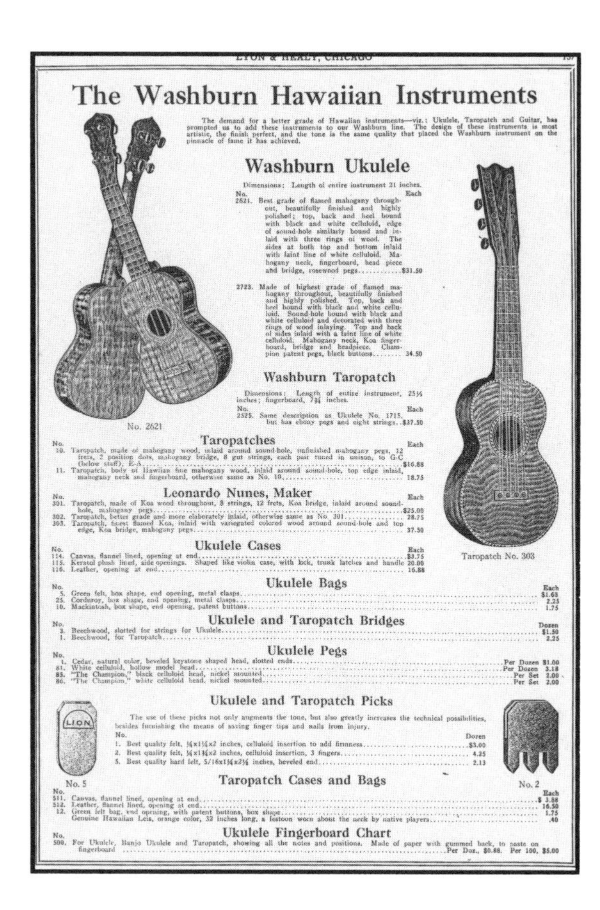

The Washburn Hawaiian Instruments

The demand for a better grade of Hawaiian instruments—viz.: Ukulele, Taropatch and Guitar, has prompted us to add these instruments to our Washburn line. The design of these instruments is most artistic, the finish perfect, and the tone is the same quality that placed the Washburn instrument on the pinnacle of fame it has achieved.

Washburn Ukulele

Dimensions: Length of entire instrument 21 inches.

No.		Each
2621.	Best grade of flamed mahogany throughout, beautifully finished and highly polished; top, back and heel bound with black and white celluloid, edge of sound-hole similarly bound and inlaid with three rings of wood. The sides at both top and bottom inlaid with faint line of white celluloid. Mahogany neck, fingerboard, head piece and bridge, rosewood pegs	$31.50
2723.	Made of highest grade of flamed mahogany throughout, beautifully finished and highly polished. Top, back and heel bound with black and white celluloid. Sound-hole bound with black and white celluloid and decorated with three rings of wood inlaying. Top and back of sides inlaid with a faint line of white celluloid. Mahogany neck, Koa fingerboard, bridge and headpiece. Champion patent pegs, black buttons	34.50

No. 2621

Washburn Taropatch

Dimensions: Length of entire instrument, 25½ inches; fingerboard, 7¾ inches.

No.		Each
2525.	Same description as Ukulele No. 1715, but has ebony pegs and eight strings	$37.50

Taropatch No. 303

Taropatches

No.		Each
10.	Taropatch, made of mahogany wood, inlaid around sound-hole, unfinished mahogany pegs, 12 frets, 2 position dots, mahogany bridge, 8 gut strings, each pair tuned in unison, to G-C (below staff), E-A	$16.88
11.	Taropatch, body of Hawiian fine mahogany wood, inlaid around sound-hole, top edge inlaid, mahogany neck and fingerboard, otherwise same as No. 10	18.75

Leonardo Nunes, Maker

No.		Each
301.	Taropatch, made of Koa wood throughout, 8 strings, 12 frets, Koa bridge, inlaid around sound-hole, mahogany pegs	$25.00
302.	Taropatch, better grade and more elaborately inlaid, otherwise same as No. 301	28.75
303.	Taropatch, finest flamed Koa, inlaid with variegated colored wood around sound-hole and top edge, Koa bridge, mahogany pegs	37.50

Ukulele Cases

No.		Each
114.	Canvas, flannel lined, opening at end	$3.75
115.	Keratol plush lined, side openings. Shaped like violin case, with lock, trunk latches and handle	20.00
116.	Leather, opening at end	16.88

Ukulele Bags

No.		Each
5.	Green felt, box shape, end opening, metal clasps	$1.63
25.	Corduroy, box shape, end opening, metal clasps	2.25
10.	Mackintosh, box shape, end opening, patent buttons	1.75

Ukulele and Taropatch Bridges

No.		Dozen
3.	Beechwood, slotted for strings for Ukulele	$1.50
1.	Beechwood, for Taropatch	2.25

Ukulele Pegs

No.		
1.	Cedar, natural color, beveled keystone shaped head, slotted ends	Per Dozen $1.00
81.	White celluloid, hollow model head	Per Dozen 3.18
85.	"The Champion," black celluloid head, nickel mounted	Per Set 2.00
86.	"The Champion," white celluloid head, nickel mounted	Per Set 2.00

Ukulele and Taropatch Picks

The use of these picks not only augments the tone, but also greatly increases the technical possibilities, besides furnishing the means of saving finger tips and nails from injury.

No.		Dozen
1.	Best quality felt, ¼x1¼x2 inches, celluloid insertion to add firmness	$3.00
2.	Best quality felt, ¼x1¾x2 inches, celluloid insertion, 3 fingers	4.25
5.	Best quality hard felt, 5/16x1¼x2¼ inches, beveled end	2.13

No. 5

No. 2

Taropatch Cases and Bags

No.		Each
511.	Canvas, flannel lined, opening at end	$3.88
512.	Leather, flannel lined, opening at end	16.50
12.	Green felt bag, end opening, with patent buttons, box shape	1.75
	Genuine Hawaiian Leis, orange color, 32 inches long, a festoon worn about the neck by native players	.40

Ukulele Fingerboard Chart

No.		
500.	For Ukulele, Banjo Ukulele and Taropatch, showing all the notes and positions. Made of paper with gummed back, to paste on fingerboard	Per Doz., $0.88. Per 100, $5.00

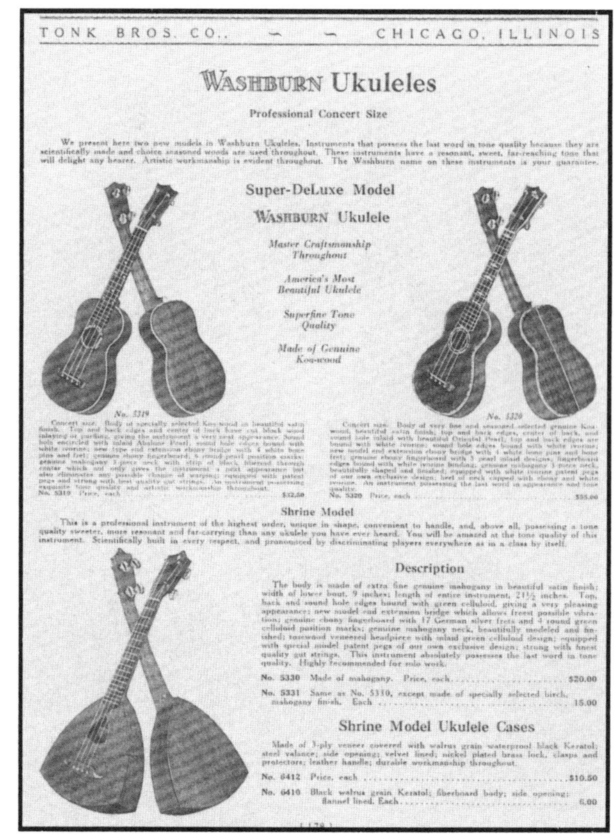

TONK BROS. CO., — — CHICAGO, ILLINOIS

Washburn Ukuleles

Professional Concert Size

We present here two new models in Washburn Ukuleles. Instruments that possess the last word in tone quality because they are scientifically made and choice seasoned woods are used throughout. These instruments have a resonant, sweet, far-reaching tone that will delight any hearer. Artistic workmanship is evident throughout. The Washburn name on these instruments is your guarantee.

Super-DeLuxe Model

Washburn Ukulele

Master Craftsmanship Throughout

America's Most Beautiful Ukulele

Superfine Tone Quality

Made of Genuine Koa-wood

No. 5319

Concert size. Body of specially selected Koa-wood in beautiful satin finish. Top and back edges and center of back have cut black wood inlaying or purfling, giving the instrument a very neat appearance. Sound hole encircled with inlaid Abalone Pearl; sound hole edges bound with white ivorine; new type end extension ebony bridge with 4 white bone pins and fret; genuine ebony fingerboard; 6 round pearl position marks; genuine mahogany 3-piece neck with strip of black fiberoid through center which not only gives the instrument a neat appearance but also eliminates any possible chance of warping; equipped with patent pegs and strung with best quality gut strings. An instrument possessing exquisite tone quality and artistic workmanship throughout.

No. 5319 Price, each $32.50

No. 5320

Concert size. Body of very fine and seasoned selected genuine Koa-wood, beautiful satin finish; top and back edges, center of back, and sound hole inlaid with beautiful Oriental Pearl; top and back edges are bound with white ivorine; sound hole edges bound with white ivorine; new model end extension ebony bridge with 4 white bone pins and bone fret; genuine ebony fingerboard with 5 pearl inlaid designs; fingerboard edges bound with white ivorine binding; genuine mahogany 3-piece neck, beautifully shaped and finished; equipped with white ivorine patent pegs of our own exclusive design; heel of neck capped with ebony and white ivorine. An instrument possessing the last word in appearance and tone quality.

No. 5320 Price, each $35.00

Shrine Model

This is a professional instrument of the highest order, unique in shape, convenient to handle, and, above all, possessing a tone quality sweeter, more resonant and far-carrying than any ukulele you have ever heard. You will be amazed at the tone quality of this instrument. Scientifically built in every respect, and pronounced by discriminating players everywhere as in a class by itself.

Description

The body is made of extra fine genuine mahogany in beautiful satin finish; width of lower bout, 9 inches; length of entire instrument, 21½ inches. Top, back and sound hole edges bound with green celluloid, giving a very pleasing appearance; new model end extension bridge which allows freest possible vibration; genuine ebony fingerboard with 17 German silver frets and 4 round green celluloid position marks; genuine mahogany neck, beautifully modeled and finished; rosewood veneered headpiece with inlaid green celluloid design; equipped with special model patent pegs of our own exclusive design; strung with finest quality gut strings. This instrument absolutely possesses the last word in tone quality. Highly recommended for solo work.

No.		
No. 5330	Made of mahogany. Price, each	$20.00
No. 5331	Same as No. 5330, except made of specially selected birch, mahogany finish. Each	15.00

Shrine Model Ukulele Cases

Made of 3-ply veneer covered with walrus grain waterproof black Keratol; steel valance; side opening; velvet lined; nickel plated brass lock, clasps and protectors; leather handle; durable workmanship throughout.

No.		
No. 6412	Price, each	$10.50
No. 6410	Black walrus grain Keratol; fiberboard body; side opening; flannel lined. Each	6.00

Tenor Ukeleles, Tiples

Washburn offered Tenor Ukuleles in the twenties and thirties that were big-bodied brothers of the fancier ukes. These are generally tuned the same as the regular ukes, although some players tune them down a half step or whole step to further accentuate the richer tone. Models included the early-'20s Style 711 and mid-'20s models 5350, 5355 DeLuxe and 5360 Super DeLuxe.

The Tiple (pronounced tip-lee or tip-lay, not ti-pull) was introduced into America in the '20s. Originally from Argentina, Tiples have 10 strings, tuned like the Ukulele; a pair of A's (one regular, one an octave lower), three D's and three F#'s (two regular, and one in the middle an octave lower), and a pair of unison B's on top. The steel strings and guitar shaped body with spruce top give it a totally different sound than the gut-stringed ukes. The Regal-made Washburn No. 5394 was available throughout the 1930s from Tonk Bros. A Bell Tiple No. 5395 was a short-lived variant of the Bell guitar.

TONK BROS. CO., — — CHICAGO, ILLINOIS

WASHBURN Tenor Ukuleles

Professional Grand Concert Size

New models in Washburn Tenor Ukuleles. These new instruments are rare beauties. They possess a deep, rich, resonant, far-reaching tone that captivates everyone. Scientifically built throughout. Choice seasoned woods, artistically finished. Each instrument is thoroughly tested and bears the approval of an expert before leaving our factory.

DeLuxe Model WASHBURN Tenor Ukulele

Grand Concert Size
Fancy Pearl Inlaid

Superfine Tone Quality

Made of Genuine Koa-Wood

Master Craftsmanship Throughout

America's Most Beautiful Tenor Ukuleles

Super-DeLuxe Model WASHBURN Tenor Ukulele

No. 5355 DeLuxe Model

No. 5355 Body is made of specially selected Koa-wood in beautiful satin finish. Top and back edges and center of back have cut block wood inlaying or purfling. Sound hole edges bound with white ivorine; ebony bridge; genuine ebony fingerboard; genuine mahogany 3-piece neck with strip of black fiberoid through center which not only gives the instrument a neat appearance, but also eliminates any possible chance of warping; ivorine patent pegs.
Price, each $40.00

No. 5360 Super DeLuxe Model

No. 5360 Body of very fine seasoned selected genuine Koa-wood, beautiful satin finish; top and back edges, center of back and sound hole encircled with inlaid beautiful Oriental Pearl; top and back edges are bound with white ivorine; sound hole edges bound with white ivorine; extension ebony bridge; genuine ebony fingerboard with 5 inlaid pearl designs; fingerboard edges bound with white ivorine; genuine mahogany 3-piece neck, beautifully shaped and finished; ivorine patent pegs.
Price, each $60.00

No. 5350 Washburn Tenor

Washburn Tenor Ukulele

Enlarged Model—Length 24½ inches

The WASHBURN Tenor Ukulele has a beautifully figured genuine mahogany back, sides, top and neck, hand rubbed satin finish all over; top and back edges bound with ivorine; new type end extension mahogany bridge which allows freest possible vibration and cannot tip or pull off; polished bone bridge pins and fret; beautifully finished genuine rosewood extension fingerboard with 17 very accurately placed German silver frets and 4 pearl position dots; polished bone fingerboard nut; beautifully modeled head equipped with special model patent pegs; ivorine design inlaid in head; patent pegs have nickel-plated brass posts mounted with ivorine buttons. Gold leaf decalcomania around lower bout. Strung with finest quality gut strings.
No. 5350 Each $30.00

[179]

The WASHBURN Tiple

Here's the instrument of the hour—The TIPLE!

Its rise to popularity was sudden. In a few short months it has won nation-wide favor. Today the Tiple is one of the leaders in the field of music.

Ukulele Fingering—The Tiple is fingered the same as a ukulele. This means that hundred of thousands can play it at once.

The Tone of a Guitar—The Tiple has a quality of tone resembling greatly that of the guitar. It brings therefore to the ukulele player the deep, rich, resonant tone of that beautiful instrument without the necessity of any further study or practice on his part.

Tuning—The Tiple is strung with ten steel strings. The F♯, D and A sets each have one string tuned an octave lower. This scheme of tuning brings harmonies that blend remarkably.

No. 5394 The "WASHBURN" TIPLE. The entire instrument made of high-grade mahogany except the top which is fine selected eastern spruce. Sides, neck and back are finished in medium nut brown color, whereas the top is natural white. Both edges are bound with black celluloid and black celluloid head plate. Correctly fretted **genuine Ebony Fingerboard.** Headpiece is veneered with rosewood and the name "WASHBURN" is inlaid with pearl. Nickel-plated patent heads **$30.00**

Harps

There is no sound on earth as lovely as that of a harp, and no instrument as beautiful. Archaeologists trace the harp's origins back to 1300 B.C. in the region now known as Egypt. The instrument has always been associated with romance, culture and class, whether played solo or with a symphony.

Harps were relatively small and without pedals until the early 1700s when a Bavarian named Hockbrucke made the first pedal mechanism, allowing notes to be raised one half step. The harp grew to its present size of close to six feet tall and in 1810 the double action mechanism was invented by Sebastian Erard, allowing one whole tone or one half tone change in pitch.

LYON & HEALY HARP. Double Action.
STYLE 22.

Lyon & Healy was America's largest dealer of both new and used harps, all imported from Europe. A huge repair department set up and adjusted the harps for Lyon and Healy as well as repairing those of customers. It was decided that a better harp could be built in Chicago, Illinois than any coming from Europe and two years and $10,000 later, Harp serial No. 501 was finished (see p.64). The year was 1889. Mr. Lyon and Mr. Healy's intention was to have George Durkee and staff build a harp sturdy enough to "go around the world without loosening a screw," as well as competing with the European makers for quality of finish, tone and aesthetic design. Success was immediate. At the World's Fair of 1893, the Lyon & Healy harp was honored with the Grand Prize, and before the turn of the century, was considered the world's finest, even when compared to the long-established European builders. A list of users in 1906 included the harpists from the Royal Operas of Berlin, Vienna, Frankfurt, and Budapest, and the courts of Spain, Portugal and St. Petersburg. Prices ranged form $350 to $900.

For a short time before WWI, the Washburn name was put on a line of harps ranging in price from $250 to $500 compared to $500 to $2,800 for the Lyon & Healy models. These Washburns were promoted on the strength of the brand name recognition and affordability. The Lyon & Healy harp was of higher quality than the Washburn, which usually designated top-of-the-line instruments. Following WWI only the Lyon & Healy name was used as the list of European and American Operas and Symphonies continued to grow. Prague, Leipzig, Copenhagen, Amsterdam, Moscow, Stockholm and Zurich were among the additions to the long list of European opera houses using Lyon & Healy harps.

In the U.S., the Lyon & Healy harp was used in almost all the major symphony orchestras, including New York, Boston, Chicago, Cleveland, Detroit, San Francisco, and Los Angeles, as well as the Metropolitan Opera and the New York Philharmonic. By the early 1900s, 95% of the world's orchestras used Lyon & Healy harps and this total domination has continued through today, with the modern harps still being made in Chicago at the same factory as the late 1800s. Even ownership by CBS from 1977 until 1985 hasn't effected the company's strength and respect in the field and the new owners have seen to it that the tradition continues. Not that improvements aren't looked for, with the new Electric Harp being a fitting example. By the way, harp #501 was used at Morgan Park High School in Chicago until the early 1980s. It was bought back by Lyon & Healy and is now on display at the old factory on Ogden Ave.

250 LYON & HEALY, CHICAGO.

THE NEW WASHBURN HARPS.

The New Washburn Harps meet the demand for a high-class Harp of light weight, at a popular price. They embody the essential points of construction which have made the Lyon & Healy the world's standard of Harp quality. The Washburn Harp, Style H (see illustration), is particularly well adapted for Orchestra and light Concert use, its light weight (about 50 pounds) making it easy to transport, while its sterling merits are bound to make it a general favorite with those who do not feel justified in purchasing the more expensive Lyon & Healy Harp.

HARPS FOR RENT

Harps may be rented of us. Six months' rental is allowed if the purchase of a Lyon & Healy or Washburn Harp is afterward made.

With the sole exception of the regular Lyon & Healy Harp, there is no other make that will give the same satisfaction as the Washburn. It is built for use—strong, reliable, with a correct scale and perfect working mechanism. For the use of small Orchestras and for light Concert purposes we recommend it with the utmost confidence.

No responsible dealer can afford to recommend any Harps excepting those made by Lyon & Healy.

OUR OWN MANUFACTURE

Send for illustrated price list containing descriptions of the various styles of Washburn Harps.

Dealers should write for our Harp Proposition. It offers a very attractive margin of profit. Washburn Harps are easy to sell because they are "right" in price, quality and appearance.

Prices on this Page are not subject to usual Discounts. Quotations to the Trade will be made on application.

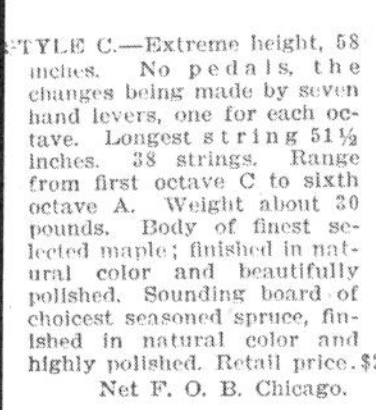

STYLE H.—Double Action

STYLE C.—Extreme height, 58 inches. No pedals, the changes being made by seven hand levers, one for each octave. Longest string 51½ inches. 38 strings. Range from first octave C to sixth octave A. Weight about 30 pounds. Body of finest selected maple; finished in natural color and beautifully polished. Sounding board of choicest seasoned spruce, finished in natural color and highly polished. Retail price. $250 00
Net F. O. B. Chicago.

STYLE H.—Double action. 6 octaves. 43 strings. Height, 66 inches. Longest string, 57½ inches. Weight about 50 pounds. Body of finest selected maple, finished in natural color and handsomely polished. Sounding board of choicest seasoned spruce, finished in natural color and highly polished. Fluted column. Carved base. Brass head plate. Nickeled tuning pins. Outfit includes Shipping Case, Canton Flannel Cover and Tuning Hammer. Retail price................$400 00
Net F. O. B. Chicago.

STYLE J.—Double action. Concert size. Extreme height, 69½ inches. 45 strings. Longest string, 60 inches. Weight about 60 pounds. Body of finest selected maple, finished in natural color and handsomely polished. Sounding board of choicest seasoned spruce, finished in natural color, highly polished and artistically ornamented. Fluted column and hand carved base. Retail price................$500 00
Net F. O. B. Chicago.

Send for List of Second Hand Harps.

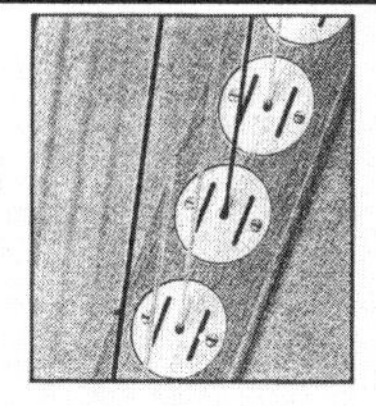

The RMC Electric Stereo Harp Pickup is the most sophisticated pickup system designed for the harp to date. Each string is sensed separately using low profile string sensors; then high-performance Stereo Active Electronics mix and preamplify the separate string signals together to produce a stereo output. The amplified sound is a true reproduction of the string vibrations, which makes it "musically expressive" to both the player and listener.

ROBERT CAMPBELL (left), president of CBS Musica Instruments, and R. Gregory Durham, president o Lyon-Healy, check out a Lyon-Healy concert harp CBS has announced the purchase of Lyon-Heal leading harp maker. Lyon-Healy concert harps se for $4,300 to $9,000 each.

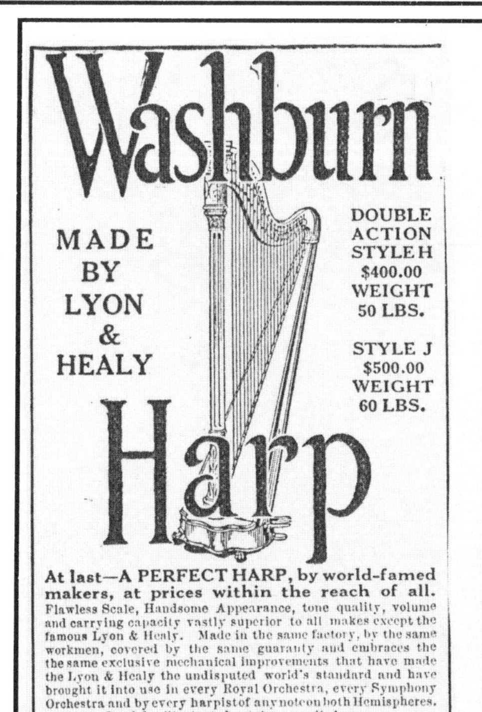

Photo Gallery

Modern Acoustics

113. R312 c.1995. Inset: Savannah D56SW c.1995
114. Golden Harvest c.1984
115. Top left: DC80 c.1990. Inset: R306 c.1993 Bottom: J50S and J20S c.1990.
116. Washburn 12-string acoustic and electric/acoustics.
117. Top left: Tanglewood Classic c.1984. Top right: Mirage Classics c.1984. Bottom: Tapicas Sevilla C200SW and Valencia C100SW c.1990.
118. Jethro Burns Artist M6SW c.1981. Inset: Jethro Burns Deluxe M5SW c.1987.
119. B-19 Flathead c.1981. Inset: B-16 Flathead c.1983
120. Clockwise from upper left: Dolly Parton, John Waite, Hank Williams, Don McClean, John Hartford, Jethro Burns, Patti Loveless, Michael Rutherford.

Photos courtesy Washburn International.

Washburn

George Washburn
Golden Harvest
Hand Made
Serial No.
831103

Washburn

Washburn

Autoharp

Modern Acoustics

American Series Flattops

With full scale acoustic guitar production set to commence in Nashville, Washburn's R & D department began preparing its new line by working with a number of independent American craftsmen. A group of custom guitars combining both traditional and progressive elements were constructed in two sizes, the standard Dreadnought and the smaller-bodied Auditorium. The Auditorium size, a longtime favorite among super-pickers for its evenness of both tone and volume, was chosen for the top of the line.

Built in the tradition of the turn of the century "Presentation" models, the R312 (see p.113) is currently available, featuring herringbone trim, a fully inlaid fingerboard "vine" and a rosette of engraved pearl leaves. White and black pearl and abalone are used for the inlays. A "Durkee"-style bridge with pearl dots set into the carved "clamshell" ends goes back to the very early days of Washburn, as does the slotted headstock and smaller body size. The choicest woods available today and a nitrocellulose lacquer finish should help this treasure age nicely and the suggested retail price (close to $5k) should keep production in the collectors item range.

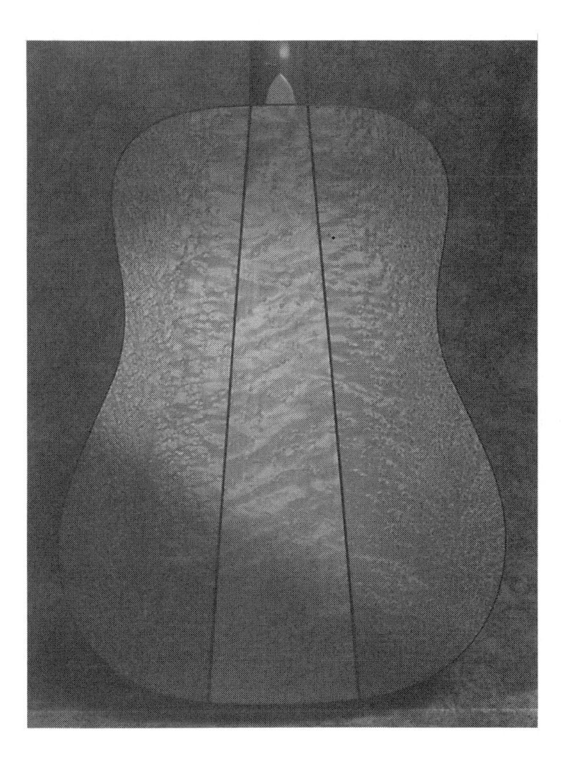

For more than half a century the Dreadnought body has reigned supreme over the steel string guitar world (see p.73). A number of prototypes built over the last few years have led to a limited production of specially made instruments that will be the basis of the new acoustic line. A brand new headstock shape, flared at the top and crowned in the center, is complemented at the other end of the strings with an equally new "butterfly" bridge. Premium grade woods are used throughout. The top model, the Savannah D56SW, features highly-figured koa for the backs and sides and a spruce top, bound in herringbone and maple (see p.113). Abalone crown inlays set off the matching koa peghead overlay and the ebony fingerboard.

The "Native American Series" is a tip-of-the-hat to this country's original "founders," with ceremonial feathers in pearl decorating the pegheads. The D55SW Cherokee uses rosewood and spruce for the body and mahogany for the neck. "Feathers" are inlaid into the ebony fingerboard at frets 5, 9, 12 and 15, as well as a pair set into the headstock overlay. A banner is inlaid across this piece with "Cherokee" engraved into the pearl. Maple binding and herringbone purfling top off this deluxe model.

A bird'seye, maple-bodied partner, the D51SW Apache, is slightly simpler in its appointments, having pearl dot inlays, no neck binding or herringbone and only one feather in its cap (headstock). Both models use a "new" Washburn logo, going back to the turn of the century.

Native American™ Series
PREMIUM WOOD
DREADNOUGHTS
WASHBURN
Cherokee
For the past one hundred years, Washburn's objective has been to build the best guitars money can buy. Our purpose strikes a chord that resounds through our new Native American Series acoustics.
As you might expect, we use only the finest hand-selected and aged timbers, complementing them with pearl, Abalone and exotic wood accents. With the meticulous workmanship of our American craftsmen, these precious materials become works of art. Tap tuning of the braces and hand applied finishes insure that these instruments will become heirlooms your grandchildren can own. Built to last decades and improving with each year, the Apache and Cherokee are not only great guitars, they are your most enjoyable investment.
Apache D51SW
Bird's-eye body, Spruce soundboard
Cherokee D55SW
Rosewood body, Spruce soundboard
5

Flattop Guitars - Solid Wood

Right from the start the '70s Washburn line included a pair of solid wood guitars, i.e., no laminated wood for the tops, backs or sides. This is generally accepted as the "proper" way to build instruments although there is some argument as to the importance of solid backs and sides (more on this, next section). Solid wood is certainly the traditional construction for quality guitars and the first new top-of-the-line Washburn models were built in this manner. The mid-'70s W600 was traditional in its appointments as well, being a Martin D45 Doppelgänger. While not the most original instrument, it was nicely assembled using rosewood, spruce, ebony and pearl. The W500 had less pearl, a three-piece solid mahogany back and a rosewood fingerboard.

The first top-of-the-line model following the sale of the new company, the D50S, was also a spruce top, rosewood back and sides, ebony fingerboard solid wood instrument, but trimmed in multi-colored marquetry around the body and soundhole. A flamed, mahogany-bodied version, the D25S was trimmed in a more traditional herringbone. On both guitars, snowflake inlays added to the delicate theme, but again, were not the most original design.

As Washburn grew in the late '70s/early '80s, their influence on the designs became stronger. A positive trend began with the release of a group of solid wood guitars that were genuine professional quality (see Jimmy Page and Don McLean, p.120). These would be the inspiration for the long line of similar instruments that has continued through today. The Prairie Song Custom featured all-wood construction, from the solid spruce top, solid rosewood back & sides, mahogany neck and ebony fingerboard to the inlaid ebony bridge and end pins to the maple binding, heelcap and position markers. Even the pickguard was wood, matching the back and sides.

A mahogany-body mate, the Timber Ridge Custom, was identical, save for the rosewood fingerboard and the highly flamed "Ovankol" mahogany for the back and sides. Both guitars were available in Dreadnought and Auditorium sizes and with 6 or 12 strings. A slightly less fancy version with dot inlays, an unbound headstock and rosewood fingerboard and bridge was available for each model, lacking the "Custom" designation.

Joining, then superseding these models at the top was the Harvest line, featuring Washburn's classic "V" shaped headstock, a brilliant piece of industrial design. The short-lived Golden Harvest featured abalone trim and an elaborate tree-of-life inlaid fingerboard (see p. 114). All the Harvests had pearl tuner buttons, abalone soundhole rings and inlaid bridges. The DL became the D70 Harvest Custom, lasting a year longer than the Golden Harvest. Football-shaped inlays were unique to this model. A mahogany-bodied SJ was equally short-lived. The Standard Harvest became the D68SW and lasted into the '90s. Both the D90SW Golden Harvest and the D70SW Harvest Deluxe, as it was now called, returned to the line for the early '90s. The rosewood Prairie Song lasted into the '90s as the D61SW, finally changing to a mahogany body c.'94 before being retired c.'95, while the mahogany body Timber Ridge and both Custom versions were discontinued in the mid-'80s.

A second line of acoustics was released in '95 with the crowned headstock shape and "butterfly" shaped bridge. Besides the U.S.-made D56SW and the Native American Series, the D44SW Golden Harvest and D42SW Harvest "All Solid Wood Series" guitars also incorporate the new look. The 44, while lacking the tree-of-life inlay of the original Golden Harvest, does feature its solid spruce top and solid rosewood back and sides, book-matched of course. The 42 has the same basic construction but uses mahogany instead of rosewood and an unbound rosewood fingerboard. Both guitars have the new Washburn logo and three awns of wheat inlaid into the headstock, with the model name engraved into the new pearl headstock banner. The new headstock and bridge apparently will be reserved for the top-line instruments, with U.S. production of the 44 and 42 joining the D56, 55 and 51SWs by the end of 1995.

Other side
Harvest
ALL SOLID
WOOD SERIES
· Harvest™
• Aged, lightweight, shaved Spruce bracing
• Finest quality, hand selected solid Sitka Spruce top
• Bookmatched, solid Mahogany back and sides (D42SW)
• Bookmatched, solid Indian Rosewood back and sides (D44SW)
• Mahogany neck with vintage, Pearl inlayed "Crown" peghead
• Indian Rosewood fingerboard with snowflake inlay
• Ivoroid body and neck binding (D44SW)
• Rosewood butterfly bridge
• Tortoise pickguard
• Nickel Grover tuners
Harvest
D42SW
Golden Harvest
D44SW
· Golden Harvest™
By adapting elements from Washburns of the 1930s, and blending them with fresh accents, the newly refined Harvest Series represents a unique approach to contemporary guitar design. The pearl Washburn "Crown" logo is inlayed in a sweeping, arched peghead. A distinct feature, the carved butterfly bridge echoes the headstock, and brands these instruments as "Washburns".

Solid Top Flattops-Dreadnoughts

As stated in the preceding section, solid wood construction is the standard by which all other methods are judged. There is a school of thought, however, that the thickness (thinness) of the top, the quality of its wood (quarter-sawn, well-seasoned, close-grained, etc.) and the material, position and shape of the bracing, bridge plate, bridge and saddle is responsible for over 90% of the guitar's character (response at different volumes, sustain, harmonic richness, overall volume, etc.). The hardness of the back and sides seems to have more influence on timbre and frequency response than whether the reflective surface is stiff plywood or resonant solid wood. The continued success of the synthetic-bodied Ovation guitars reinforces this logic. While it's probably safe to say that the absolute best sounding acoustic guitars are solid wood, the better solid-top instruments are worlds above the lesser solid wood instruments. The majority of the '50s and '60s Chicago-made solid-wood flattops and south-of-the-border classicals come to mind . . . and since not everyone has an instrument budget in the four figure range . . .

Besides the solid-wood models, the first new Washburn line c.'74 was split 50/50 between solid-top guitars and student-grade laminated toppers. The W260, W280 and W300 solid-top models all were appointed with an interesting patterned wood marquetry around the top and soundhole. Otherwise they were basic dot inlaid Dreadnoughts with the 280 and 300 having bound fingerboards and the 260 and 280 having mahogany bodies. The 300 was rosewood.

Again, besides the solid-wood models, the second new Washburn line c.'78 was split, this time 40/60 between solid top guitars and the student models. The D30S featured the herringbone/snowflake inlay motif of the better models and a rosewood body; a dot inlaid, mahogany body D26S was the other choice in

The '80s and ''90s Washburn solid-top Dreadnoughts were immensely popular guitars, (selling in great volume, especially compared to the solid-wood models) and became known as "best buys" in the mid-priced market. The all important solid top was properly braced etc., giving a sound comparable to guitars costing considerably more. Woods used for the tops were spruce and cedar, with the bodies constructed of a variety of woods. Rosewood and mahogany were the most popular, with bird's-eye maple, flamed maple, Makassar (ebony), Ovankol (mahogany), walnut and Koa also being used. Besides the traditional square shouldered models, the company has also offered round shouldered "Southern Jumbo" instruments.

Feeling the effects of late '70s guitar craft, a trio of new models for 1980, the D31S (rosewood), D29S (mahogany) and D18M (all mahogany) came with a brass nut and saddle set as original equipment. Even the bridge pins were brass . . .even the end pin was brass?!? The D27S and D26S were basically the same guitars with the more traditional "white" hardware. The 31 and 29 changed hardware in short time and all but the mahogany-topped D18 lasted through '85, being replaced by the D30S and D25S. All these models were still in the line ten years later. The solid cedar/bird's-eye maple D30S and the solid spruce/Ovankol mahogany D25S both have the rounded shoulders of Gibson's early J models, as did the last D31 and D29. The square shouldered, rosewood-bodied D21S and the D25S were originally fitted with diamond shaped inlays and a "wing" inlay at the 12th fret. In '94 the D25S switched from spruce to cedar for the top and from diamond inlays to dots. Another "Southern Jumbo"-shaped guitar joined the D25S in '95; the D27S features a spruce top and Koa back and sides. The D21S became the Prairie Song for '95 and is fitted with mini fleur-de-lis fingerboard inlays and a fancy pearl headstock fleur-de-lis decoration. The D30S did not fare as well and was omitted from the newest catalog. Its rosewood-bodied sister, the cedar-topped D29S, was only available c.1991.

Late '80s additions D28S and D20S also lasted into '95 with the D28S recently being discontinued. This model was fitted with a three piece rosewood back similar to Martin's D35 and had a snowflake inlaid fingerboard. The flamed maple bodied D20S shared the diamond/wing pearl inlay of the D21 and 25S. Its model number was used on a new model in '94, the WD20S. This mahogany-bodied guitar introduced the "Veil Process" finish, a very thin coating designed to let the wood breathe and age faster. The cedar-topped, rosewood body WD40S also introduced this finish, but the model was very short lived, possibly because of the public's association with the name "WD40" as a lubricant spray. Another recently discontinued model was the D32S of the late '80s. The body was made from beautifully grained Makassar ebony. Very exotic!

In recent years the overall quality and originality of the solid top line has gone up considerably. This has made room for long running student models D13 and D12 to become the solid-topped D13S and D12S while competing price-wise with a number of laminated top guitars from other companies. Another way of looking at these upgrades is "they could, so they did"; the mass production process (started by Washburn long ago) allowing the use of solid tops on all but their least expensive guitar.

D-31S Dreadnaught
• Select Solid Spruce Top
• Select Rosewood Sides and Back
• Natural Hardwood Purfling
• Mahogany Neck with Diamond Reinforcement
• Truss Rod Adjustable Through Sound Hole
• Brass Nut and Saddle
• Brass Bridge and End Pins
• Precision Cast Gold Plated Machine Heads - 16:1 Ratio
• Equipped with Washburn L-100 Strings
D-29S Dreadnaught
Features are the same as D-31S with the exception of the following:
• Mahogany Sides and Back
• Tortoise Shell Pickguard
• Equipped with Washburn L-100 Strings
• Also Available in 12-String - D-29S-12
D-18M Dreadnaught
• Select Mahogany Top, Sides and Back
• Steel Reinforced Mahogany Neck
• Natural Rosewood Bridge, Fingerboard and Peghead Overlay
• Tortoise Binding with Wood Purfling
• Brass Nut and Saddle
• Brass Bridge and End Pins
• Individual Enclosed Gold Plated Tuners
• Equipped with Washburn L-100 Strings

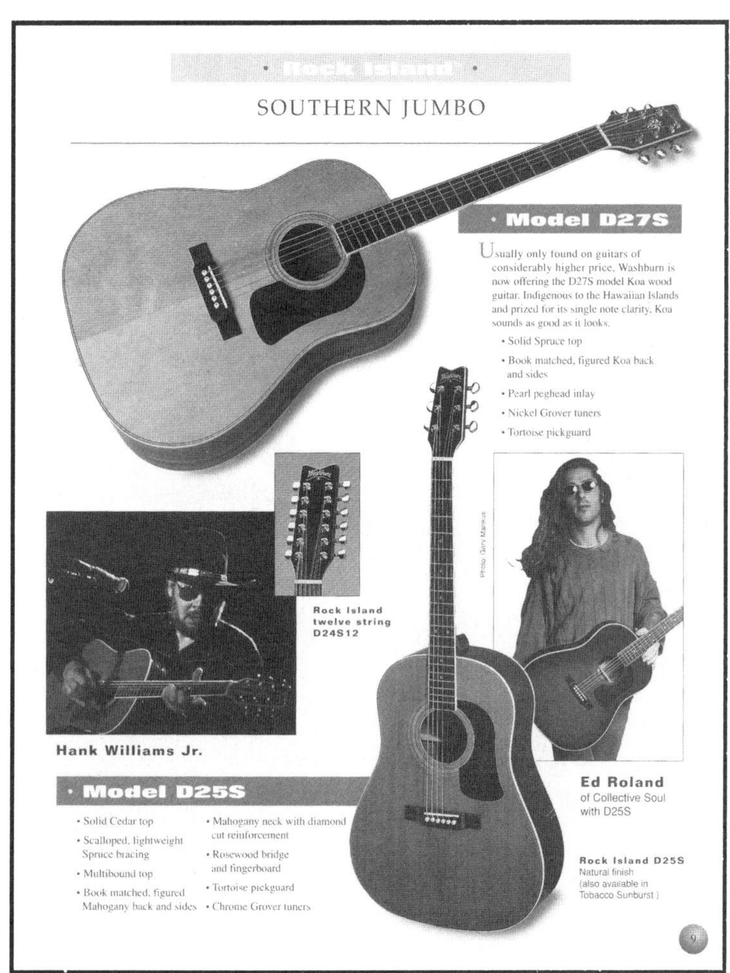

• Rock Island™ •

SOUTHERN JUMBO

· Model D27S

Usually only found on guitars of considerably higher price, Washburn is now offering the D27S model Koa wood guitar. Indigenous to the Hawaiian Islands and prized for its single note clarity, Koa sounds as good as it looks.

- Solid Spruce top
- Book matched, figured Koa back and sides
- Pearl peghead inlay
- Nickel Grover tuners
- Tortoise pickguard

Rock Island twelve string D24S12

Photo: Gary Mankus

Hank Williams Jr.

Ed Roland of Collective Soul with D25S

· Model D25S

- Solid Cedar top
- Scalloped, lightweight Spruce bracing
- Multibound top
- Book matched, figured Mahogany back and sides
- Mahogany neck with diamond cut reinforcement
- Rosewood bridge and fingerboard
- Tortoise pickguard
- Chrome Grover tuners

Rock Island D25S
Natural finish
(also available in Tobacco Sunburst)

9

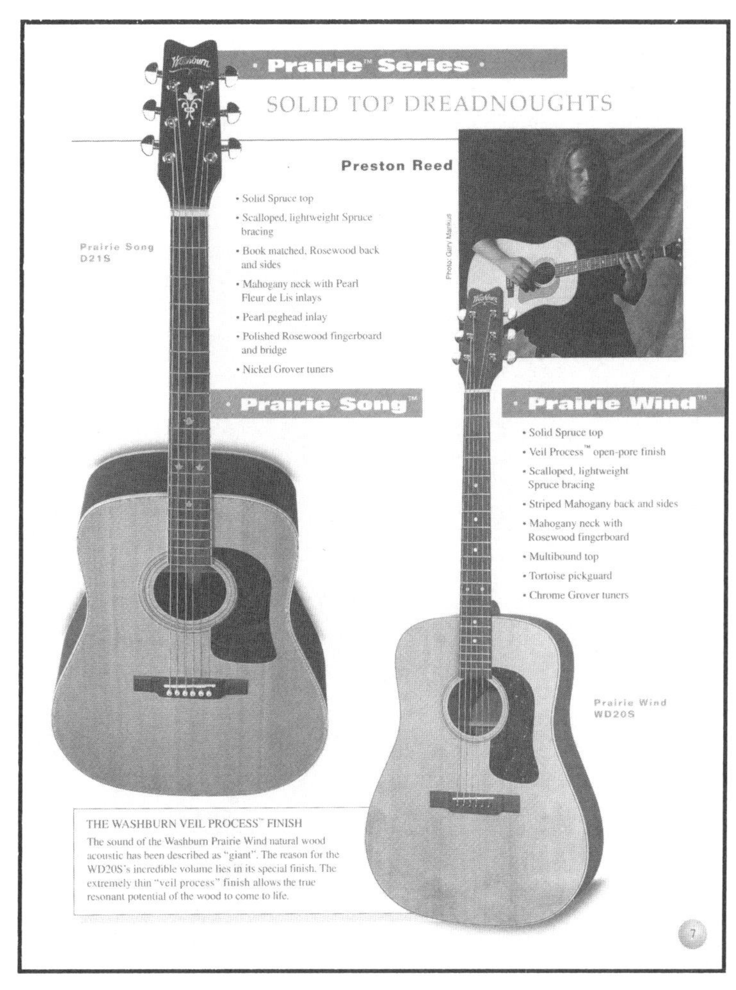

· Prairie™ Series ·

SOLID TOP DREADNOUGHTS

Prairie Song D21S

Preston Reed

Photo: Gary Mankus

- Solid Spruce top
- Scalloped, lightweight Spruce bracing
- Book matched, Rosewood back and sides
- Mahogany neck with Pearl Fleur de Lis inlays
- Pearl peghead inlay
- Polished Rosewood fingerboard and bridge
- Nickel Grover tuners

· Prairie Song™

· Prairie Wind™

- Solid Spruce top
- Veil Process™ open-pore finish
- Scalloped, lightweight Spruce bracing
- Striped Mahogany back and sides
- Mahogany neck with Rosewood fingerboard
- Multibound top
- Tortoise pickguard
- Chrome Grover tuners

Prairie Wind WD20S

THE WASHBURN VEIL PROCESS™ FINISH

The sound of the Washburn Prairie Wind natural wood acoustic has been described as "giant". The reason for the WD20S's incredible volume lies in its special finish. The extremely thin "veil process" finish allows the true resonant potential of the wood to come to life.

7

Solid Top Flattops
Folk, Auditorium and Jumbo Sizes

Different styles of music and the appropriate techniques used to perform them warrant a variety of different sounding and responding instruments. There is no one perfect guitar and the wise player will try a variety of models in search of what's right for him or herself. Aesthetically, some people simply don't want "another Dreadnought"; it would be a sad day when the acoustic guitar joined the numerous other musical instruments that use one "standard" approach to construction, e.g. trumpets, clarinets and to some extent, violins, cellos and standup basses.

The first new Washburn folk guitar (c.'74)was a bottom-of-the-line instrument, the W200, and the new owners (c.'78) also had folk models at the bottom, the F15, F20 and F25. They did, however, offer the option of ordering folk versions of their top instruments, designated F50S, F30S, F28S and F26S.

Steve Goodman

Following the late '70s offerings, the early '80s top-of-the-line Prairie Song Custom and Standard models were available in the Folk Style, as were the Timber Ridge Custom and Standard. The solid-top F27 and F26 were Folk/Auditorium size counterparts to their Dreadnought siblings, as were the laminated-top F15 and F12 models. All of these 14th-fret neck joint, solid headstock instruments were discontinued in the early '80s and the Auditorium size would not return until the steel string version of the 1890's Model 306 was reissued in 1993 as the R306 (see p.115). This charming 12-frets clear, slotted headstock instrument featured a rosewood fingerboard and bridge instead of the original model's ebony and a cedar top instead of spruce, but visually was close to the original with its appropriately sized rosewood body and slotted-headstock mahogany neck. The inlays and "Durkee" bridge were correct with the exception of a compensating tilt to the saddle and the straight-on alignment of the bridge pins (see p.67). A mahogany-bodied, dot-inlaid model R301 with a standard bridge has recently joined the line below the 306, and the Presentation model R312 now sits at the top of the entire Washburn line. A larger-than-D-sized Jumbo was available c.'91-'93 with either a cedar top and walnut back and sides (J20S) or a spruce top and bird's-eye maple body (J50S). The oval soundhole gave these guitars a unique look as did the oversized body (see p.115). A cutaway electric version (J21CE) placed the J-body into a "whole nuther class" for '94, but the solid top Jumbo has recently returned as the cutaway acoustic J28SC (see following page).

Flattop Cutaway Models

Cutaway bodied steel string guitars have been around for quite awhile; early '30s Kay Krafts and Epiphone Recording models, postwar CF100s and FT Deluxes, etc. It wasn't until the '80s, however, that the cutaway flattop really caught on. With the introduction of the Festival Series of electric/acoustics c.1980, Washburn began offering its unique Cutaway bodies which are noticably different from a standard flattop. In the mid '80s, a traditional student grade model was upgraded with both a cutaway and an electric pickup, the D12CE. This combination would become somewhat standard for Washburn, as most of their cutaway flattops have had pickups and most of their electrified flattops have had cutaways.

An acoustic model flattop with an outrageously clever cutaway design was unveiled at the Summer of '87 NAMM show and heads turned. The production models DC60 (spruce top, mahogany body) and DC80 (cedar top, rosewood body) featured luthier Stephen Davies' "Stephen's Extended Cutaway," making comfortable playing above the 12th fret a reality. A compensated saddle made the intonation of the higher frets bearable, as compared to a simple angled bridge saddle which makes no compensation for the wound-third, plain-second differences. While interest amongst the trade was high, the buying public was somewhat cold to the idea. Following the addition of electronics (first as an option) in the early '90s, the models were discontinued following a five to six year run. (A smart buy if you can find one used.)

A new acoustic flattop with a standard Venetian cutaway is available as the Jumbo sized J28SC. This model and its electric brother J28SCE feature the new headstock logo and bridge design of the U.S. models and a visually pleasing set of abalone crown inlays.

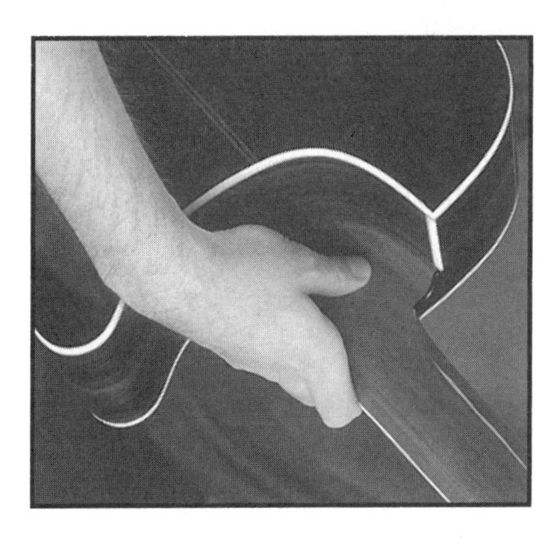

12-String Flattops

The doubling of individual strings into "courses" has added volume and richness, (aka chorus) to stringed instruments almost since their inception. Octave strings in place of unisons took the idea a step further, as on lutes, tiples and 12-string guitars. To go with the first new Washburn 6-string acoustics, a pair of 12-string Dreadnoughts were offered, the WD240-12 and WD300-12. Both guitars had mahogany necks and bodies, rosewood fingerboards and bridges and spruce tops, the 300's top being solid. The bridges on these guitars were adjustable for height.

For '78, five of the seven flattop models were also available as 12 strings. The rosewood body D50S12 and D30S12 and the mahogany body D26S12 all came with solid spruce tops. The D25-12 and D20-12 had laminated spruce tops. The upgraded models of the '80s included solid wood 12-string versions of the rosewood/spruce Prairie Song and Prairie Song Custom. The binding and pickguards were also solid wood. A pair of solid-top models with mahogany bodies, the D29S12 and D26S12, matched their 6-string counterparts, with the D29S12 having a brass nut and saddle. The D25-12 and D15-12 were rosewood and mahogany bodied respectively, both with laminated tops.

The top-of-the-line Prairie Song Custom model was short lived while the standard P.S. lived on into the '90s as the D61SW12. In '85, the D25SN12 replaced the 29S and 26S solid-top 12-strings and the D12N12 replaced the laminated D2012 and D15-12. The D12 would gain a cutaway and pickup, becoming the D12-12CE and leaving the solid top D25S12 as the bottom-of the-line 12-string acoustic for the second half of the '80s. 12-string versions of the solid wood D32 with Makassar ebony back and sides (D32-12) and herringbone trimmed D28 (D28-12) were added c.'87.

A most interesting late '80s addition was the 24-fret DC60-12 Lexington 12-string, featuring the Stephen's Extended Cutaway. This progressive guitar was more like a custom instrument, with its oval sound hole and outrageous upper bout. Unfortunately, the whole Stephen's equipped line was discontinued, c.1993.

An acoustic D1212 was added at the bottom of the 12-string line and was joined by the D1312 in '92. The D32S12, D28S12 and D25S12 were dropped, being replaced by the D24S12. The top of the line D61SW12 was retired, leaving just the D24S12, the D1312 and the D1212 for '94. The current line has been reduced to just two models, the D24S12 and the D12S12, now with a solid spruce top.

Student Line

Guitars made of laminated woods have a number of things going for them. Number one is they are cheaper to make and easier to guarantee (solid spruce and rosewood split easily). Number two is they will take a great deal of abuse, inevitable in certain conditions (extreme climate exposure; young, irresponsible, kids; the rigors of busking, aka panhandling, where a quality guitar detracts from tips; etc). Number three may surprise you . . . an old recording trick is to use a plywood guitar on rhythm tracks when a very percussive sound is desired, more as a drum than a harmonious device.

The two Washburn factions of the '70s both offered plywood guitars with pearl inlaid around the border (If they could do it for so cheap over there, how come it was/is so extravagantly expensive over here?). The W250 (c.'74) specified a "laminated spruce top" as did the lesser W220 and W200, while the new company's was "select spruce top" on it's D25, as well as its lesser D20 and D15 (c.'78). It's interesting that the first hierarchy publicly "admitted" the usage of plywood while never mentioning the overseas connection, and the second group announced their association with the orient but to this day still uses the "select spruce top" phrase for laminated. Some laminated wood is actually cross-grained plies of the same wood while others are a thin veneer on top of mysterious layers of "wood." Is this chapter going to delve into the history of the inner layers of Washburn's Student line? Let's move on. . .

The D12, now with a solid top, was introduced by 1980 and held the bottom-of-the-line spot until the release of the D10 in 1990. Other models were the D14, c.'80-'92, the 13, c.'88, now with solid top, the short-lived D15, and the maple D24 of the early '80s. A very bottom of the line D8 was only available c.'94 and was offered with mahogany or spruce tops.

The new D10 has the distinction of being the world's best selling acoustic guitar, a fact Washburn is and should be proud of. Getting decent playing and sounding, affordable instruments into the hands of beginners is an honorable feat, as anyone who had to start on a monstrous, untunable, fingertip eating box with cables can attest to. One other note in defense of the ply, it does not feed back easily when amplified! (see Festival Series)

Classicals

Although imported classical guitars were ubiquitous commodities during the '60s & '70s, for some reason the Beckmen era Washburn line did not include a single nylon-stringer. Considering the generic selection of steel-string guitars, banjos and mandolins bearing the Washburn name in '74, the addition of generic classical guitars would have been a logical step. When the company changed hands, all the lines were revamped to include newly designed models, and a small line of classicals were added. At the top of the line were replicas of instruments by two of the all time finest makers, Ignacio Fleta (C120S) and Hermann Hauser (C140S).

Master Classic Hauser Design
• Handcrafted Following the Original German Master's Design
• Solid Aged Spruce Top
• Solid Rosewood Sides and Back
• Mahogany Neck with Ebony Fingerboard
German Silver Frets
Deluxe Gold Plated Tuners
• Equipped with Washburn H-300SC Strings
Master Classic Fleta Design
• Handcrafted Following the Original Spanish Master's Design
• Select Solid Spruce Top
• Rosewood Sides and Back
• Mahogany Neck with Ebony Fingerboard
• German Silver Frets
• Deluxe Gold Plated Tuners
• Equipped with Washburn H-300SC Strings
Fleta Specifications
Scale Length = 25 5/8"
Neck Width at Nut = 2"
Neck Width at 12th = 2 7/16"
Length = 39 2/8"
Width = 14 11/16"
Depth = 3 7/8"
Hauser Specifications
Scale Length = 25 5/8"
Neck Width at Nut = 2 1/16"
Neck Width at 12th = 2 7/16"
Length = 39 2/8"
Width = 14 7/16"

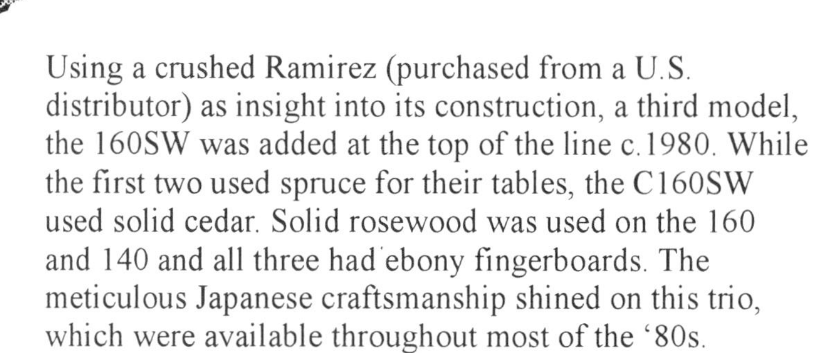

Using a crushed Ramirez (purchased from a U.S. distributor) as insight into its construction, a third model, the 160SW was added at the top of the line c.1980. While the first two used spruce for their tables, the C160SW used solid cedar. Solid rosewood was used on the 160 and 140 and all three had ebony fingerboards. The meticulous Japanese craftsmanship shined on this trio, which were available throughout most of the '80s.

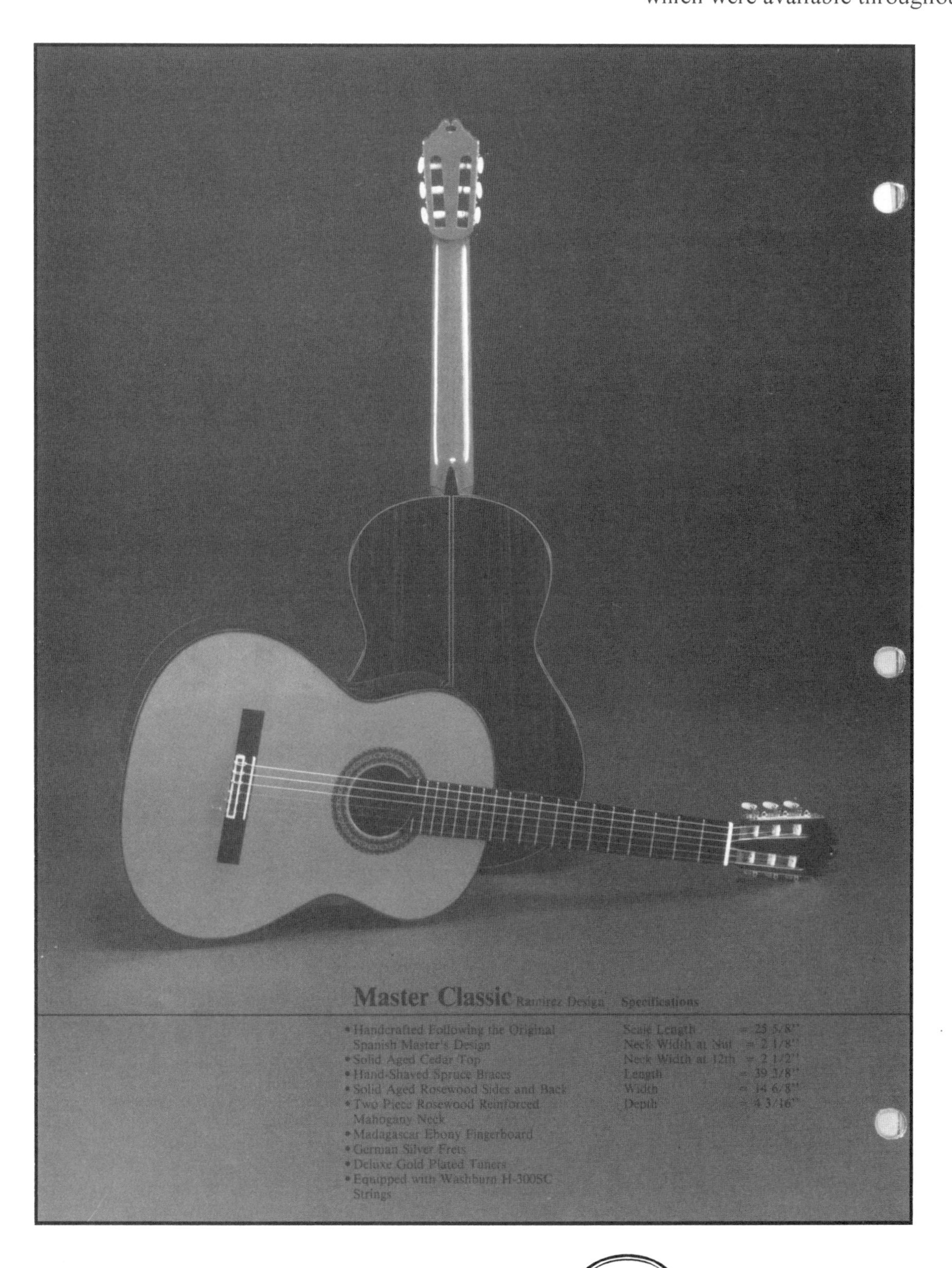

Master Classic Ramirez Design
Specifications
• Handcrafted Following the Original Spanish Master's Design
• Solid Aged Cedar Top
• Hand-Shaved Spruce Braces
• Solid Aged Rosewood Sides and Back
• Two Piece Rosewood Reinforced Mahogany Neck
• Madagascar Ebony Fingerboard
• German Silver Frets
• Deluxe Gold Plated Tuners
• Equipped with Washburn H-300SC Strings
Scale Length = 25 5/8"
Neck Width at Nut = 2 1/8"
Neck Width at 12th = 2 1/2"
Length = 39 3/8"
Width = 14 6/8"
Depth = 4 3/16"

For the '90s Washburn was less traditional, offering a small line that included two electric cutaway models, the solid-top C84SCE and the laminated C64CE. A solid cedar-topped C94SCE joined the C84, c.'94, and soon replaced it (see p.117). Jacaranda back and sides, a Fishman transducer, the Equis II preamp and (GASP) an adjustable truss rod (they work fine on steel strings don't they?) were the major upgrades on the C94. Two traditional models, the solid-top C80S and the student model C40 complete the offerings, all designed by Enrique Tapicas.

The C80S was originally one of three solid top Tapicas guitars. For a short time at the beginning of the '90s, two solid cedar-topped instruments, the C200SW and C100SW, bridged the gap between the serious replicas of the '80s and the stripped-down line of '95 (see p.117). These guitars had ebony boards, bone nuts and saddles and ornate marquetry trimmings. A previous C100S model was available from the late '70s to the mid '80s as a starter solid top guitar.

Besides the company's original student grade C60, 50, 40, 30, 20 and 10 models, an interesting but short-lived Flamenco model was available as a complement to the Ramirez, Hauser and Fleta styles. The CF110S had the traditional Flamenco solid headstock with friction pegs, cypress body, solid cedar top and clear tap guard.

Mandolins

Beckmen Musical Instruments offered a pair of pear shaped mandolins, one with a carved spruce top (WM40) and one with a laminated top (WM70). On the guitars and banjos, a higher number meant a better instrument; it's odd that the WM70 student model featured a blonde top, a bound peghead, block inlays and rosewood back and sides, features associated with better models. The top-of-the-line carved-top WM40 had solid mahogany back and sides, but was finished in sunburst, lacked the headstock binding and was fitted with dot inlays, all features of student models.

These were replaced by '78 with a noticeably better line, featuring the new Jethro Burns models. Styled after Gibson's F5, the M5S and M4S shared carved spruce tops, maple backs, sides and necks and ebony fingerboards. The Deluxe (5) came with gold hardware and elaborate fingerboard and peghead inlays, while the Standard (4) was fitted with dots. A third Burns model, the M6S was soon added at the top of the line and is easily recognizable by its "rope" purfling around the top edge (see p.118). The biggest difference was the solid wood used for the sides and carved back, which soon became standard on the 4 and 5. The 6 was discontinued in the mid-'80s but the 4 and 5 made it into the '90s, outlasting Mr. Burns who passed away in 1989 at the age of 79.

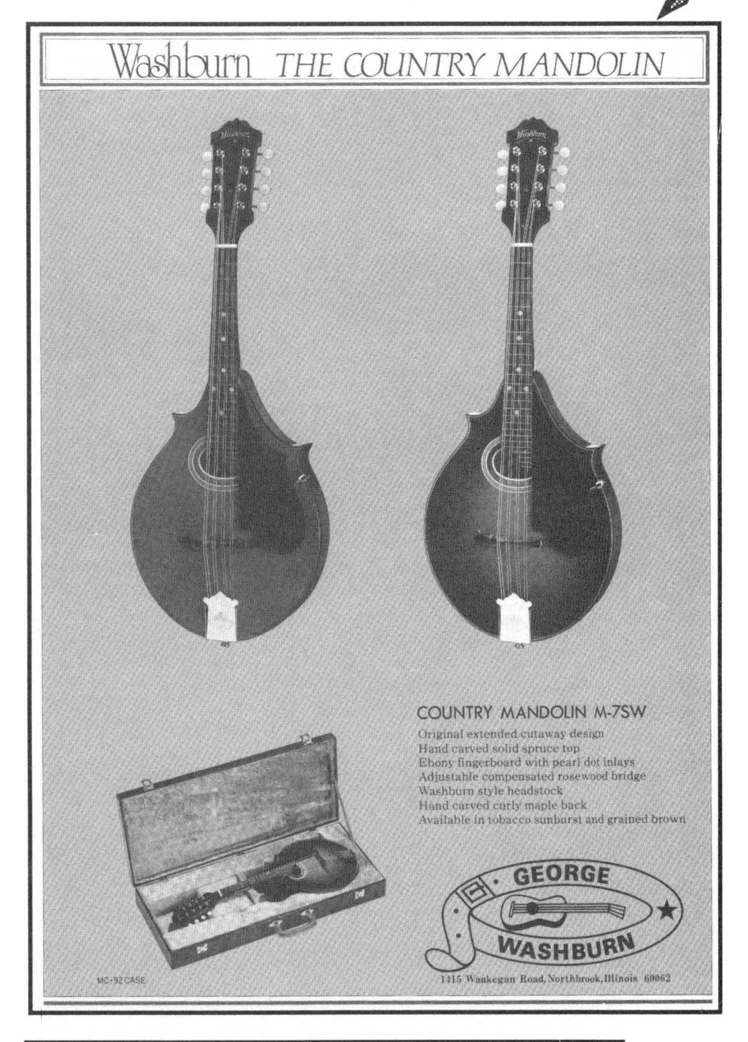

Washburn THE COUNTRY MANDOLIN
COUNTRY MANDOLIN M-7SW
Original extended cutaway design
Hand carved solid spruce top
Ebony fingerboard with pearl dot inlays
Adjustable compensated rosewood bridge
Washburn style headstock
Hand carved curly maple back
Available in tobacco sunburst and grained brown
GEORGE
WASHBURN
1415 Waukegan Road, Northbrook, Illinois 60062
MC-92 CASE

Following the discontinuation of the 6, a third Florentine mandolin joined the 4 and 5. The M3SW, originally was a pear-shaped model and later changed to an f-style with dot inlays. Dressed up with fancier inlays, today it is the top mandolin by Washburn. The 4 and 5 both were offered into the mid '90s, before Jethro's artist models were also laid to rest. The 3 continues the tradition with carved tops and backs and solid wood construction.

Washburn has always offered a series of pear-shaped instruments featuring solid spruce tops. For '78, an oval hole M3S brought back the peghead and body of the Lyon & Healy Style C of the late-teens, early-'20s. By the early-'80s, a Deluxe version, the M3SW-DL, with bound headstock and abalone trim around the sound hole and top, joined the M3. The oval hole was retired by the mid '80s, with the M3 taking on the f-style body.

At the bottom of the line for '78 was the f-holed, pear-shaped M2. The snakehead neck and laminated top construction were only seen on this early model. Solid spruce and the Style C headstock were soon standard and in the mid-'80s a similar model, the M1 was added. The 2 was soon dropped, but the M1 solid top remains in the line to this day.

A short-lived reissue of the late-teens/early-'20s Lyon & Healy Style B was available in the early '80s, built with carved tops and backs. Called the "Country Mandolin," the M7SW had a higher number than the Burns models only because all the other numbers were being used. This is not to suggest they were not nicely designed, having the two point, asymmetrical body shape of the old As and Bs and the stylish peghead of the old Bs and Cs. The black binding and oval soundhole also reached back to the '20s, as did the solid spruce and book-matched solid maple.

Banjos

The first banjos from the new Washburn company c.'74 included a "professional" model and four mahogany student instruments, all 5-string resonators. The top-of-the-line WB180 featured geared pegs, maple construction and fancy inlays. The WB100 with guitar tuners and the WB120 with banjo pegs both had block inlays with rounded edges. The WB150 and 160 were dressed up with engraved armrests, bowtie inlays and ornate truss rod covers.

Following the change in ownership a new series was released that included what would become Washburn's flagship banjo, the B16 flathead. Endorsed for years by folk artist and former Smothers Brothers Show regular John Hartford, the model is still in the line, basically unchanged, going on twenty years later.

A twenty hole, bell brass tone ring a 14-ply maple rim and double adjustable tension rods were the basis of this serious banjo. Flamed maple was used for the resonator and neck, with ebony for the fingerboard. Ornate pearl inlays and quality parts (planetary pegs with geared 5th string, Shubb compensated bridge, Eagle Claw and Kirschner tailpieces) topped off this gem. The earliest models had a natural finish, which was quickly changed to sunburst. In the mid '80s a fancier headstock inlay was added. A raised head model, the B18, was offered for a few years alongside the flathead B16, but was dropped in the early '80s. Aside from the tone ring and the slightly different inlay patterns, the 16 and 18 were identical.

At the student end of the line were the B14, 12 and 10. The B14 sported fancy inlays while the B10 had guitar pegs and old-style tension brackets. Both the 12 and the 10 had dot inlays. The inlays changed at least twice before both the 14 and 12 were retired in the early '90s. The 10 became the 9 in the early '80s, losing the fingerboard binding. The B9 is still in the line, offering the entry level complement to the long running B16, the only other Washburn banjo currently offered.

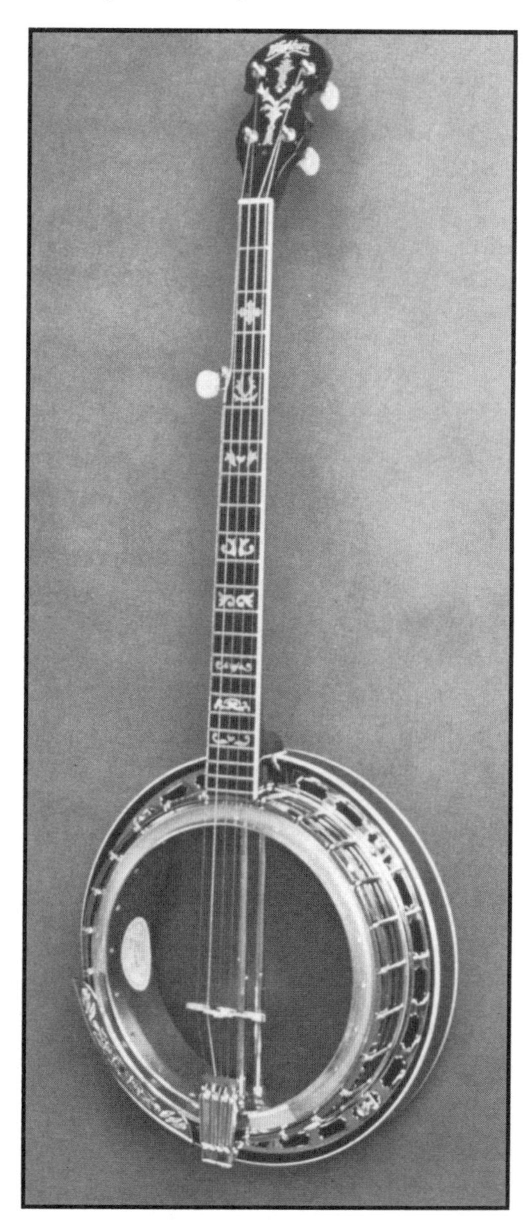

A short lived, top-of-the-line model B19 was offered in the early '80s, sporting an engraved pearl ram's head inlaid into the peghead with animal motif inlays in the fingerboard (see p.119). A carved heel and extra marquetry further set the 19 apart from the 18 and 16. A very striking instrument with its inspiration in the ornate banjos of the early 1900s.

A pair of "Mystic" banjos were a short-lived addition in the mid-'80s, offering the spring tension rim to shell connection. Similar to the technique pioneered in the '20s (and often including ball bearings), 24 high tension springs were dropped into 24 small holes drilled into a three ply maple shell. The springs applied an even pressure to the tone ring/head contact point, compensating for fluctuations in the flat surfaces of regular shell and tone-ring. The B23, aka the Mystic DL, and the B21 Mystic were short-lived with the neck of the 23 added to a standard pot to become the second B19, which lasted into the early '90s. Top-of-the-line, but less fancy than the original B19, the later version sported different fancy inlays and a carved heel. The back of the headstock was also carved.

All the aforementioned banjos were/are five-string models, today's standard. For a short time at the start of the B18 and 16 models, special-order versions were available in yesterday's standards, the Tenor and Plectrum styles. Going back even further, an old-timey, open-back frailing banjo, model B11, was offered for a short time in the early '80s but quality-wise was similar to the bottom-of-the-line B10.

In recent years the banjo has been bypassed by Washburn's R & D department. Although the company started out supplying folk instruments in the '70s, the '80s and '90s saw Washburn focus on the guitar, using the slogan "What a great guitar should be." It will be interesting to see if the banjo and mandolin survive as acoustic instruments . . . perhaps R & D can transform these distinctive sounds into functional electric instruments for the 21st century.

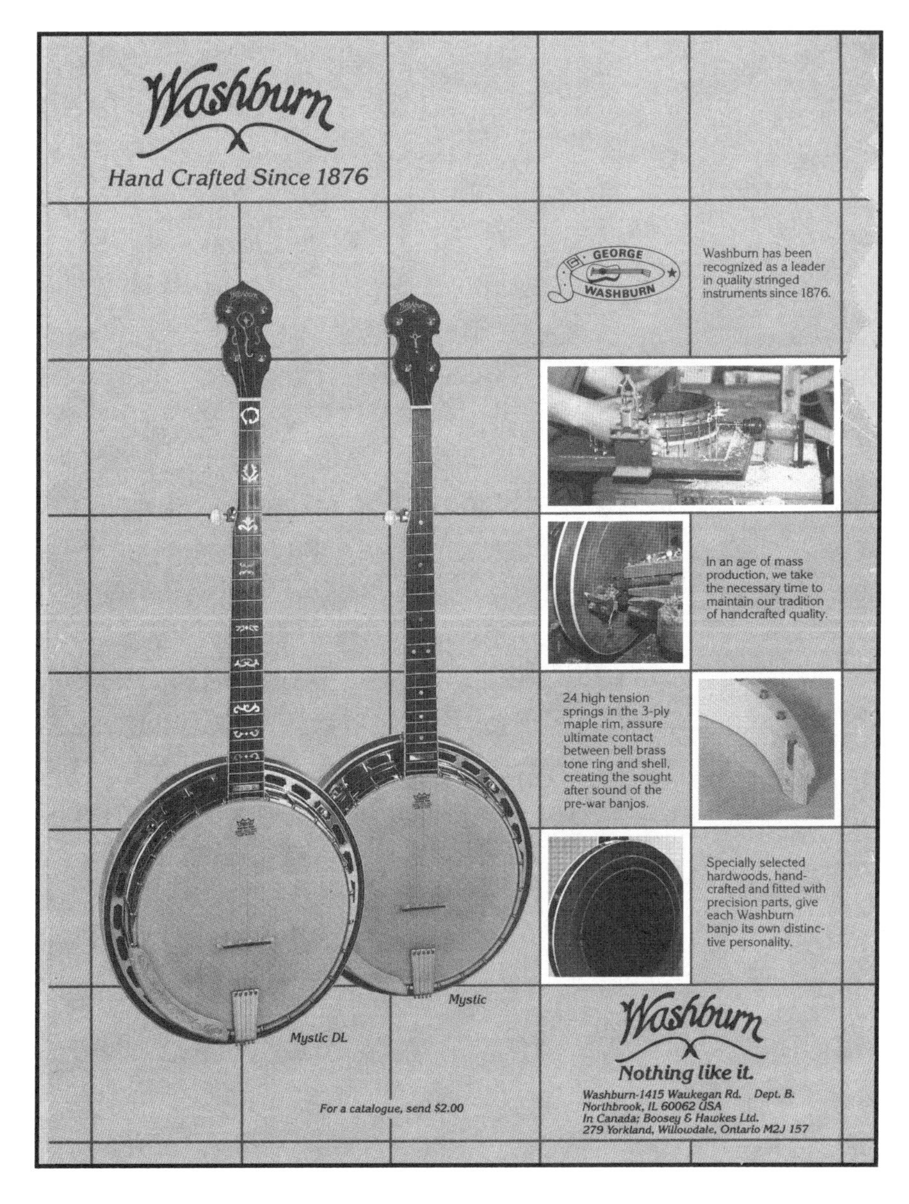

Photo Gallery

Modern Electrics

145. Venom (custom-built for Joe Perry) c.1995.
Inset: Marilyn (custom-built) c.1994
146. Festival Series: Top left and right: Monterey Artist, Artist and Studio c.1983. Bottom: EA50 Forum c.1989.
147. Left: EA36. Right: Nuno Bettencourt Model c.1995.
148. Left: D17CE c.1993. Right: Prairie Song D21S c.1995.
149. Left: Mirage DL c.1993. Right: SBT20 and SBT21
c.1989. Bottom: SBF80 c.1993
150. Orleans J10 c.1995. Inset: J12 prototype c.1995.
151. Top: HB35DL and HB35 c.1981. Bottom: HB35 c.1992.
152. Top: MG154 c.1992. Middle: MG100 c.1994.
Bottom: MG94 c.1992.
153. Top: Artist A30 c.1995. Bottom: SB100 c.1992.
154. Falcon c.1978
155. Rudy Sarzo Models X3 c. 1985. HM20V c.1986
(extreme shape). Ace Frehley AF40V c. 1986. Stage BBR
c.1985 (black w/red).
156. Top: LS103 c.1992. Middle: N4 c.1992.
Bottom: Challenger I EC29 c.1989.
157. KC90 c.1990. Inset: MG401 c.1995.
158. Top: XB1000 c.1994. Bottom: B20 and B5 c.1984.
159. AB40 c.1991. 5-string AB25 c.1995.
160. Clockwise from top left: Charlie Drayton, Hutch Hutchinson, Darryl Jones and Bob Glaub, Steve Stevens, Nuno Bettencourt, Clarence “Gatemouth” Brown, Joe Perry, and the Bellamy Brothers.

Washburn
USA
DESIGNED BY GROVER JACKSON

Washburn
Washburn
Washburn
Washburn

Washburn
Washburn

Washburn

Washburn
George Washburn

WASHBURN
WASHBURN

HB 35
Washburn

Washburn USA
Washburn
Washburn USA

Washburn

washburn
Falcon

washburn

Washburn
USA
Washburn

PG
55R
Professional Series
WASHBURN
Washburn

Washburn

Washburn

Washburn

Washburn

AEROSMITH

Electric Instruments

THE FINEST ACOUSTIC PREAMP SYSTEM

EQUIS II™

Washburn is a dominant force in the specialized field of electric-acoustic instruments with more than 20 years of experience. The EQUIS II™ preamp system represents a major breakthrough in electric- acoustic guitar technology. Never before has any system been so well thought out for not only the performing or studio musician, but for the engineer, as well.

EQUIS II features noiseless gain with combined, variable and fixed frequency equalization. What sets EQUIS II apart from all other systems is its choice of outputs. EQUIS II is equipped with a conventional 1/4 inch output jack controlled by the on-board EQ. An XLR output allows the guitar to send a completely independent, pre-EQ signal directly to a mixing console without the need for an external direct box.

The state of the art Equis II system boasts a battery life of over 1000 hours, up to ten times longer than other systems. The degree of accuracy with which these instruments reproduce their acoustic tones when amplified clearly establishes Washburn as the leader in electric-acoustic guitars.

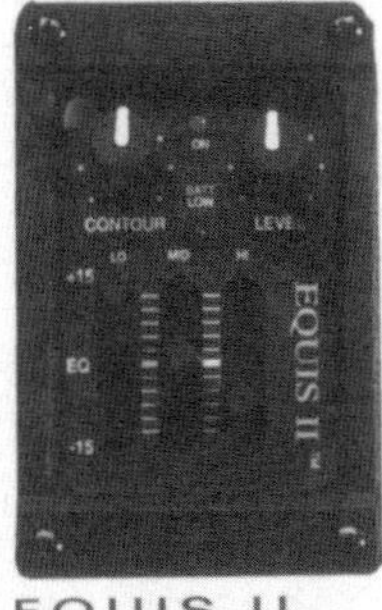

EQUIS II
Volume, Mid range "Contour" and 3 -Band EQ controls

Dual output jacks and 9V battery compartment

Festival Series

Washburn's biggest influence on the professional market has traditionally been its 6 and 12-string guitars that sound like flattop acoustics when played through an amp or P.A. system. The countless "name" players using these guitars is testimony to their usefulness. The first try for the company was a winner, the Festival Series of '79-'80 and still going strong. The most important guitars of the series were the Woodstock and Monterey thin body guitars. All the Festival models had flat tops, oval soundholes and Florentine cutaway bodies. The backs have always had an arch to them. A transducer built into the bridge was connected to volume and tone controls. This was the 3200 system.

The Woodstock used laminated mahogany for the top, back and sides and was available in 6 and 12-string versions. The more expensive Monterey was similar but had a bound fingerboard and peghead, diamond inlays and a solid cedar top. At the top of the line was the Tanglewood full body depth model, also with solid top. Although it was top of the line, the thin bodies would gain the positive notoriety amongst purists who were still trying to amplify the acoustic guitar. Although not listed, a flyer from 1980 showed a fancy version, the Artist, on the cover. This model had wing inlays on the fingerboard and pearl trim around the soundhole and outside edges of the top.

Woodstock Thin Body Design
Festival Series
6 and 12 String Guitars
• Mahogany Top, Sides and Back
• Mahogany Neck with Rosewood Fingerboard
• Deluxe Washburn Tuners-13:1 Ratio
• Washburn Compensated Bridge with Bone Saddle
• Washburn Original 3200 Sound Generator
• Gain and EQ Controls
• Equipped with Washburn L-100 Strings
• Available in Mahogany, Tobacco Sunburst and Wine Red Finishes

Bob Dylan with The Grateful Dead

In the next few years the solid wood tops would be saved for the electrified acoustics. The Tanglewood was as much an acoustic as it was a Festival and was discontinued in the mid '80s, shortly after adding the nylon-string Tanglewood Classic to the line. The solid-top, thin-body Monterey was also discontinued, leaving just the laminated top Woodstock EA40 and 40-12 in the line for '85. Spruce was now the standard wood for the tops, with mahogany an option. The growing line of solidbody acoustics and flattops with pickups allowed for the refining of the top Festivals. A second thin model, the EA20 was added and featured a mahogany top. The solid spruce top EA45 Tanglewood and EA44 Monterey returned c.'87 and were fitted with the EQ300 system using sliders instead of knobs. The EA40 also had this feature, while the EA20 continued to use the volume and tone knobs.

By the end of the decade the whole Festival line used the slider EQ setup. The EA30 joined the line and was available as a 12-string. The solid top EA44 and 45 models were again retired, being replaced at the top of the line by the EA50 Forum with Magma Finish and pointy headstock. This model only lasted around a year before being replaced at the top of the line by the Marquee EA45 with regular peghead and an outrageous looking top featuring "sound channels" instead of the oval soundhole. These sound channels were also used on the hollowbody bass guitars, and would continue to be used on the top Festival models.

John Jorgensen

In an interesting name game move, the Monterey moniker was given to the new EA30, this time a laminated top guitar. The Tanglewood name was also used again, this time on a nylon string guitar with a slotted peghead. To further confuse things, the EA44 and 45 model numbers returned in '92 on thin and full depth Festivals with solid cedar tops. The EA46 with sound channels was demoted to become the EA36. The EA30 and 40 were dropped, with a new Nuno Bettencourt signature EA22 in black with abalone borders and wing inlays replacing them. At the top of the line was the short lived EA48 with solid cedar top and lots of abalone trim. A 12-string version of the EA20 was available.

Robert Plant

1993 would see the EA41 nylon and the fancy EA48 both dropped and the Tanglewood name tagged back on the solid top EA45. The Woodstock name, which had been used on the EA40 previously, was now given to the EA44. '94 would see the addition of the deep body EA10 as a complement to the thin body EA20. The 12-string model went the way of the classical and for '95 we have another confusing move in the name game. The EA20, stable in the line for going on 10 years, had been referred to off and on as the Newport. With the retirement of the solid top EA44 and 45, the Woodstock name again went to a different model, the EA20. The Newport name went to the EA10. The EA36 Marquee was again top-of-the-line, with a limited edition oval sound hole "Melissa" model offered as tribute to long time Festival user Gregg Allman. The black guitar has the name Melissa engraved into the fingerboard.

Gregg Allman

Ya got all that? While the names and model numbers have been so convoluted that trying to keep track year by year would be ludicrous, suffice to say that in the 15-plus years the Festival line has been available there has almost always been a laminated model in thin and deep bodies and most of the time there has been a deluxe model with solid top construction. The laminated-top-with-sound-channels Marquee and the EA20 with oval sound hole have been stable since their inception. It appears that many of the professional users have intentionally opted for the laminated top models due to their electrical qualities and that's what these guitars were designed for, to sound good at high volumes. Many are the pros that have a penchant for classic electric models from the '50s and '60s and wouldn't think of playing a new solid body, yet they use brand new Festivals . . .because they do their job so well.

Electrified Flattops

While the Festival guitars were the answer to many performers' prayers, they were somewhat job specific. For the player who could not afford separate acoustic and electric flattops or wanted a single guitar that could perform double duty at moderate (or less) volumes, Washburn began offering electrified acoustics in the mid-'80s. The D60E was a stock Timber Ridge acoustic, with solid spruce top, full depth solid mahogany body, etc, plus the addition of the 3200 transducer system. A second model, the D22E was a more affordable choice.

A pair of cutaway flattops with full depth bodies were offered, both with electronics built in. This combination would be the norm, as most Washburn electrified flattops are fitted with cutaways and almost all the cutaway acoustics have come with pickups. The first models c.1985 were the D23CE and the D12CE. A 12-string version of the D23CE was also offered. Both the 6 and 12-string D23s were dropped, with the 12-string option going to the D12. The D22 was replaced with an electrified version of the stock D21.

D-60E Timber Ridge
D-23CE-12 Missouri
D-23CE Missouri
D22E Virginian
D-12CE

NATURAL ACOUSTIC SOUND····· In order to achieve the best amplified acoustic sound, you've got to start with a superior sounding acoustic guitar. At the heart of every Washburn is the blend of premium, select woods and patient hand crafted quality. With the addition of our performance proven Washburn 3200 sensor system, technology [illegible] craftsmanship combine to produce a superior acoustic-electric gu[illegible] that offers smooth playability and uncompromising natural acoustic sound.

SBF-25B Mirage Pro
SBF-24N Mirage Standard
SBC-50B Mirage Classic DL
SBC-20TS Mirage Classic

SOLID BODY FOLK AND CLASSIC GUITARS······ the premier live and studio performance

MIRAGE STEEL STRINGS
- Slim, cutaway design
- 14th fret neck joint
- Fast mahogany neck
- Rosewood bridge with compensated saddle
- Washburn 3200 tone sensor
- Mirage pro features additional humbucking with active midrange boost control

MIRAGE CLASSICS
- Slim, cutaway design
- 14th fret neck joint
- Contemporary classic neck
- Rosewood bridge with compensated saddle
- Washburn 3200 tone sensor
- Mirage deluxe classic offers additional active midrange boost control

Washburn
230 Lexington Drive
Buffalo Grove, IL 60089
U.S.A.
A LEGEND IN PERFORMANCE

John Hiatt

As the '80s came to an end, these instruments became more popular and the line was expanded. The solid spruce/rosewood D61SWE replaced the D60E and a new pickup system, the Equis II, was soon added. A cutaway, solid D29CE also was equipped with this system, as was the D21SE as it was now called. By '92 all the models had cutaway bodies. These ranged from the D10CE, D12CE (the D1212CE was dropped) and D17CE with laminated tops to the solid spruce/rosewood D61CE and D68CE.

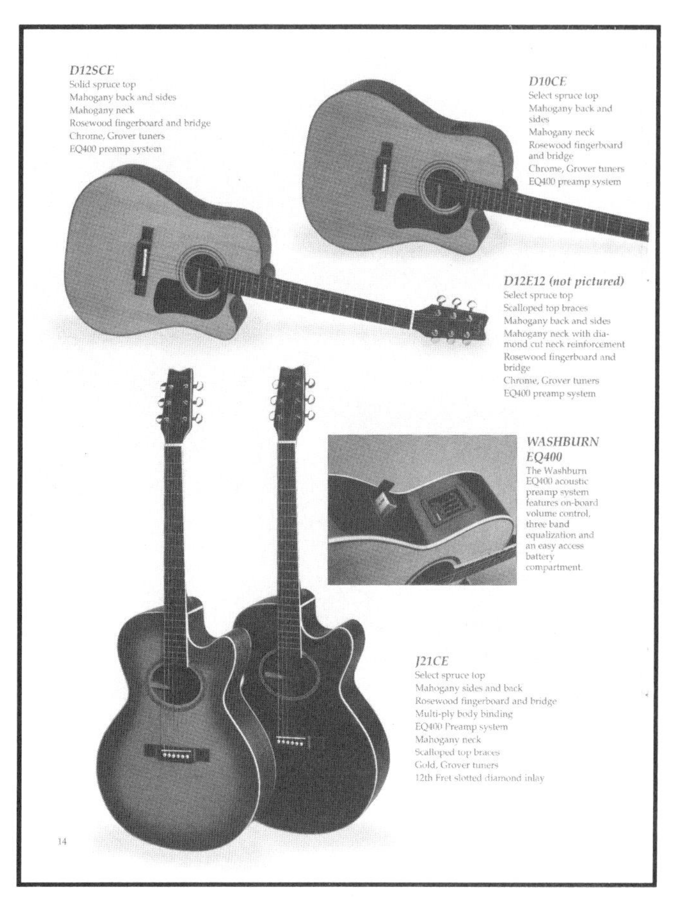

These two solid-wood guitars were joined at the top of the line by the electrified versions of the Stephens Cutaway acoustics, logically named the DC60E and DC80E. The 80 was quickly dropped and the 60 lasted another year before these future collectibles were both gone.

The solid wood D61 and 68SCE guitars were last seen in the '94 catalog and soon joined the DC60 & 80Es. The D10CE had been added at the bottom of line and the long running D12CE became the solid top D12SCE. A short-lived 12-string version, the D12E12 was added as was a 12-string D1712CE. Another short lived addition was the rounded body J21CE. This would be replaced by the J28SCE, a totally new guitar with solid spruce top, fancy inlays and a sculptured bridge. This beautiful instrument is by far the top of the line which has recently been somewhat reduced. The D17CE Timber Ridge, as it is now called (different from earlier Timber Ridge), is joined by the D10CE, the D12SCE and the WD20SCE which had joined the line in '94. This model features the "Veil Process" open pore finish, a solid spruce top and the Fishman transducer with the Equis II pre-amp.

Solid Body Acoustics - Folk and Classical

Following the immediate success of the Festival series, Washburn released another instrument c.1984 with the sound of an "acoustic" flattop steel string, this time with a solid body. The Mirage guitars looked like cutaway acoustics from the front, with a round sound hole and wooden pin bridge. The body, however, was less than 2" deep. The DL was the standard model, available in a variety of colors and equipped with volume and tone controls. These were mounted on the side of the guitar, on the bass side of the upper bout. The Washburn 3200 transducer system was built into the bridge. The Pro had the addition of a Middle control for the acoustic pickup and three knobs on the face of the guitar. These controlled a humbucker magnetic pickup mounted near the bridge, offering even more versatility from a single instrument.

A 12-string version of the DL was also available, as were a pair of nylon string Mirages. Again, a cutaway body that from the front looked like a regular acoustic, but with a depth of less than 2". A slotted peghead and standard classical tie bridge kept a somewhat traditional feel for the player and the sound was surprising realistic, depending on the amplification used. The Mirage Classic models were equipped with volume and tone controls, while the Classic DL had the additional "Middle."

The Mirage Series became the SBF (Solid Body Folk) and SBC (Solid Body Classic), with the DL becoming the SB24, the Pro SB25, the Classic SBC20 and the Classic DL the SBC50. By '87 only the SBF24 survived. This was joined by the SBT21, shaped like a Fender Tele with a pointy headstock, no pickups and three knobs. These were for volume, tone and "Fat," aka midrange. Gone was the soundhole and traditional 3-on-a-side headstock. A short-lived Fender Strat-shaped SBS20 model joined the SBT21 before both were retired c.1989. The SBS was virtually identical to the SBT except for the body shape. The SBF24 gained the middle control and for a short time had the three controls mounted on the face of the guitar instead of the shoulder. In '90 the SBC20 solid body classical returned, but it did not stay in the line very long.

The SBF24 was replaced by the SBF80 by '92 and this model is still in the line. The 80 features a flamed maple top on a traditional flattop body, save for the less than 2" depth and the Florentine cutaway. Gone is the faux sound hole of earlier models. A 12-string version, the SBF80-12 was available for a short time c.1990 and is mysteriously no longer offered. The use of Fishman brand transducers with easily accessed controls, and the more traditional size and feel of a flattop, make this latest version the ultimate guitar for players needing an acoustic sound at high volumes, sans feedback problems.

Classic Solid Body

Mirage Classic DL Natural

Mirage Classic Natural

Mirage DL Tobacco Sun Burst

Mirage Classic DL Black

Mirage Classic Tobacco Sun Burst

Individual gain and E.Q. controls permit fast, accurate settings. Active electronics add to the power and sensitivity of the instrument.

Instrument Humidifier

On the Mirage Classic DL the addition of a midrange cut-boost selector permits total control of the tone spectrum. The true (natural) sounds of a fine classic are now avalabe to todays performer.

Washburn Strings

Washburn Contoured Shoulder Strap

Washburn has eliminated all previous performance barriers associated with the nylon string guitar. The Mirage Solid Body Classic produces a crystal-clear natural sound without body resonant feedback, while providing sustain previously unobtainable in a classic.

When you're going for the best in sound and performance, go for a trusted name ··········Washburn.

Washburn

1415 Waukegan Road
Northbrook, IL 60062
U.S.A.

Washburn instruments are distributed world-wide.
Specifications subject to change without notice.
"Washburn" is a trademark of Fretted Industries.

Printed in Japan.

Sammy Hagar

ELECTRIC ACOUSTIC
SOLID BODY ELECTRIC ACOUSTIC
The SBF80 is the ultimate high-volume electric acoustic. The SBF80 represents the most accurate reproduction of a true acoustic at concert volumes. The frequencies that give a traditional acoustic it's warm character are the same frequencies that cause body resonant feedback when amplified. The SBF80's unique pickup and electronics capture those frequencies without a hollow body, so the player can pour on the bass and low-mids without fear of feedback.
SBF80
Book matched, flamed sycamore top
Computer channeled, semi-solid, mahogany body Mahogany neck
Rosewood fingerboard and bridge
Slotted, diamond fret markers
Chrome, Grover tuners
Multi-ply binding on body, neck and headstock
Active electronics
Fishman USA pickup
KASIM SULTON
Kasim on Meatloaf's "Bat Out of Hell II" tour with his cherry sunburst SBF80.

Rick Vito

Hollowbody Archtops

Washburn began to court the Jazz player in the early '80s with the short-lived J4 f-hole, deep bodied, single pickup instrument. Leaving the market for a short time, the company would try again in '89.

The J6 has been in the line ever since, albeit with a number of changes to the model. The first style was an L5 look-alike using laminated maple for the top instead of carved spruce. The tailpiece, Venetian cutaway body and the layout of the electronics were dead ringers but the fingerboard and peghead were Washburn. A new "W" tailpiece of thin tubular metal replaced the two piece L5 style the following year and in '93 the top went to spruce. Sycamore replaced maple for the back and sides the following year and for '95 the J6 has a new cast "W" tailpiece and fancier peghead decoration and logo. The new tailpiece is much heavier than the previous trapeze-style and is reminiscent of Rickenbacker's "R" tailpiece. The company has somewhat disrespectfully named the model "Montgomery," assuming they're referring to Wes and not the city in Alabama. The late great jazz artist was proud of his association with Gibson, even though they wouldn't give him a signature model when he was consistently at the top of the charts and the polls (they did give Trini Lopez his own model). In a mid '60s ad, Mr. Montgomery posed with a Fender amp sans guitar while his brother stood by with Fender bass and amp, a very credible fellow, Wes was.

To go with the "Montgomery," Washburn is offering the "Orleans," probably named in honor of the birthplace of Jazz and not John Hall's band from the '70s. The J10 has an "Arched, tuned spruce top with voiced bracing" although no mention is made as to whether it is laminations of spruce to reduce feedback or carved from solid wood. A floating pickup/wooden pickguard

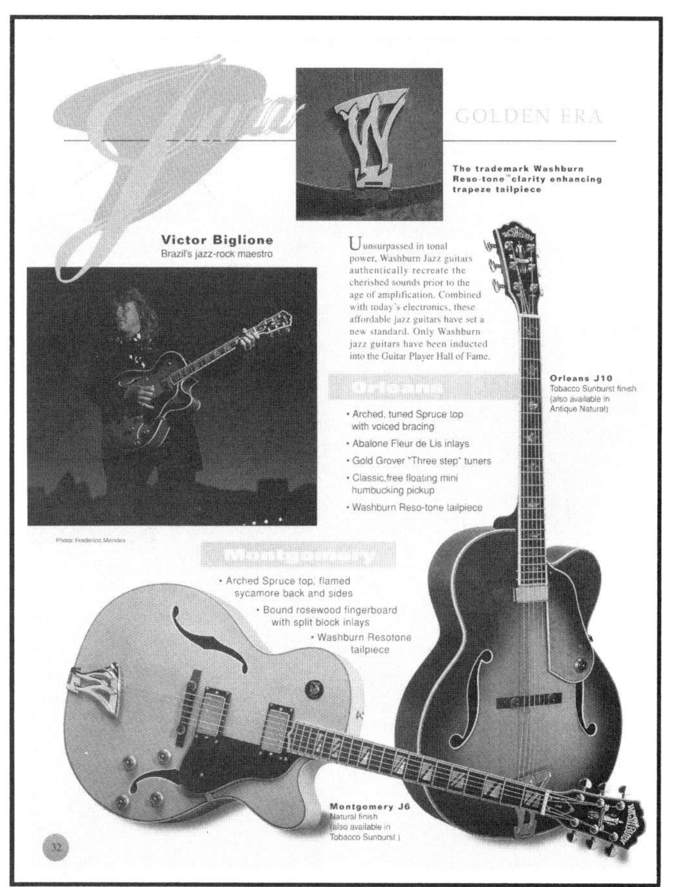

assembly with volume control has a classy look and the abalone fleur de lis inlays and peghead inlays are quite striking. Gold Grover Imperials are also a nice touch. The J10 model number had been used c.1989-90 on a carved spruce top Florentine cutaway deluxe model with ebony board and pearl tuner buttons. These were only available for a short time. A carved-top J12 acoustic is set for release in early 1996, available with a floating pickup.

Semi-Hollow Electrics

Following, WWII, Gibson began using laminated maple for the top of their hollowbody electrics and "electric" guitars began replacing "electrified" guitars. In 1955, they announced the thin-body, hollow electric ES225 which offered the more comfortable feel of the new solidbodies, with the sound of the traditional hollowbody electric (Lyon and Healy had offered a thin-bodied guitar before WWI, see p. 72). 1958 saw the release of two of the greatest guitar designs of all time. The Gretsch 6120 Chet Atkins with Filtertron Humbuckers and bracing between the top and back crossed the sound of the hollowbody and the solid body. Gibson's dot neck ES335 with PAF humbuckers and a solid block running down the center, took this one step further allowing a stop tailpiece and Tune-a-matic bridge to be mounted directly into solid wood. This design is still one of the most favored and most imitated in the history of the six-string.

From Guild's Starfire 4, 5 and 6 to the Fender Starcaster to the Yamaha that turned heads in the late '70s, numerous companies have offered variations on this winning combination. 1983 saw Washburn providing a new twist, adding a bridge with strings-through-the-body construction. The Fender Telecaster has a unique sound, even acoustically, because of this feature and hard tail Strats, early P-basses and early Music Man Stingrays have all found players that swear by the design.

Washburn's HB35 was a dot neck model with exposed coil humbuckers. Coil taps connected to the volume controls added variety to the sounds. A deluxe version, the HD35DL, featured a multiple bound, curly maple body with "wing" inlays and gold hardware. A new wiring arrangement added a switch to the standard four knobs and selector arrangement. Instead of two volume pots and two tones, the DL had Master Volume, Master Tone and a quasi-parametric EQ with controls for Frequency and Gain. Blonde and Burgundy were added options for '84, as was a vibrato tailpiece assembly, a novel twist. Public response was slow, and the model was soon discontinued.

A more traditionally configured HB35 returned in '89, set up with standard stop tailpiece, tune-a-matic bridge and electronics. Block inlays and gold hardware were now stock. A more ornate model, the HB60 had multiple-ply binding and pearl and abalone split-block markers on an ebony fingerboard. Pearl tuner buttons and a bound tortoise shell pickguard were the finishing touches on this short-lived model. The 60 and 35 combined in '90 to become the third edition HB35. This model has been associated with Clarence Gatemouth Brown and his variety of musical styles. A new all pearl (no abalone) split block marker fingerboard reverted to rosewood and the pickguard lost its binding. The selector switch was moved to the upper bout's bass side. Flamed sycamore became an option in '93 (HB35S) and standard in '94, at which time maple began to be used instead of mahogany for the necks. With the standard HB35 having evolved into a rather fancy model, room was made for a new model in '94, the dot marker, single-bound maple-top HB30 with chrome hardware and exposed coil pickups.

A very short-lived model, the HB50, was available in '89 only. A rounded edge on the back side was new, as was the choice of mahogany instead of maple. The bird's-eye maple tops had half as many f-holes (1) and knobs (2) as the HD35.

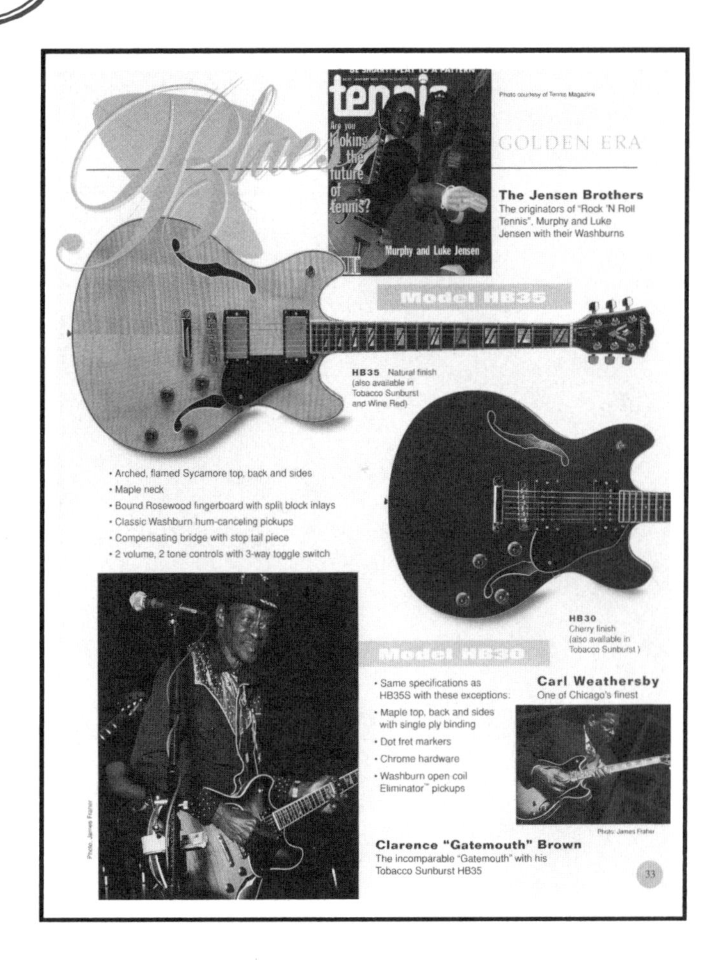
Blues GOLDEN ERA

Photo courtesy of Tennis Magazine

The Jensen Brothers
The originators of "Rock 'N Roll Tennis", Murphy and Luke Jensen with their Washburns

Model HB35

HB35 Natural finish (also available in Tobacco Sunburst and Wine Red)

- Arched, flamed Sycamore top, back and sides
- Maple neck
- Bound Rosewood fingerboard with split block inlays
- Classic Washburn hum-canceling pickups
- Compensating bridge with stop tail piece
- 2 volume, 2 tone controls with 3-way toggle switch

HB30
Cherry finish (also available in Tobacco Sunburst)

Model HB30

- Same specifications as HB35S with these exceptions:
- Maple top, back and sides with single ply binding
- Dot fret markers
- Chrome hardware
- Washburn open coil Eliminator™ pickups

Carl Weathersby
One of Chicago's finest

Photo: James Fraher

Photo: James Fraher

Clarence "Gatemouth" Brown
The incomparable "Gatemouth" with his Tobacco Sunburst HB35

33

Solidbody Electrics
Chicago-Made

With the future of Washburn's electric guitars in the capable hands of Grover Jackson, the Chicago factory is turning out some of the most accurately designed and manufactured guitars ever. The combination of computer controlled machinery , experienced hands (many from the Hamer factory), the best hardware available (Wilkinson, Schaller, Sperzel, Duncan, Lawrence, Switchcraft, CTS etc.) and Jackson's vision (he changed the way guitars felt and played in the '80s) should make the project a success.

Back in '91, the company opened a small/medium factory in an old icehouse on the North side of Chicago that had been used for woodworking for the previous thirty years. This was nearly two years before Jackson entered the picture. The factory ambitiously produced a fairly large number of different models, from the Mercury Series to the reissue/upgrade of the original Washburn solid bodies of the late '70s.

The N4 Nuno Bettencourt model was available in alder, swamp ash or padauk and featured the Stephen's Extended Cutaway. These guitars had previously been made in Japan. The Stephen's cutaway was also seen on the LS93 Fender Strat copy. A more traditional Tele copy was available in Ash (LT92) or Alder (LT82). Another signature model was the two humbucking pickup Steve Stevens model SS80. With Frankenstein graphics it became the SS100.

The Wing series SB100 was reminiscent of the early Washburns and the Hamer double cutaways. An arched, curly maple top, tune-a-matic bridge with stop tailpiece and no neck-through the body construction separated the SB10 from the early Falcons and Hawks. The SB50, with two single coil "soapbar" pickups and a flat top was more Hamer than early Washburn. The Mercury Series featured a curly maple top on four of its five models. A piece of 3/8" maple followed the contours of the body which was dressed away at the "elbow" area. The MG154 and MG142 used mahogany for the bodies while the MG112 and MG104 used alder. The 154 and 104 were fitted with two humbuckers with a Strat pickup in between and Floyd Rose by Schaller vibrato assemblies. The MG142 and MG122 had two humbuckers and a tune-a-matic/stop tailpiece set up. The three pickup MG94 came with a maple neck and a solid alder body with no maple cap. All these MG guitars had a somewhat pointed shape to the headstock.

When Jackson arrived in Chicago in March of '93, things quickly came to a halt. This was his "baby" now and he knew how he wanted it to operate. By July of '93, the N4 and only the N4 was being produced (Serial numbers from 9307_ _ _ on were built under the Jackson team). Some custom guitars were built and to this day artists working with the company have instruments made there.

The MG series was reinstated having new 22-fret necks with adjustment for the truss rod at the body instead of the nut as on earlier models. A more rounded headstock shape similar to the old Danelectro/Silvertone "Dolphin" style is another giveaway feature of the new models. Today's models include the Artist MG122 and the Pro MG100. The 122 has two pickups and a maple top, while the Pro has three pickups mounted directly into a swamp ash body. Both models employ the Wilkinson VS100 vibrato assembly which offers the best of both fixed and floating bridges. Variations on the 100 in '94 were the MG120 with maple top, the MG90 with oiled mahogany body and the MG112 with Gotoh Floyd Rose and two canted Duncans. The MG102 was a 122 with a swamp ash body.

B.B. Chung King

Jennifer Batton

A few of the Strat and Tele copies were made in '94, and while they were very well done, the line has headed in a more original direction. Washburn's past is again touched upon with the Eagle SB20, very similar to the '93 SB100, the new model having its selector switch in the middle of the controls instead of near the bottom edge of the top. The Stage Series Artist A30, with flamed maple top and the Pro A20 in black are close to the originals, but with a Shaller Floyd Rose.

Today there are three Nuno Bettencourt models from Chicago, the alder N4A, the swamp ash N4SA and the outrageous N8SA double neck 12/6. The 6-string neck is a regular N4 but the 12-string half features octave strings that secure at the nut and are adjusted by knobs placed between the bridge and the bottom strap button.

The latest signature model is for Pantera's Dimebag Darrel who insisted on the exact feel of his old Dean model. Even the "V" headstock had to stay so stay it did. It is available in three colors, Black Jack, Dime Slime and Dime Bolt.

At the top of the new line is the custom MG900 Venom with a bound body topped with quilted maple. Two snakes are inlaid into the ebony fingerboard, with fangs exposed! The first example was built for Joe Perry of Aerosmith. He was also the recipient of a custom doubleneck that he immediately added to his live arsenal. Again, the "Presentation guitar" idea goes back to the turn of the century Washburns.

Michaelangelo

Derrick Trucks

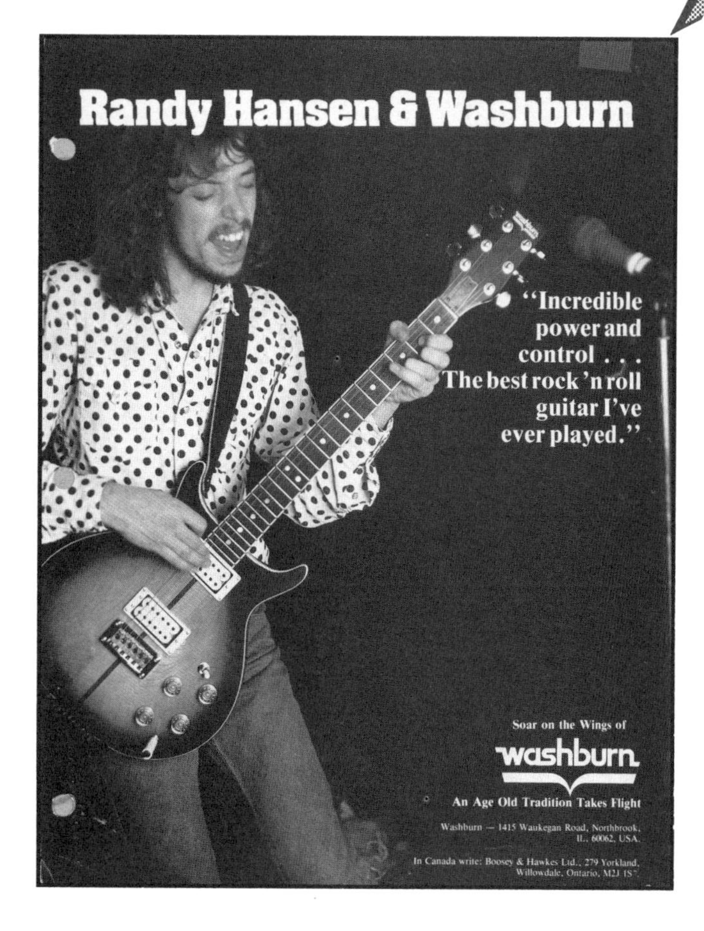

Solid body electrics

Washburn expanded into the electric guitar market in 1978 with the release of the Falcon and Hawk models. These "Wing Series" guitars featured neck-through body construction with the top model Falcon having a five-ply neck and the Hawk having three. The Falcon had a bound ebony fingerboard. Both models had strings-through body bridges, dual humbuckers, brass saddles and nuts and push/pull volume controls that activated coil taps for each pickup. A deluxe model was added in '80 and was available in three variations. The Eagle could be had with rosewood or maple tops or in gleaming white with pearl trim around the top and "wing" inlays. An inexpensive version with a bolt-on neck was known as the Raven. It was replaced by the T-Bird with three in-line control knobs by '83. By '85, pointy headstocks were in and the Wing series was out despite being used at the time by some of the more credible endorsers. The style returned in '92, sans neck-through-body and brass. The SB30 had a flamed maple top while the SB20 was ash. A tune-a-matic/stop tailpiece replaced the strings-through-body the following year as the SB80 model, which was dropped in '94. The Chicago factory built a version for its initial run and a second version under Jackson, the SB20 Eagle. The SB10 Hawk and the flat topped, strings-through-the-body Raven complete the current offerings.

Nancy Wilson

Shortly after the Wing Series was released, another body shape entered the line, c.1980. The "Stage Series" guitars had a reverse Firebird-esque shape with hockey stick pegheads and were available in two styles, the bound A20 and the unbound A10. Both had two humbuckers and strings through the body. A vibrato assembly was optional. Two models, the A15 with three single coil pickups and the A5 with two very strange looking single coils were added in '83 and the BBR black body/red trim treatment was available around '85. The Wonderbar vibrato was now standard on all the Stage models, just before they were discontinued, c.1986.

A whole line of Stages was re-released in '95, with the Chicago-made curly maple topped Artist A30 at the top followed by the Pro A20 of solid mahogany. The Deluxe A10 has a sycamore top and Floyd Rose licensed vibrato while the Special A5 has a strings-through-the-body bridge. All four of the new Stages share the same headstock logo, which seems to be the only justification for the words "WASHBURN USA" (with "Stage Series Reissue" underneath). The 30 and 20 are U.S.-made, the production models 10 and 5 are not. Although "Washburn USA" is a blanket expression for an American company, it suggests U.S. manufacture and hopefully will be saved for such.

Howard Leese

The success of the Jackson guitars in the mid '80s was a big influence on Washburn's electrics, as well as most of the other manufacturers. A wedge shaped, 2 pickup RR2V was joined by the three pickup RR11 and RR12. These were copies of Randy Rhoads' Jacksons. A triple-coil RR40 model was the last of these c.'87. An even more outrageously shaped guitar ran concurrently with the RR models. The HM20V is most famous for being the featured guitar in Robert Palmer's MTV hit video "Addicted to Love." A third heavy metal/pointy headstock guitar was the Ace Frehley signature model, Washburn's first signature on a guitar and the only one besides Jethro Burns' mandolins and the Rudy Sarzo basses and guitars. (see page 155) The AF40V had a pointy body, four points to be exact and a lightning bolt that extended half way down the neck and the body. These lasted into the late '80s.

While all the guitars discussed to this point were original designs (except the RR models), the mid-'80s saw the release of a number of "copies." Not dead-ringer copies like some of the '70s guitars by Ibanez, Tokai, et al, but "Washburn" versions of a number of guitars that are considered classics. Granted, most of these instruments have become generic objects or shapes and are now industry standards used by countless companies. The '84 FV20V (curly maple top), FV10V (bound body, three knobs) and FV2V (unbound body, two knobs) used the popular Flying V shape. The word "popular" is the key here: Washburn built what the kids wanted and had incredible growth figures to show for it.

The most blatant copy was the WB64 Steinberger-like guitar with headless construction. Good for strapping on your back while traveling by bike or motercycle, these were offered for a short time c.'85. The RS10 had the body of a Paul Reed Smith with a joined neck and curly maple top. While the controls were laid out in a similar fashion, the Washburn had a Floyd Rose licensed vibrato with locking nut and a pointy headstock, somewhat out of context on this guitar. The RS8 was finished in solid colors and had fancy inlays. Released in '87, the RS models were short-lived but their arched tops would live on in the '89 KC series.

Two of the most copied guitars of all time are the Gibson Les Paul and the Fender Telecaster and Washburn took its turn with both. The WP100 ad WP80 were Les Paul Custom clones and the WP90 and 50 were Les Paul Standard surragates available c.'89-90. The Tele was taken on in '85 and was amongst the first non-original Washburns. The BBR black and red Tour 24V was Tele-esque while the '85-'87 triple pickup/Wonderbar/Floyd-equipped WT4 and WT10 with pointy headstock were Tele in body shape only. A more compatible group of features were added to the WT100 and 90 c.'89, an arched maple top with a tune-a-matic and strings-through-the-body were interesting approaches and the more traditional headstock was a welcome sight. A very straight Tele copy, the WT552, mysteriously appeared in the '94 catalog as a mate to the Chicago-made LT82 but both are now gone.

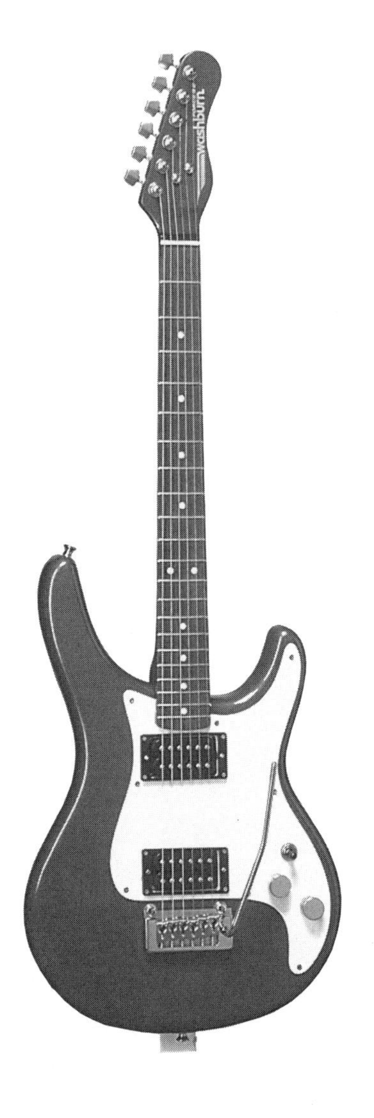

The 84 "Force" series Force 30V used a "Strat-ish" body, pickguard pickup assembly (3 single coils) and the familiar controls. The one humbucker Force 31V and two humbucker Force 32V with custom colors and matching headstocks come across as less plagiaristic and can be looked at as the inspiration for a continuous run of guitars referred to here as the Standard Series. These were joined/replaced by the less expensive Force 2 and 2V (two humbuckers) and Force 3 and 3V (Strat electronics). "BBR" treatment (black finish, red trim) was a Washburn original and was used on the Force 6 (two humbuckers).

The Force series of '85 featured the Washburn "hockey stick" peghead at one end and the Washburn "Wonderbar" springless vibrato at the other. Two humbuckers on a pickguard-less body made the G20V guitars originals. The G10V and G5V had the one humbucker/two single coil treatment.

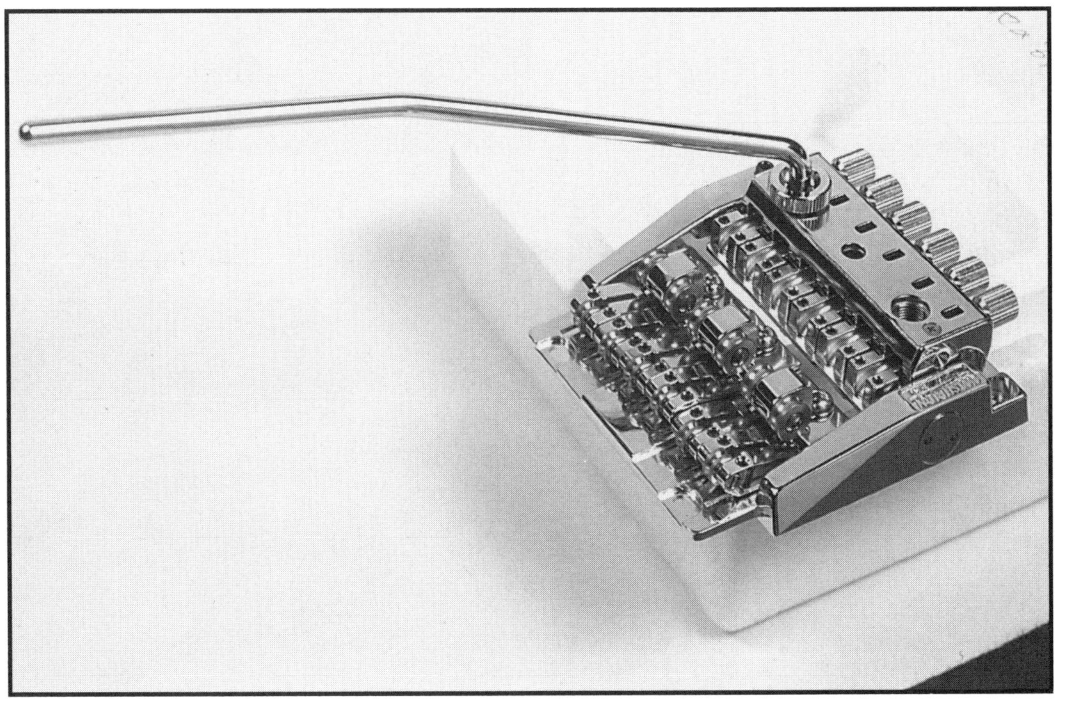

For '86-'87 the G Series took on a Jackson-ish headstock and, on certain models, the inlay design. The G40V had a triple coil pickup, the G23 had three single coils. The G10V was a dot-inlaid, one humbucker/two single coil model. The '87 G15, 8 and 5 all had the one humbucker/two single coil setup while the dot inlay G4 left out the middle pickup. The G3 had three single coils, the G2 changed from three pickups to a single pickup with volume and tone controls, the G1 lost the tone control and the Wonderbar. The G Jr. had the one humbucker/two single coil set-up. All but the Jr. were equipped with Floyd Rose-ish vibratos and locking nuts. Bolt-on necks and EMG-style pickups were also standard.

These were replaced c.'89 by the KC series of arched top and back Strat-ish shaped bodies. The top of the line KC100 had a set neck, while the KC70 with similar pickup configuration (one humbucker two single coils with individual on/off/on switches) lacked the active electronics. The KC60 lacked the middle pickup, the KC40 came with exposed coil pickups and a 5-way selector and the KC30 was fitted with three single coils. All the guitars had locking nuts and Floyd Rose licensed whammys. The KC45 had a Bad Ass-style tailpiece, the 20 a standard Strat whammy and the 10 a single humbucker. All the KCs had a new style headstock that was a serious step away from the mid '80s skewers. The line changed numbers in '90 with the neckset 100 dropped and the others slightly changed. The KC90 had exposed-coil Duncan humbucker/two single coil set ups as did the Duncan-less KC40. The KC70 had EMG-ish pickups and the Floyd Rose-ish vibrato common to all. The KC44 was a 40 with two humbuckers and single coil in the middle and the 42 was a 40 with a reverse headstock. The KC20 came with a standard vibrato.

Robbie Robertson

'92 saw the release of the Mercury Series in place of the KCs. The fingerboards went to 24 frets and pickguards were added to all but the bottom two models. The top of the line MG74 and the MG70 both had maple tops and clear pickguards, the 74 having gold hardware. The MG40, 42, 43 and 44 were essentially the same guitar with different pickup rigs. The 40 used one humbucker and two single coils, the 42 two humbuckers, the 43 three single coils and the 44 two humbuckers with a single coil in the middle. The MG24 with standard vibrato used this configuration while the MG20's front pickup choice was a single coil. The MG series was used as the basis of the first Chicago-built guitars of '92 and the '93 standard line added a two-pickup MG72 and dropped the 43 as well as the 24 and 20. A tune-a-matic bridge model MG52 and the MG30, a 40 with a pickguard, were added to the line.

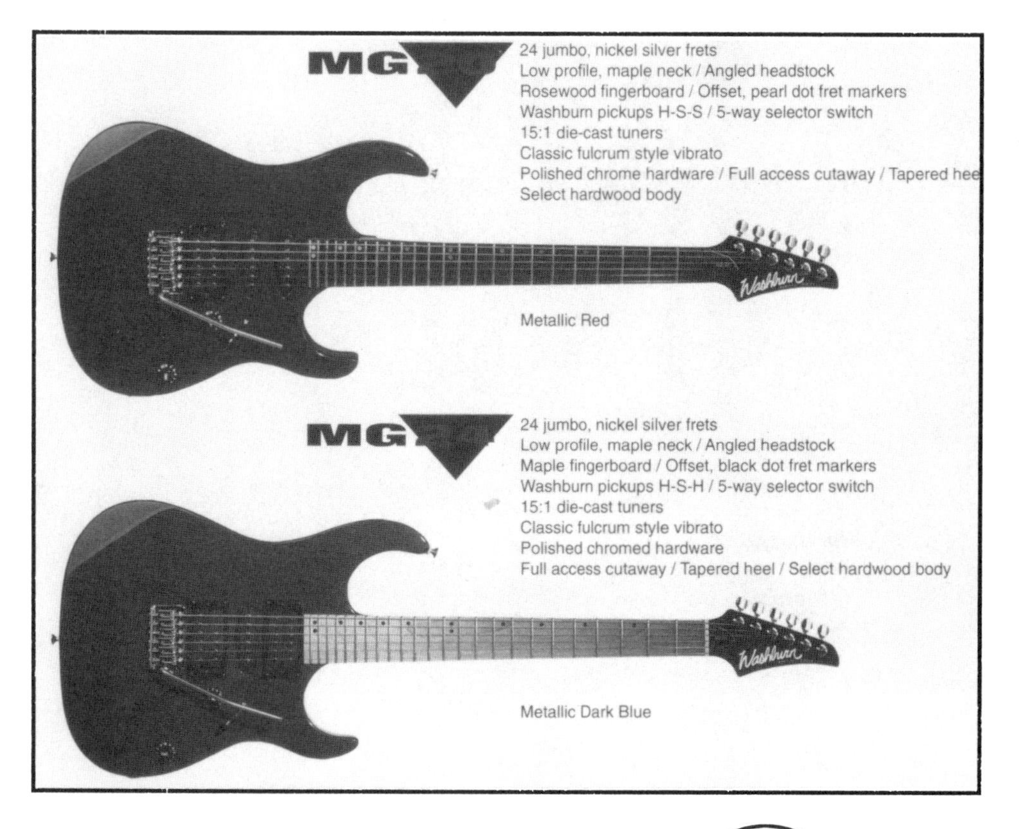

MG
24 jumbo, nickel silver frets
Low profile, maple neck / Angled headstock
Rosewood fingerboard / Offset, pearl dot fret markers
Washburn pickups H-S-S / 5-way selector switch
15:1 die-cast tuners
Classic fulcrum style vibrato
Polished chrome hardware / Full access cutaway / Tapered hee
Select hardwood body
Metallic Red
MG
24 jumbo, nickel silver frets
Low profile, maple neck / Angled headstock
Maple fingerboard / Offset, black dot fret markers
Washburn pickups H-S-H / 5-way selector switch
15:1 die-cast tuners
Classic fulcrum style vibrato
Polished chromed hardware
Full access cutaway / Tapered heel / Select hardwood body
Metallic Dark Blue

'94 saw a new Chicago line, again with the Mercury name. The new Jackson-designed rounded headstock carried over to the standard models which all had new model numbers that would last one year. Are you ready? The bound body MG821 had two humbuckers and the unbound MG701 came with a humbucker and two single coils. A new tailpiece, the amazing Wilkinson VS100, was used on these locking nut-less guitars. The MG 700 used a Floyd Rose-licensed tailpiece and locking nut, as did the no-longer-American-made Steve Stevens model (SS40). The humbucker/two single coil MG300 and the two humbucker/single coil middle pickup MG340 also used the Rose. A tune-a-matic MG522 and standard vibrato by Schaller MG401 completed the line for '94. Things were simplified in '95 with the Mercury series stripping down to two Chicago models and two standard models, the MG200 Special and the MG401 Deluxe. The 401 has the Wilkinson tailpiece and a pickguard while the 200 has direct mounted pickups and a standard vibrato. To encapsulate all this in one sentence, the '84 Force guitars were semi-pro quality, the '95 descendants Mercury series guitars are very professional in their quality.

VINTAGE NICKEL GOTOH LOCKING TUNERS

6105 DUNLOP FRETWIRE

C.L.A.S.™ SYSTEM

Washburn International's exclusive Convergent Linear Alignment System™ insures a perfectly straight string path through the nut for flawless tuning. C.L.A.S. eliminates string binding in the nut and maintains string pitch when the tremolo is used.

Deluxe MG401
Antique Natural finish

Lloyd Holley
Guitarist for the grind-core rappers, Collapsing Lungs

Deluxe

- Book matched, figured Ash top
- Solid Alder body
- Wilkinson VS100 tremolo
- Grover tuners
- Chrome hardware
- Direct mounted Washburn Eliminator™ pickups
- Neck: 511 Middle: 512 Bridge: 523
- 5-way switch
- Volume and tone control with coil tap

GROVER JACKSON

Recognised as the pre-eminent guitar builder, Grover Jackson has influenced an entire generation of guitar players.
Grover's legacy continues today wth Washburn's Mercury Series™ guitars. The Mercury's streamlined, double cutaway body and clean lines are Grover's trademark. Fitted with modern hardware and equipped with high powered electronics, the Mercury Series is the new standard for today's musician.

Grover Jackson
Washburn USA

Special MG200
Black finish

Special

- Standard fulcrum tremolo
- Grover tuners
- Chrome hardware
- Direct mounted, Washburn Eliminator™ pickups
- Neck: 411 Middle: 412 Bridge: 423

Tony MacAlpine
Jazz-shread virtuoso

23

An interesting series from the late '80s were EC models introducing the Stephen's Extended Cutaway. A single pickup was all that would fit between the bridge and the end of the fingerboard on the 36-fret EC36. That was five more frets than Danelectro's Guitarlin of the late '50s and for many guitarists very difficult to actually play, although mandolinists have dealt with tight frets for hundreds of years. A two pickup model with 29 frets, the EC29 was a bit more practical, as well as being more versatile sound-wise. Custom finishes in outrageous patterns set these unique instruments off visually. The EC26 Atlantis introduced the "bolt on" Steven's device method of gaining access to the high frets. These guitars were all short-lived with the 26 lasting into the early '90s and acting as inspiration for the N4 models that replaced it.

Extreme had but one album when Washburn began working with "wunder kid" Nuno Bettencourt in '89. The following year the N4 and N2 models were released. The N4 featured the Stephen's Extended Cutaway bolt-on neck joint with a 22-fret rosewood board neck. A Floyd Rose vibrato with locking nut and two Duncan pickups connected to a selector switch and a single volume control were the operational devices. A reverse headstock accented the smaller than normal Strat-like body shape. Any effects/benefits from having a reverse headstock (ala Hendrix) were negated by the locking nut, but visually it was outstanding. The little "sharkfin" where the neck flares to meet the body was also visually intriguing. The early N2 used Washburn pickups and Floyd but lacked the Extended Cutaway, although the "sharkfin" was painted on with "Nuno" in place of the usual "Stephen's" logo. Both the early N4 and N2 had the model numbers on the headstocks.

A Bill Lawrence bridge pickup replaced the original Duncan, a Shaller Floyd replaced the original and the model number was deleted from the headstocks c.'92. The N2 also deleted the "Nuno" Sharkfin and was offered in padauk as well as alder in '93. The Chicago factory had taken over production of the N4 by this time. The N4 and N2, both stable in production, have been joined by a new custom doubleneck and a solid finish N1 with a standard vibrato. On this model, which is equipped with a standard nut, the effects of the reverse headstock come into play. Like the N2, it is constructed with a standard four-bolt neck joint.

Solidbody Basses - Early Models

Raven Sunburst
Raven Wine Red
Scavenger Black
Scavenger Ivory
Raven
Scavenger
Wing Series
• Solid mahogany body with carved arch-top
• Detachable rock maple neck
• Strings through body anchored in back
• Polished rosewood fingerboard
• Humbucking pickups
• Precision die cast bridge with brass saddles
• Deluxe machine heads
• Individual volume and tone controls with pickup selector
• Solid mahogany body with carved arch-top
• Detachable rock maple neck
• Strings through body anchored in back
• Polished rosewood fingerboard
• Single coil split pickup
• Precision die cast bridge with brass saddles
• Deluxe machine heads

Following the release of the Wing Series guitars in the late '70s, a matching bass was released. The prototype Vulture and the subsequent production model Scavenger had strings-through-the-body construction, an arched top solid mahogany body, a bolt-on maple neck with rosewood fingerboard and a split pickup, ala Fender's P-Bass. Joining the short-lived Scavenger was the Stage Series B20 with "hockey stick" peghead and the mutant reverse Firebird body. The neck-through-body and strings-through-body construction were serious efforts to make a serious bass, as was the ebony fingerboard and ash body with bound curly maple top. Brass saddles and nut were still in vogue and the PJ pickup arrangement was quite functional. The B20II was finished in black with brass binding and inlays, a brief experiment.

Pete Way

Early-Eighties Standard Basses

The B20 was joined in '83 by the Force Series B40, also with neck-through-body and strings-through-body construction. The ash body had two deep cutaways with a longer bass side horn than treble side. The horns were both rounded as were the edges of the body, which tapered from the center to the outsides. Three fixed bands of parametic EQ were available one at a time which, combined with the PJ pickup set, made for a versatile bass. A pair of P-Bass clones, the bound body B8 and the standard B4, rounded out the growing bass line. A single-pickup B5 Stage with pickguard and no binding was originally equipped with a split pickup and by '85 switched to a black plastic-covered rectangular pickup, as did the B8 and the soon to be retired B20.

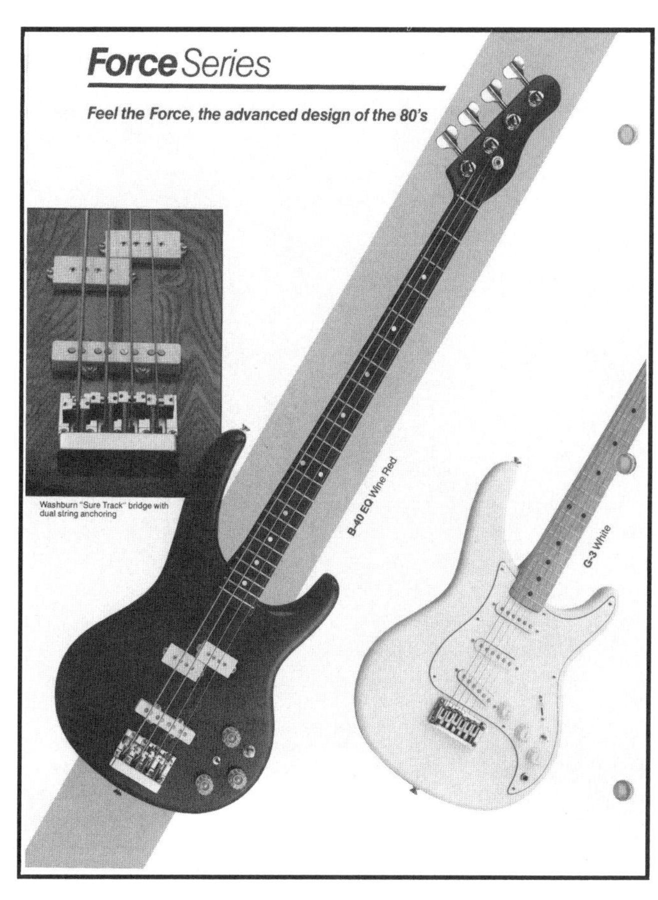

Misc. '80s Basses

The new humbucking pickup was used on all the mid-'80s basses including the B40 and a trio of new and short-lived models. Two of the instruments were simply copies of two hot new styles, the B60 being similar to the headless Steinberger models and the B42 licensing the English Status bass, also headless. The Bantam B62 Steinberger-esque double neck bass had fretless and fretted four string necks, a versatile combination. The third new bass was a Washburn original, designed with Rudy Sarzo of Quiet Riot, who had been a Washburn endorser since his days with Ozzie Osbourne in the early '80s. The two pickup B70 and single pickup B50 featured active EQ, a four pointed body with Japanese sun graphics and the hockey stick peghead, also with graphics. Red and white or black and white were the options. A trio of 26-fret basses were built with the Stephen's Extended Cutaway. The B100 had a solid flamed maple body, the B90 a flamed maple cap and the B80 with solid colors of extreme designs. The active PJ set was identical on all three. The Status bass, popular in Europe, was given another go as the B60 and the black walnut B70, lasting into the early '90s.

Late-'80s Standard Basses

The B40 was replaced with the pointy headstock B30 featuring PJ pickups in the EMG-style. Solid colors were now stock on all the basses which by '87 included the similarly equipped B15 with Select EMGs and the twin J-bass pickup B20 (unrelated to earlier B20) and B10. A single P-bass pickup powered the B2. An interesting fretless model B32, with a low impedance active pickup built into the bridge, was offered for a short time and, like the rest of the basses of this era, came with a pointy headstock. By the end of the decade a milder shape was used on the B20 and 10.

Bhakiti Kumalo

'90s Standard Basses

In the early '90s, the B20 became the XS4 and the B2, the XS2, both featuring scalloped cutaways. The new acoustic/electric basses joined the line at this time. The XS4 became the Mercury MB4 and the XS2, the MB2 c.'92. For '94, a new line of Jackson-designed Bantam basses replaced the Mercury Series, which had replaced the XS Series, which had replaced the B Series. The XB400 with two humbucking pickups was new, while the XB200 replaced the MB4. A new headstock design and a bit of streamlining to the body gives these basses a look all their own.

Misc. '90s Basses

Besides the standard basses of the '90s, Washburn offered two others, one of which was an all-new design. Classically styled, the single cutaway B200 looked something like the Les Paul Recording bass of the '70s and featured a set-neck, two pickups and bound fingerboard, headstock and carved maple top. It was dropped as the line was trimmed down in 1995. The MB8 differed from the standard Mercury Series basses with its flamed sycamore top and twin Status pickups and electronics. An upgraded model for '94 was the SB800.

5, 6 and 8-String Basses

In the late '50s, Danelectro began offering 6-string versions of its standard 4-string basses. The extended upper range allowed the bassist to play guitar parts or "lead" bass but, while doing this, the band lost its bass player. Fender and host of others, however, followed suit with Fender offering a less guitar-like 5-string having a "C" string on top tuned a 4th above the G. Many 6-string bassists began tuning their top two strings to C and F instead of the guitar's B and E, allowing a continuous run of bass licks and patterns. In the '80s, the extended range moved down from low E to low B, using a very heavy, specially-made low string. One problem with the low notes relates to the human ear's inability to distinguish pitch below 50 Hz. This is why the upright bass settled with the low E instead of the low C one octave below the cello. Another reason was the difficulty in building an instrument capable of reproducing a fundamental frequency below the approximate-40Hz E. Which brings up the main problem with today's electric basses having an extended low range: most bass rigs are unable to reproduce the ultra-lows. And that's for live music. To reproduce these lows on a home stereo, not to mention boom boxes and most car stereos, would require special sub-woofers for all. This would be progress, as many of today's consumer-oriented "Hi-Fi" speakers have a boost in the mid-bass range to compensate for a lack of deep bass, instead of the flat-response systems found in higher-end equipment. Artistically, the musician should be able to use any sounds available to them, and many progressive players have worked the lower notes into their repertoire and style, swearing by the '80s and '90s 5 and 6-string basses. The "feel" portion of the frequency range is a very important, though often neglected, part of the bass.

Washburn offered the solidbody B105 in the late-'80s, which became the XS5 which became the MB5 which was superceded by the new XB500. The 6-string MB6 with the low B and high C strings was added to the line c.'93 and was quickly replaced by the XB600. The XB500 and XB600 are now fitted with a pair of specially wound humbucking pickups.

Hagstrom's 8-string bass of the mid-'60s (as used by Noel Redding) was inspiration to Hamer's late-'70s 8-strings (as used by Cheap Trick's Tom Petersson) which was inspiration to a short-lived Washburn Stage 8-string. All of these instruments have four standard strings and four octave strings.

XB500
Natural Material Finish
Same specifications as XB400 with the following exceptions:
Washburn Eliminator™ 5-string J style pickups
Custom 5-string bridge
XB600
Same specifications as XB400 with the following exceptions:
Washburn Eliminator 6-string J style pickups
Custom 6-string bridge
Black Finish

Chicago-Made Basses

At the top of the line for '94 was the short-lived single pickup XB1000 (see p.158) which has been replaced by the two humbucking pickup XB900. This Chicago-made instrument features Bartolini pickups, treble, mid and bass pots, a Wilkinson bridge, 24 frets and a beautiful solid ash body with a thin matte finish. Both of these models were designed by Grover Jackson.

Basses-Hollow

Gregg Allman Allen Woody

No Washburn instrument has dominated a field like the electrified acoustic bass guitars of the '90s. With Jules Shear's brainchild, "Unplugged," offering a respite from the over-processed sounds of the '80s, guitarists and bassists alike began to pursue a warmer, richer, more natural tone. The arched top, Venetian-cutaway AB40 featured a solid spruce top, quilted ash back and sides and an ebony fingerboard on a maple neck. The flat-topped, Florentine cutaway AB20, still in the line, has laminated woods, giving a sound & response many electric bassists find more comfortable (i.e. many jazz guitarists prefer Gibson's laminated ES175 to their carved top L5CES). Both the AB40 and 20 featured a uniquely styled sound hole; "Sound Channels" as the company called them. The controls of the 40 were mounted to the top, while the 20 used the Equis II system with sliders mounted on the instrument's side. Early endorsers included Charlie Drayton, Hutch Hutchinson, Darryl Jones and Bob Glaub.

Rowland Sully

David Rhodes

A pair of special interest basses, the AB45 and AB20FL were 5-string and fretless versions of the AB40 and AB20, respectively. In '94 the solid spruce top AB40 became the laminated sycamore AB30 with the Equis II electronics package. A Fishman pickup, considered the industry's best, became the standard unit on both the 30 and the 20. A lower priced model, the AB10 lacked the Fishman pickup and was originally issued with an oval sound hole which quickly changed to the parallel slats of the others. The AB25 5-string, similar to the 20, replaced the 45.

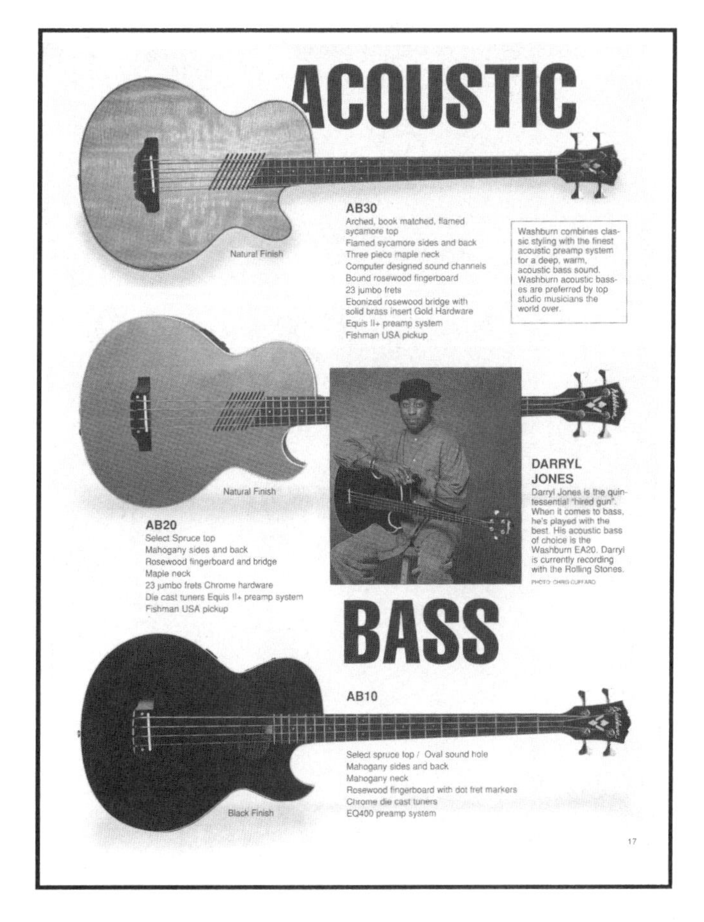

The '95 AB30 includes a magnetic pickup joining the Fishman Transducer. The controls have returned to the top, with separate Treble and Bass controls, as well as a blend control for the pickups. This new twin-pickup AB30 should be even more appealing to electric players.

As the 21st Century approaches it will be interesting to see if the solid body bass continues it's domination, or if an acoustically traditional bass sound, now available at loud volumes, becomes more widespread.

Washburn: The Next 100 Years . . .

As owner and chairman of Washburn International, I would like to personally thank you for allowing me to share with you the history of this grand company. Crafting affordable, quality instruments has been our goal since the onset of my involvement with Washburn. Some designs, though considered radical at the time, have become industry standards, and are now an integral part of the world music scene. Recognized for their musical instrument innovation, the Washburn luthiers, with the aid of advanced technology, are building our finest instruments ever. As we approach the 21st century, we will continue our tradition of excellence. Expect the Washburn legacy to continue.

Rudolf Schlacher

The Washburn SBF80